Shakespeare's Body Language

RELATED TITLES

Early Modern Theatre and the Figure of Disability
ISBN 9781350017207
Genevieve Love

Emotional Excess on the Shakespearean Stage: Passion's Slaves
ISBN 9781408179673
Bridget Escolme

The Hand on the Shakespearean Stage: Gesture, Touch and the Spectacle of Dismemberment
ISBN 9781474234269
Farah Karim-Cooper

Playing Indoors: Staging Early Modern Drama in the Sam Wanamaker Playhouse
ISBN 9781350109506
Will Tosh

Stage Directions and Shakespearean Theatre
ISBN 9781350118812
Edited by Sarah Dustagheer and Gillian Woods

Shakespeare's Body Language

Shaming Gestures and Gender Politics on the Renaissance Stage

Miranda Fay Thomas

THE ARDEN SHAKESPEARE
LONDON • NEW YORK • OXFORD • NEW DELHI • SYDNEY

THE ARDEN SHAKESPEARE
Bloomsbury Publishing Plc
50 Bedford Square, London, WC1B 3DP, UK
1385 Broadway, New York, NY 10018, USA
29 Earlsfort Terrace, Dublin 2, Ireland

BLOOMSBURY, THE ARDEN SHAKESPEARE and the Arden Shakespeare logo
are trademarks of Bloomsbury Publishing Plc

First published in Great Britain, 2020
Paperback edition first published 2021

Copyright © Miranda Fay Thomas, 2020

Miranda Fay Thomas has asserted her right under the Copyright,
Designs and Patents Act, 1988, to be identified as author of this work.

For legal purposes the Acknowledgements on pp. xi-xiii constitute
an extension of this copyright page.

Cover image: Samantha Spiro as Katherina and Simon Paisley Day as
Petruchio in The Taming of the Shrew (© Manuel Harlan)

All rights reserved. No part of this publication may be reproduced or
transmitted in any form or by any means, electronic or mechanical,
including photocopying, recording, or any information storage or retrieval
system, without prior permission in writing from the publishers.

Bloomsbury Publishing Plc does not have any control over, or responsibility for,
any third-party websites referred to or in this book. All internet addresses given
in this book were correct at the time of going to press. The author and publisher
regret any inconvenience caused if addresses have changed or sites have
ceased to exist, but can accept no responsibility for any such changes.

A catalogue record for this book is available from the British Library.

A catalog record for this book is available from the Library of Congress.

ISBN: HB: 978-1-3500-3547-8
PB: 978-1-3502-2814-6
ePDF: 978-1-3500-3549-2
eBook: 978-1-3500-3548-5

Typeset by Integra Software Services Pvt. Ltd.

To find out more about our authors and books visit
www.bloomsbury.com and sign up for our newsletters.

*For Oisín,
and for the academic precariat*

CONTENTS

List of Illustrations ix
Acknowledgements xi
Note on Texts xiv

Introduction: Embodying Shame 1

1 Thumb-biting: Performing Toxic Masculinity in *Romeo and Juliet* 23

2 Figging: Spanish Anxieties and *Ancient* Grudges in Pistol's *Henriad* 45

3 Spitting at Richard: Taming the Beast in *Richard III* 71

4 Spitting at Shylock: Shameful Conversion in *The Merchant of Venice* 93

5 Horning: Fragile Masculinity in *Othello* 115

6 Handwashing: Feminine Shame in *Macbeth* 141

7 Kneeling: Passive Aggression in *Coriolanus* 161

8 Stillness: Female Constancy in *The Winter's Tale* 187

Epilogue 199

Notes 203
Bibliography 229
Index 246

LIST OF ILLUSTRATIONS

1 Carved bone pendant, c. 200 BC. 5

2 Gesture plate, featuring 'improbitatem objicio' and 'Stultitiae notam infigo', from John Bulwer's *Chirologia and Chironomia*, 1644, 189. 46

3 Jan Sanders Van Hemessen, *Die Verspottung Christi*, painting, 1544. 55

4 Frans Franken II, *The Mocking of Christ*, oil on copper, c.1581–1642. 57

5 Limbourg brothers, 'The fall and the expulsion from Paradise', from *Très Riches Heures du Duc de Berry*, vellum, 1415–1416. 59

6 William Blake, *Vanni Fucci 'Making Figs' against God* (1824–1827), illustration for *The Divine Comedy* by Dante Alighieri (*Inferno* XXV, 1–15), pen and ink and watercolour over pencil and traces of black chalk, with sponging, 52.7 × 37.2 cm (sheet) 61

7 View of the Sistine Chapel ceiling painted by Michelangelo di Lodovico Buonarroti Simoni (1475–1564). 62

8 Meister von Messkirch, *Verspottung Christi* (*Mocking of Christ*), tempera and oil on wood, c.1535–1538. 107

9 Johann Koerbecke, *Mairenfelder Altar, linker Flügel außen unten rechts: Verspottung* (*Mocking of Christ*), painting (tempera on panel), 1457. 108

10 From the title page of *The Resolution of the Women of London to the Parliament*, woodcut, 1642. 115

11 Gesture plate, featuring 'Innocentia ostendo', from Bulwer's *Chirologia* (London, 1644), 151. 149

12 Henry Peacham, *Titus Andronicus*, drawing, c.1595. 162

13 Lucas van Leyden, *Esther before Ahasuerus*, engraving, 1518. 173

14 *The Annunciation*, charcoal drawing by Federico Barocci (1528–1612), Italy, sixteenth century. 175

15 *The Assumption and Coronation of the Virgin*, 1510 (1906), Albrecht Durer. 176

16 *Temptation of Eve*, lintel by Gislebertus or Gisleberto 177

ACKNOWLEDGEMENTS

My primary thanks are to my PhD supervisors, Sonia Massai (King's College London) and Farah Karim-Cooper (Shakespeare's Globe). Their guidance on my doctoral dissertation has resulted in this book, and they were an enviable support network at each and every stage. They remain personal heroes. My PhD examiners, Gillian Woods and Evelyn Tribble (who also provided a very helpful reader report for this manuscript), were exemplary in their generosity, and I owe them a debt of gratitude for helping me to take my thinking to the next level. Lyn and I went on to co-convene a seminar entitled 'Shakespeare and Gesture' at the 2018 meeting of the Shakespeare Association of America in Los Angeles, and I extend further thanks for her support there, as well as to the congress organizers and our marvellous seminar participants, whose work helped further shape my own thoughts on the topic this book discusses.

My thanks are due to the team at Arden who have helped edge this book into the world, in particular Margaret Bartley for her initial enthusiasm, Mark Dudgeon for his patience, and the endlessly helpful editorial assistants I have worked with: Susan Furber was so helpful when this manuscript was in its very early stages, and the fabulous Lara Bateman saved my sanity on multiple occasions as the book was entering publication.

My work in this book has been immeasurably improved by fellow academics, who have read and commented on it, namely Brett Greatley-Hirsch, Ellie Rycroft, Susan Anderson, and my anonymous readers. All other errors remain my own. Thank you to Ewan Fernie, who had already written his own book on Shakespeare and shame, for productive discussions when this book was in its infancy. An especial thank-you to Danielle Clarke, who made me incredibly welcome at University College Dublin (UCD) when I emigrated to Ireland. I would like to extend further thanks to the Drama Department of Trinity College Dublin, who have recently welcomed me to their team, in particular Melissa Sihra and Nicholas Johnson. To the students I taught at UCD, King's, Greenwich, Central School of Speech and Drama, St Anne's College, Oxford, and Shakespeare's Globe: thank you for hours of interesting discussion, keeping me on my toes, and inspiring me to keep writing.

The gratitude I extend to the early modern community of scholars and practitioners I have met since 2010 is beyond words. Beloved teachers, erstwhile colleagues, conference confidantes, adored actors, motivational mentors, members of the academic precariat, and true friends: your strength, wisdom, and kindness have kept me here. Take a bow Hailey Bachrach, Sally Barnden, Anna Blackwell, Claire M. L. Bourne, Dominic Brewer, Judith Buchanan, Thea Buckley, Robin Craig, Hannah Crawforth, Kabrina Davey, Callan Davies, Natalya Din-Kariuki, Michael Dobson, Sophie Duncan, Derek Dunne, Jen Edwards, Ken Fincham, Kim Gilchrist, Mikey Goodman, Kate Graham, Jane Grogan, Andrew Hadfield, Robbie Hand, Ellie Hardy, Ronan Hatfull, Mia Hewitt, Megan Holman, Gwilym Jones, Simon Kane, Jonas Kellermann, Andy Kesson, Pete Kirwan, Duncan Lees, Sarah Lewis, Georgie Lucas, Hannah Manktelow, Giulia Mari-Allan, Erin McCarthy, Harry McCarthy, Emer McHugh, Gordon McMullan, Nicole Mennell, Lucy Munro, Richard O'Brien, Sarah Olive, Stephen O'Neill, Pat Palmer, Joanne Paul, José A. Pérez Díez, Eoin Price, Nam Rao, Anne Sophie Refskou, John Roe, Kirsty Rolfe, Nina Romancikova, Richard Rowland, Elizabeth Scott-Baumann, Will Sharpe, Bill Sherman, Natasha Simonova, Emma Smith, Helen Smith, Simon Smith, Patrick Spottiswoode, Robert Stagg, Daniel Starza-Smith, Hilary Tones, Will Tosh, Tim Treloar, Nash Trevelyan, James Wallace, Emma Whipday, and Nora Williams-Platt. Equally effusive and loving thanks also to Nicola Kirkby, Maureen England, and Nina Pritchard. Especial thanks to Leo Grant and Will Hadwen, for lifelong friendship and unconditional kindness.

To my family, Janet and Glyn Thomas, and Pearl and Dennis Stephenson: thank you always for your unwavering support and encouragement. To William Wall and Liz Kirwan: thank you for being both new readers and new family. Thanks also to newfound brother Illan Wall, sister Bríd Spillane, and nephews Ruán and Odhran.

Finally, to my husband Oisín Wall: thank you for inspiring me every day with your own diligence and wit (how do you write like you're running out of time?) and for believing in me when I lose hope. This book owes its completion entirely to your support and love: it is yours. I would also thank our wonderful dog, Winnicott, but he has no concept of what a book is. Please don't chew this.

NOTE ON TEXTS

All quotations from Shakespeare are from the Arden third series editions, except where stated. Quotations from Christopher Marlowe are taken from Frank Romany and Robert Lindsey's edition of *The Complete Plays* (Penguin, 2003). Any other cited material published before 1700 is taken from facsimile texts available via Early English Books Online (http://eebo.chadwyck.com) except where stated.

Introduction: Embodying Shame

This book explores how shaming gestures operate in Shakespeare's dramatic works. A shaming gesture is an action of non-verbal communication, performed with the deliberate intention of inflicting humiliation upon someone else. When Sampson bites his thumb at the Montague servants in the first scene of *Romeo and Juliet*, he is taunting them, making a vulgar insinuation with his hand in order to provoke them into a fight. When Lady Anne spits on Richard III's attempts at wooing her, her spittle marks him out as someone shameful, unclean, and in need of taming. And when Hermione's statuesque stillness in the final scene of *The Winter's Tale* unites a long-lost family, the passivity of her natural gesture brings catharsis and peace to Leontes' anger, shaming him into a more respectful relationship.

Gestures are embodied social metaphors: they are the epitome of the political as the personal. A gesture encapsulates a variety of understood meanings or intentions, and the signs they produce serve as a microcosm of the wider society which endowed them with original signification. The performative nature of society is played out through the gesticulations that codify the tensions and incitements within a particular group of people at a particular point in time. Despite some notions of gesture being a universal language, the language of the body is inherently produced and explicated by the society in which it is found. Far from being universal, it is instead highly specific to the tensions in the performance of social relationships.

The shaming gestures featured in this book are essentially symptoms of a wider cause: the gender politics of Shakespeare's age. These gestures, the cause of humiliation to many, embody a broader set of social norms and taboos rooted in traditional ideas about gender roles and gender performance. Put simply: one of the most effective ways to mock or shame someone already insecure about themselves was to question their gender identity. Modern-day audiences of Shakespeare's plays will naturally bring their own social contexts and expectations to the theatre: in some cases, this will lend greater sympathy to characters' behaviour; in others, greater frustration. While this book takes as its focus shaming gestures which are rooted in customs of the early modern period, it is my intention to read such moments through the lens of present-day feminism. In each chapter I historicize the gesture in question and the society from which it emerged, but I also write primarily from the perspective of an intersectional feminist ally and regular theatregoer.

Masculinity and femininity are parts we are often handed at birth; throughout our lives, we are reviewed on our performance of these roles and judged for any deviations from the script. Consequently, gender and shame are both embodied in performance. By this, I mean that they are rooted in the way that bodies move through society and are responded to by that society. Gender is not about biology, chemistry, or the contents of one's underwear. It is an external manifestation of an internal identity consistent with what we might call character: an ongoing public performance of a personal truth. When these manifestations come into conflict with others' preconceived ideas about identity, such gender performances can be refuted and negated by another performance: the act of shaming.

The role of shame is in constant play in Shakespeare's work, but it is used to enact a variety of different dramatic ends: sometimes comic, sometimes tragic; sometimes it is used incidentally to the main plot of the play, sometimes it is used with devastating consequences. But the character who is being shamed with such gestures becomes an unwilling spectacle. Punishment was frequently public-facing during the early modern period. Items such as whipping posts, pillories, and stocks were visible reminders in early modern communities that wrongdoing would result in humiliation in front of one's peers; indeed, since the medieval period, criminals were 'paraded through the streets and pelted with rubbish'.[1]

Shame is the freezing of the self in an unfavourable public image: once you have been exposed to the gaze of those who see you in a negative light, your own control over how your selfhood is fashioned is destabilized. It is for this reason why the emotion of shame can be so psychologically painful. In *Cymbeline*, when Imogen comments that '[t]he breach of custom / Is breach of all' (4.2.10–11), she stresses the vast importance of social decorum. Her stepmother, the Queen, says in turn of Imogen that '[s]he's such a lady / So tender of rebukes that words are strokes, / And strokes death to her' (3.5.39–41). As has been observed by Jennifer Jacquet, the emotion of shame can be felt almost physically, with her noting how shame 'may be nonviolent, but that does not mean [it is not] painful'.[2] In fact, the experience of shame can travel in both directions, and the desire to inflict shame on others can reveal a prior emotional wound in those who would rather humiliate their peers than face their own inadequacies.

Towards a semiotics of shaming gestures

When a non-English-speaking tourist visits Shakespeare's Globe on London's Southbank today, what do they make of the way the actors use their bodies? If they do not understand the language of the play, how might they infer meaning through gesture and movement? Would they recognize an actor conveying certain emotions, or would something be lost in translation? For that matter, how might a native Londoner visiting the Globe for the first time in 2019 see such action, given that it is motivated by a 400-year-old story? Inevitably, the performance of a Renaissance play in an historically informed setting, such as Shakespeare's Globe, elicits a different kind of movement from an actor, due to such varying elements as the way Renaissance costumes physically restrict the body, the size of the audience, and the open-air stage, not to mention what the early modern script itself might prompt. If an Italian tourist were to visit the reconstruction of Shakespeare's Globe today, and view a performance of, say, *Henry V*, they would certainly recognize the gesture made by Pistol in 3.6. Furious that Captain Fluellen will not intervene to save the life of Bardolph, Pistol cries, 'Die and be damned, and *fico* for thy friendship!' (3.6.56), making an obscene gesture as he does. While modern audiences certainly understand from the scene's context and tone that the gesture serves as an offensive one, the associations behind such a gesture may well be lost to them. However, the *fico*, or the fig gesture, is still used in Italy today as a vulgar insult.

The gesture's origins date back over 2,000 years. The amulet shown here (Figure 1) is a variation on the *fascinus*: a Roman symbol of the divine phallus. While the right half of the pendant depicts a penis, the left shows a body part which, on the surface of things, seems far less vulgar: a clenched first, with the thumb pushed between the index and middle finger. However, this gesture is the *fico* or fig. Such pendants were carried by Roman soldiers as a good luck token designed to ward off 'evil powers',[3] and the one pictured dates from around 200 BC. Yet the gesture's ability to cause offence lasted from Roman Britain to well into the seventeenth century, and while the thumb-sign is no longer regularly used as a vulgar gesture in Britain today, its power as symbol remains in the cultures of continental Europe. The cultural history of the *fico*, and other such shaming gestures, provide a fascinating insight into the societies from which they originated. Somewhat

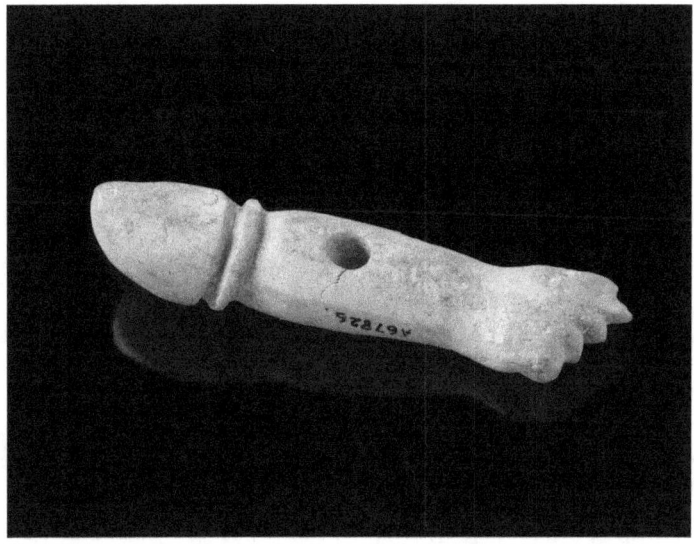

FIGURE 1 *Carved bone pendant, c. 200 BC. Science Museum, London (Object A67826, Image 10697402).*

unsurprisingly, such insults are often rooted in 'images of the parts of the body thought of as shameful',[4] as is evident in the example of the Roman fascinus. But what is intriguing about the pendant is that it contains both the offensive body part itself *in addition to* the gesture, which becomes a synecdoche for it. In a single object, the gesture's association with the vulgar power of male sexual dominance is confirmed. The value of such a connection should not be overestimated, for as the theorist Michel de Certeau observes, 'Of all the things everyone does, how much gets written down?'[5] Gestures are most often learned through habit, with their meaning inferred by social context. They become part of an ephemeral network, the gestures written upon the air but remembered by the observer, and operating within mutual cultural understandings. In his studies of movement, Jacques Lecoq notes how '[t]he body reflects society, its milieu and its period'.[6] In this case, the amulet is carved from bone: a very literal embodiment of where such gestures are rooted. But gestures are not merely the body's language; they also encapsulate the values and tensions of society itself. In this way, the body natural's gestures respond to the actions of the wider body politic.

In this book, I read a variety of gestures across the whole of Shakespeare's dramatic canon, from the thumb bites of *Romeo and Juliet*, the fig employed by Pistol in *2 Henry IV* and *Henry V*, the spitting in *Richard III* and *The Merchant of Venice*, the *cornutu* cuckold horns in *Othello*, Lady Macbeth's handwashing in *Macbeth*, kneeling in *Coriolanus*, and Hermione's passive statue in *The Winter's Tale*. My work thinks about how shaming gestures adapt as Shakespeare begins to write in the Jacobean period; by the end of his career, scenes of shaming are far less overtly vulgar, but instead focus on spectacles of kneeling, confrontation and passive aggression, reflecting the changing political rhetoric and visual culture of the Stuart era. The gestures I examine all occur in fraught situations where there is tension between the characters, and it is important to consider why a gesture is used at such moments: Do the words spoken by characters in the lead up to a gesture only take us so far? Have the characters said all they can say and have to resort to something more physical as a reaction?

The study of gesture in the Renaissance period has often centred on classical notions of rhetoric. Texts by Cicero and Quintilian offer advice on how an orator may position the hands or the rest of the body while speaking in public, and these key Roman authors would have created the essential syllabus for sixteenth-century grammar school boys.[7] Shakespeare and the actors in his company would have been tutored 'in the long tradition of Quintilian's rhetoric with its emphasis on careful speech and studied gesture',[8] as well as pithy Ciceronian epithets on delivery such as 'action is truly the body's speech'.[9] Renaissance schoolboys would also have learnt much from Thomas Wilson's *The Arte of Rhetorique,* published in 1553, which was Tudor England's most seminal work on oratory.[10]

In particular, the third book focuses on elocution and style, saying that gesture 'shal not onely delite men with the sight, but perswade them the rather the truth of our cause'.[11]

These sorts of gestures provide a useful context for my own research, yet they are not the gestures analysed in this book. Instead, I study gestures which are far ruder and much more insulting, not ones that, in Thomas Wilson's words, 'delite men with the sight' at all. But Wilson's *Arte of Rhetorique* also quotes Tullie to tell us that 'the gesture of man, is the speache of his bodie'.[12] Gesture is its own language and can communicate certain ideas or opinions in an efficient way, and the emotions elicited by such gestures are just as telling. In his *Anatomie of Abuses* (1583), Phillip Stubbes warned against viewing 'such wanton gestures, such bawdie speeches: such laughing and fleering: such kissing and bussing: such clipping and culling: Suche winckinge and glancinge of wanton eyes'.[13] An audience's viewing of such gestures was, to Stubbes' mind, a dangerous thing. Evidently, 'such wanton gestures' do not merely taint the performer of such actions; they also tarnish the observer of them. Renaissance writers such as Michel de Montaigne have written on the ability of hands to show shame as well as 'sweare', 'condemne', 'injure', 'despise,' and 'mocke',[14] and John Bulwer's *Chirologia and Chironomia*, the seventeenth century's most impressive collection of gestural codes, notes how hands can 'reprove', 'affront', 'offer injury', 'admonish', 'reproch', 'mocke', 'insult', 'chide', 'upbraid', 'contemn', and 'disdain'.[15] While I explore the movements of hands in this book, I also consider the gestural implications of spitting and kneeling. From head to toe, the Renaissance body was used to evoke shame in the minds of those on the receiving end of these gestures.

Up until now, the analysis of gesture in Shakespeare has considered it from a rhetorical angle. The gestures explored in this book are less oratorically orientated: their 'vulgarity' as rude or shaming gestures has left them in the footnotes, but their lower-class origins do not make them less worthy of study. Rather, their marginality reveals much more about the social tensions of the period and what the 'civilizing process' (as described by Norbert Elias) was trying to repress. So if Shakespearean scholars are analysing verbal language, the language of gesture must also be considered in order to understand the human behaviour of the early modern period. Non-verbal communication plays a central role in social behaviour, and it is through the performance of these reproaches that we are able to understand the behavioural boundaries of any community, including Renaissance England. To quote the historian Keith Thomas, 'to interpret and account for a gesture is to unlock the whole social and cultural system of which it is part'.[16] If we look for the underlying associations behind gestures from previous eras, we can better understand the motivations behind such societies. The actions they make perform a particular set of ideas and ideals, and through these we can learn about the past from which they emerged. Lecoq notes how

> Gestures too can be modified to the point where they become symbols. Although created rationally, symbolic gestures may join together in rituals which make use of more or less styli[z]ed images, seeking to transcend visible signs so as to make contact with the invisible.[17]

By focusing in on the taboos of this period, and how they are epitomized in the form of shaming gestures, we can closely examine some of the tensions of this particular historical moment. In her writing on Shakespeare's use of the hand, Farah Karim-Cooper notes the fundamental importance of studying gestural movement on the early modern stage: 'How much is written there that we have forgotten how to read?'[18] The gestures in Shakespeare's work are only recently being explored to their full historical, theoretical, and performative potential by scholars, and there is rich meaning to be read in these otherwise non-verbal dramatic moments.[19]

As this book will show, Shakespeare's inclusion of gesture in his plays was not only a conscious decision reflecting his belief in the performative nature of early modern life, but also one which has major implications for reimagining social interaction as well as cultural tensions in the Renaissance period. What is more, reading Shakespeare's gestures unlocks how the political is manifested within the personal. Karen Newman has previously written that

> [t]he task of a political criticism is not merely to expose or demystify the ideological discourses which organize literary texts, but to reconstitute those texts, to reread canonical texts in non canonical ways which reveal the contingency of so-called canonical readings, which disturb conventional interpretations and discover them as partisan, constructed, made rather than given, natural, and inevitable.[20]

This mission to read 'canonical texts in non canonical ways' is one I adopt through the reading of gesture, rather than words; I am less interested in the literariness of Shakespeare's texts than the practicality of their performance. A practical approach to analysing stage movement should not be considered incompatible with social critique; in fact, it seems that carrying out the former is impossible without invoking the latter. A gesture becomes an expressive symbol through its location within a particular social context; in other words, a gesture only functions as a communicative tool when the meaning behind the movement is understood by others.

Gestural communication is effective because it can encompass a variety of different associations within the same action: thus one sign becomes a sign of many things, all connected with *but not reducible to* the social idea that is being expressed. This plurality adds to a gesture's effectiveness rather than detracting from it, particularly in the example of shaming gestures: so long as at least one shaming interpretation is possible for a spectator to read of a gestural sign, the action has served its intended purpose. Other spectators may bring different shameful associations or readings to the gesture, but provided they are all situated within the same *intention* (in this case, the intention to humiliate), the gesture's function remains intact, regardless of the difference in individual interpretive distinctions.

Shame and the spectator's gaze

Shame is used as a form of social control in Thomas More's *Utopia*, although the symbols which convey such shame are different from what we might expect. Materials which are traditionally valued, such as gold and silver, are used to create 'chamber-pots and other vessels that serve for most vile uses'. Not only this, but such metals are also used to

> make great chains, fetters, and gyves wherein they tie their bondmen. Finally whosoever for any offence be infamed, by their ears hang rings of gold, upon their fingers they wear rings of gold, and, in conclusion, their heads be tied with gold. Thus by all means possible they procure to have gold and silver among them in reproach and infamy.[21]

Of course, More's *Utopia* is a work of fiction rather than a travel guide to a real land. However, it provides us with an example of how the values of shame, and the accessories to it, are culturally defined symbols. *Utopia* is a fiction, but then so too are the associations we all have with shame: they are scripted by culture and learned through the process of everyday existence until the fiction becomes a fact of life. More's account also reveals how a crucial part of shame is that it is observed by others who make the connection between a symbol and something to be embarrassed about. Jennifer Jacquet, in her book *Is Shame Necessary?*, pinpoints how '[e]xposure is the essence of shaming', because shame 'aims to hold individuals to the group standard' (as opposed to guilt, which is where an individual fails to meet their own standards).[22] Such a view aligns itself with Michel Foucault's discussions on public punishment in previous centuries, at a time when

[p]eople were summoned as spectators: they were assembled to observe public exhibitions and *amendes honorables*; pillories, gallows and scaffolds were erected in public squares or by the roadside; sometimes the corpses of the executed persons were displayed for several days near the scenes of their crimes. Not only must people know, they must see with their own eyes. Because they must be made to be afraid; but also because they must be the witnesses, the guarantors, of the punishment, and because they must to a certain extent take part in it.[23]

The theoretical perspective of the shaming process, then, is rooted in a consideration of the public sphere and its desire to 'civilize'. Foucault sees how such disciplinary moments serve to turn the shamed body into an 'object of a representation', with the individual marked out in front of society.[24] Through this method, Ewan Fernie argues that the shamed person experiences 'the disintegration of selfhood', bringing with it 'a strong sense of exposure, producing an urgent desire to be concealed and hidden'.[25] While I agree that shame produces this desire, I query whether such an experience is analogous with the disintegration of the self. Shame is the freezing of the self in an unfavourable public image, in the sense that once you have been exposed to the gaze of those who see you in a negative light, your own control over how your selfhood is fashioned is destabilized. It is for this reason why the emotion of shame can be so psychologically painful.

Shame is used as a tool to keep people in line, and while many of these examples emerge from the way in which society deploys shame as a 'civilizing' emotion, it operates in the same way when it is used to reveal tensions or frustrations through the making of an obscene gesture. The gesture, aimed at an individual who does not meet the mark in the eyes of another, inflicts shame on such a person. While ostensibly vulgar, such actions are not considered outright violence; in this sense, a clenched fist becomes a *symbol* of aggression rather than the act of aggression itself. However, it is the sheer ability of these gestures to *provoke* a potentially violent response from the other which renders them a danger to civilized society. The shaming gesture does not hide a malicious intent behind a symbol. Rather, it communicates such an intent and does so in the sight of others who will see a reputation being damaged.

On the other side of shame, we have honour (or, as Cassio in *Othello* would have it, '[r]eputation, reputation, reputation!' (2.3.258)). C. B. Watson notes how Shakespearean theatre is filled with men 'intoxicated' with reputation and 'outward repute';[26] I would add that his theatre is equally filled with men's concerns over the reputations of women as a paternalistic extension of their own self-worth. Such 'outward repute' even led to visible symbols representing a man's good reputation in parish churches, such as tombs, memorials, and portraits.[27] Honour was vital in the early modern period, both in terms of how other people viewed each other and in terms of how individuals viewed themselves. It meant that self-perception was rooted in one's public standing. Therefore, a crucial condition of shame is that it requires an audience. This is part of the 'observer effect', or the objectification of the spectator's gaze, and thus creates the humiliating experience of public exposure. Directing a shaming gesture at someone interferes with that person's capacity to self-fashion their own identity: when publicly shamed, one becomes objectified by the gaze of the spectators witnessing the incident.

Reading gesture

Hamlet's advice to the players indicates the necessity of using effective gesture in performance in addition to speaking the lines of the script with a degree of naturalness. In fact, he even demonstrates the wrong way to gesticulate: 'do not saw the air too much with your hand, *thus*, but use all gently' (3.2.4–5, my emphasis). The key is not to 'o'erstep ... the modesty of nature' (3.2.19), but this direction evokes its own problems.

the war-mongering Spanish with 'fiery' Italian temperaments – either by mistake or in order to tarnish all foreigners with the same brush of gesticular oddity – or if the hand sign was also widely used in places such as Verona. However, the available evidence labels it as a particularly Spanish gesture. John Walter asserts that it was imported to early modern England from Spain.[40] It is also recorded in *The Reports of Sir George Croke, Knight*, which records an incident whereby an Irish Dominican friar on trial in Spain 'most insolently put finger into his mouth and scornfully bit his thumb' as 'a token of scorn and disdain in the highest degree'.[41]

Raymond Tallis explains the fascination of hand signs from overseas: 'if foreigners are funny, their gestures are even funnier. The funniness of foreigners' speech comes primarily from the fact that we cannot understand them; the funniness of their gestures comes from the fact that we can half-understand them.'[42] Perhaps this is at least partly why Shakespeare chooses to begin *Romeo and Juliet* with a thumb-bite: a gesture both recognizable due to its arrival in England and vaguely incomprehensible due to its specifically European origins. Stephen Greenblatt believes that we are intrigued by distinctive physical customs from other cultures because 'the body in its malleability, its inability to remain fixed and unchanging, its equally intense beauty and grotesqueness, is the site of what we might call an intractable theoretical [O]therness'.[43] It is precisely this Otherness that sets *Romeo and Juliet* in motion: for the audience, it is seeing a European gesture parodied on stage; for the Montagues and Capulets, it is the Otherness of the two families that fuels their feud.

In fact, the use of the vulgar thumb gesture can be read alongside Tybalt's style of duelling to suggest that there are hints of the Capulet family as being Spanish in origin or at least in quality. Charles Edelman notes an oddly English contempt displayed by Mercutio for the 'foreign' elements of Tybalt's Spanish style of fencing, which is furthered by Ralph Berry's intriguing reading of their fatal duel as one being fought on national as well as social grounds:

Imitating nature is in itself paradoxical: the act of acting itself, if done with insufficient skill, demonstrates the very pretence it attempts to conceal.

If performing gesture can lead to difficulties, the same can be said of reading gesture. The critic Jean-Claude Schmitt has hit upon the problem of analysing expressive movements by noting how gestures 'belong to an ephemeral world. Usually they do not leave any traces for historians'.[28] Gestures are very much performed 'in the moment', and yet their impact may be felt long after the event. As well as being used to shame us, gestures may be used to persuade us, to anger us, or upset us. But unless we are filming or recording these movements in some way, the only evidence of these gestures that remains is the emotions we feel. There is, of course, a distinction between gestures which are performed in theatrical scenes and gestures which are alluded to in reported speech rather than seen first-hand. As I have written elsewhere, *Julius Caesar* provides us with examples of how reported gestures can reveal the performativity and potential disingenuity of political action, but they can also corroborate evidence about an honest character.[29]

Another difficulty inherent in this kind of research is that the lack of stage directions in Shakespeare texts means that evidence of gestures can often only be inferred through the dialogue spoken by the characters. A practical problem emerging from this is the question of when modern editors should add in stage directions to Renaissance plays. David Bevington observes how many editors copy the stage directions from edition to edition 'as though they were canonical (most are not)'.[30] Usually, the best way to examine how gesture works in Shakespearean drama is to analyse his language as coded action by reading the text to see what is implied by way of physical movement. Often in a text, it is possible to read a line which indicates that a gesture must be happening: for instance, as Othello and Iago make a vow to take revenge on Cassio and Desdemona, Iago says 'do not rise yet', which implies that Othello must be kneeling (3.3.465). Instances like this are a common way of pinpointing the use of gesture in a Shakespeare scene; in fact, the Renaissance anti-theatricalist Stephen Gosson observes that '[p]layers action, doeth answere to their partes'.[31]

Gesture, of course, is all around us, and we regularly use it without really being aware that we are doing so. In his book *Gesture: Visible Action as Utterance*, Kendon observes how the body's movement is crucial in how we interact with each other, particularly in the way such actions reveal 'the nature of [our] intentions and attitudes'.[32] Consequently, Kendon suggests that gesture 'is a label for actions that have the features of manifest deliberate expressiveness'.[33] This working definition is augmented and clarified by Farah Karim-Cooper, who writes that gestures are not only 'units of bodily meaning' but ones which 'are produced by a given set of social conditions and their meanings tend to depend upon the contexts within which they occur'.[34] Such social conditions and meanings shift, of course, within different theatrical contexts such as genre, acting styles, and changing repertory tastes. Just as Marlon Brando's acting style in the 1950s contrasts heavily with Al Pacino in the 1970s, we must imagine that a comic actor such as Richard Tarlton in the 1580s would have a far different gestural style than, say, Nathan Field's acting in the first twenty years of the seventeenth century. Gestural performance will also be affected by genre, and in different contexts, gestures will receive different reactions. A teasing jest accompanied by the *cornutu* horns may garner laughter in a comedy, but the same action performed cruelly in a tragedy may result in a far deadlier outcome. As this book will show, cultural shifts also affect what gestures are performed and how effective they are perceived to be. As my discussion moves from the Elizabethan to the Jacobean period, we shall see how in Shakespeare's final works the efficacy of more passive-aggressive shaming gestures becomes more potent. Gesture is shaped and re-shaped by the context of the moment, taking into account local custom, social appropriateness, and its audience.

Gender and decorum

Throughout this book, I explore the gender politics associated with ideas about shame and the uncivil body. At times, terms such as 'feminine', 'masculine', and 'feminizing' are used, and it is crucial to specify that in doing so, I am applying the Renaissance period's associations with gender difference, and not my own. While reading these shaming gestures, I explore gender politics as a powerful fiction that writes itself upon the body. Stephen Greenblatt argues that power

> is not only the ability to levy taxes or raise an army but the ability to enforce submission, manifested in those signs of secular worship – bowing, kneeling, kissing of rings – that European rulers increasingly insist upon. If these signs always have an air of fiction about them – and indeed in England they become increasingly fantastic until they reach the aesthetic mania of the court of Charles I – so much the better, because [...] one of the highest achievements of power is to impose fictions upon the world and one of its supremest pleasures is to enforce the acceptance of fictions that are known to be fictions.[35]

Greenblatt's labelling of gestures such as bowing and kneeling as 'fictions that are known to be fictions' is in keeping with my decision to read shaming bodily action as 'embodied metaphors', for such acts write a story of power relations on the body itself.

The gendering of the body, and therefore of power itself, is a crucial factor in the fashioning of authority. Historians such as Elizabeth A. Foyster write how the construction of gender identity is in constant negotiation with society's expectations, values, and ideals. The ideals of early modern masculinity and femininity are often to be found in texts such as conduct books and broadside ballads, which provided a didactic function in terms of describing gender roles. While women were ideally sexually virtuous, faithful, dutiful, and usually silent, men were supposed to head up the household hierarchy over spouses, offspring, and servants.[36] Foyster also reminds us that the Renaissance political theorist Sir Robert Filmer 'drew analogies between the power of the king in the state and that of the father in the family'.[37] Additionally, patriarchal authority took its cue from biblical scripture, with conduct manual writers such as William Gouge quoting verses such as 'wives submit yourselves unto your divine husbands, as unto the Lord'.[38] Of course, such evidence is really only representative of gender ideals rather than a reflection of reality, meaning that they leave us 'with evidence of the theory rather than the practice of patriarchy'.[39] However, such everyday actions as gestures and the way they codify gendered norms may well reveal the practice of such theories. Because gender roles were so frequently defined in terms of male and female honour, unpicking the social behaviour associated with such ideals means that we can see how such prescriptive codes of behaviour were brought to bear upon gestural moments which evoke shame: honour's opposite number.

Judith Butler considers how gender identity can be subverted when she argues that

> [i]f the inner truth of gender is a fabrication and if a true gender is a fantasy instituted and inscribed on the surface of bodies, then it seems that genders can be neither true nor false, but are only produced as the truth effects of a discourse of primary and stable identity.[40]

The idea of gender being a fabrication reveals its ability to be malleable, especially as such an identity only needs to appear on the outside of a body. While such an outlook may feel to some like a relatively recent conception of gender identity, Will Fisher urges us to re-evaluate our assumptions. In the early modern period, he notes, it was proverbial 'to say that what "God makes [...] man shapes"'.[41] Given that the body was understood through the Galenic tradition of humours, 'male and female bodies were not understood to be two discrete entities that were fundamentally different from one another; instead, they were viewed along a continuum'.[42] In this regard, certain acts could lead to a reassessment of one's outward gender presentation. Indeed, in 1573 the French Renaissance surgeon Ambroise Paré produced a manual entitled *Monsters and Marvels*, which gave advice to early modern medical practitioners on how to discern if a hermaphrodite should be gendered male or female. In addition to addressing bodily characteristics, Paré also advises that the performance of gender be considered, recommending that one should observe whether or not they display 'other actions like those of males and females'.[43] It was therefore acknowledged that gender identity should not focus exclusively on the genital organs, but on how such an individual chooses to present their gender through characteristics such as voice, personality, and bodily movement. But while this offers individuals a means of potential liberation from a gender assigned at birth, the traditional association of particular performative characteristics as 'masculine' or 'feminine' ensures that any attempt to conform to a particular end of the gender binary is still rooted in the need to 'pass' as a male or female, limiting one's gender identity to traditional norms. While gender can be said to be a performance, society's expectations serve to prejudge, and potentially shame, such presentations which do not meet pre-existing expectations.

Shakespeare's body language

Shakespeare deals with shame and how it can be conveyed from the start of his theatrical career until its end, and his treatment of the emotion develops significantly over this period. This study focuses on the work of Shakespeare for two reasons. Firstly, because no one has explored in depth the shaming gestures on stage in this period, and his is the largest body of work surviving from the age. Secondly, because Shakespeare's career straddles both the Elizabethan and Jacobean periods, meaning that his work provides insight into social tensions during the reigns of both monarchs. Shakespeare's works give us the opportunity to directly compare gestural practices under Elizabeth I and James I and how the potency of particular signs is predicated upon them being performed at a specific historical moment. Karim-Cooper has focused her study on gesture to Shakespeare for more performative reasons, noting how his work is 'preoccupied' with the movement of the hand.[44] I concur with her assessment, and extend this argument further by considering not merely gestures of the hand but also spitting and kneeling. This book makes mention of almost all of Shakespeare's dramatic works and provides an in-depth exploration of ten plays spread across his career, representing the varied genres of comedy, tragedy, history, and romance: shame, and the gestures that cause and reflect it, are to be found in each one.

In *Titus Andronicus*, Lavinia is brutally raped and mutilated, and she dies at the hand of her father, Titus, who asks Saturnius beforehand,

> Was it well done of rash Virginius
> To slay his daughter with his own right hand,
> Because she was enforced, stained and deflowered?
> (5.3.36–8)

Saturnius answers in the affirmative, because 'the girl should not survive her shame' (5.3.40). Titus takes this as his cue, with the lines '[d]ie, die, Lavinia, and thy shame with thee, / And with thy shame thy father's sorrow die' (5.3.45–6). Lavinia's initial violation by Chiron and Demetrius is 'obscene' in two senses of the word. Not only is it a horrific event but it takes place *off*-stage. She is exposed to more than enough voyeurism over the rest of the play, of course, and her mute, bloodied figure stands for the embodiment of ravaged female shame. Such incidents are too brutal for the remit of this book; in focusing on gesture, I explore the provocation of shame rather than the physical force of it spilling over into direct violence. Yet it is useful to consider *Titus Andronicus* as a case at the beginning of Shakespeare's career and compare it with how he depicts the shaming process in his later plays. This especially changes how such a process is gendered and, by the end of this book, we shall see how passive-aggressive moments of stasis performed by women can be powerfully evocative when shaming men.

Chapter 1 explores the thumb-bite which begins *Romeo and Juliet*. Its analysis explores the factors of the play's continental setting upon this gesticular braggadocio, while also offering a case study on how toxic masculinity shapes the motives and expectations of men with something to prove. Chapter 2 concerns the Spanish fig gesture as employed by the character of Pistol in *Henry IV* and *Henry V*. Given the anti-Spanish sentiment at the time of these plays' composition, Pistol's use of a Spanish gesture at a moment of heightened national security in order to assert his pride as an Englishman is particularly curious. By analysing the origins of the vulgar and phallic thumb gesture, I consider its associations with both national identity and sexuality, given the very real threat of invasion by the Armada and the fear that England's body politic would be impregnated by Spanish forces. Chapters 3 and 4 address the gesture of spitting in conjunction with two characters seen as 'outsiders' in Renaissance culture: the disabled figure of Richard III and the Jewish figure of Shylock. I argue that spitting is necessarily a 'feminizing' act, given the association of Jewish characters with female traits such as menstruation, and the need to curb what Ian Frederick Moulton terms the 'unruly masculinity' of Richard III.

Chapters 5 and 6 look at Shakespeare's Jacobean plays, *Othello* and *Macbeth*, and consider the cuckold's horns (or *cornutu*) and handwashing in relation to personal paranoia. In Chapter 5, I consider how the cuckold's horns are a feared symbol of shame in *Othello*, a symbol that undermines a husband's masculinity and standing in the community, in addition to the insecurity it breeds upon Othello as a soldier. Similarly, in Chapter 6, the study of Lady Macbeth – a soldier's wife – explores the fear of being found out. Allison P. Hobgood argues that while modern critics have focused on guilt as 'the play's master passion', to do so 'reflects a modern, post-psychoanalytic hierarchy of the passions'.[45] By considering the scene of her sleepwalking and washing her hands of the bloody deed of murder, I explore the shameful emotion of 'fear-sickness' and how symbols become slippery and uncertain upon the early Jacobean stage, given the relocation of the site of monarchical power from the iconography of Elizabeth to the emerging visual culture depicting the new authority of James. My final two chapters contend that more traditionally feminized acts, such as kneeling and passivity, take on a new power during the reign of James I. While many of the gestures discussed in this book have their roots in masculine aggression or the desire to 'feminize' unruly behaviour, this final chapter considers how shaming gestures in Jacobean drama not only incorporate more passive forms of shaming but reveal how successful such gestures can be. In Chapter 7 I examine Volumnia's act of kneeling in order to shame her son in *Coriolanus*, and in my final chapter, I reassess Hermione's stillness as a statue in *The Winter's Tale*. In both chapters, I argue for the efficacy of passive-aggression in Shakespeare's later female characters, and how their appropriation of humbling body language plays the patriarchy at its own game, calling the bluff of their would-be oppressors. In addition to providing close-readings of these gestural moments, I include wider histories of these gestures, focusing on their appearances in wider culture. I also offer mini case-studies of how these gestures have been performed in modern productions, although the examples I include in my chapters are not meant to record a full history of how these gestures have been enacted in each play's history, but rather serve to create an impression of how these scenes have been previously approached at different moments of performance.

Shakespeare's Body Language moves through his plays in a roughly chronological order, and in doing so, charts an emotional journey from pain and resentment to new beginnings and reconciliation. While my research begins with the vulgarly phallic thumb gestures, it ends with kneeling and stasis: passive movements which are designed to shame people into positive action, and are extremely effective in doing so. This book covers a head-to-toe of shaming gestures: spitting from the face, moving with the hands, and submission of the legs. It reveals a previously unseen history of how social tensions are embodied within gesticular action and how such gestures are used as a powerful form of control to humiliate others within the body politic of early modern England.

1

Thumb-biting: Performing Toxic Masculinity in *Romeo and Juliet*

Two households, both alike in dignity, in Mississippi where we lay our scene. A belligerent young upstart named Sampson has just given his rival the finger. Does he bite his thumb? No; instead, he makes a gesture that the contemporary audience can more easily recognize. So began Cornerstone Theatre's 1989 production of *Romeo and Juliet*, which modernized the play's famous gesticulatory opening salvo between the Montagues and Capulets.[1] Such an emendation is reasonably unusual. More often, the thumb-biting is retained in modern performance, with directors taking pains to alert the audience to the gravity of the Elizabethan insult. For instance, the promptbook from Peter Hall's 1947 production reads 'crowd freeze to silence' after Sampson makes the gesture.[2] Michael Boyd's version for the RSC in 2000 had Abram's enquiry into the thumb-biting spoken 'very quietly, as the scene took on a sudden deadly earnestness'.[3] And in Daniel Kramer's surrealist production for Shakespeare's Globe in 2017, the thumb-bite was pantomimically amped up, with the Montague servant recoiling backwards from the insult. This latter gesture was performed directly in front of a tableau of Lady Montague and Lady Capulet giving birth to the star-crossed lovers, implying how the children of each family are born into a pre-existing cycle of masculine violence.

Different methods of performing the thumb-bite gesture will depend on a variety of factors: whether the performance is staged indoor or outdoor, the size of the auditorium, the demographic of the audience, the stylistic expectations of a particular theatrical institution, in addition to the contextual social mores of the production and its relationship to the world of the play. For instance, if Cornerstone's 1989 production of *Romeo and Juliet* had toured to countries such as India or Pakistan, or cities such as Naples, Italy, the thumb-biting gesture would not necessarily have needed amending. The 'cutis' gesture, as it is known there, is still used today and involves 'mak[ing] a fist then flick[ing] the thumb off the front teeth'.[4] However, the history of obscene thumb gestures in general can be traced all the way back to ancient Rome. While Desmond Morris and his colleagues observe that Shakespeare does not leave any clues as to why the thumb-bite in *Romeo and Juliet* should be so provocative,[5] gestural experts such as Fritz Graf maintain that the vulgarity of using the thumb to point with is still recognizable today.[6] Often, it is not so much the gesture itself as the characters' responses to it that indicate to a modern audience the ramifications of what occurred. However, by examining the connotations of thumbs as well as the codes of public sparring, it becomes possible to unlock the gesture's underlying social assumptions. What is more, such associations reveal the potent gender politics that are coded within such gestures, provoking the consideration that such actions represent a microcosm of the wider tensions within the plays themselves.

Let us turn to the act of apparent masculine bravado in question. Walking about the streets of Verona are Samson and Gregory, servants of the house of Capulet, who soon catch sight of Abraham, a servant of the Montagues:

SAMSON

My naked weapon is out. Quarrel, I will back thee.

GREGORY

How, turn thy back and run?

SAMSON

Fear me not.

GREGORY

No, marry, I fear thee!

SAMSON

Let us take the law of our sides; let them begin.

GREGORY

I will frown as I pass by and let them take it as they list.

SAMSON

Nay, as they dare. I will bite my thumb at them, which is disgrace to them if they bear it.

ABRAHAM

Do you bite your thumb at us, sir?

(1.1.32–44)

Samson and Gregory's verbal exchanges crescendo into the enactment of the gesture, but it is worth noting that while this opening scene contains the first example of brawling within this violent play, the buildup to it is rooted in cowardice. While Samson is apparently spoiling for a fight, Gregory knows him better: as someone who will flee at the sign of any real trouble. In fact, as soon as Gregory points this out, Samson ducks behind the legal precedents for engaging in street fighting: 'let us take the law of our sides; let them begin.' Yet when Gregory offers to frown at their enemy, Samson has a better idea: to bite his thumb. Rather than openly starting a brawl, Samson's tactic is to rile up his opponent in as nondescript a way as possible by using a gesture which can be mistaken for a perfectly innocent action. His so-called virulence is far more impotent than it looks; while excited at the prospect of getting into a fight, he baulks at the possibility of actually putting his manhood on the line. Gestures are, in this sense, the shadow of action: from a distance, they may look as important, but ultimately, they lack substance.

Yet potential alterations to the thumb-biting scene are extant within the variant texts of the play before modern actors and directors even get their hands on it. The first quarto of 1597 renders the exchanges more impersonal: instead of naming the characters, the text refers to them as '1 Capulet serving-man', '2 Capulet serving-man', and '1 Montague serving-man'. There are fewer exchanges between the servants of the two houses, and less verbal quibbling.[7] In addition, by anonymizing the names, we do not get a sense of the characters as having motives in their own right as opposed to, say, the motives of their house masters. By contrast, 1599's second quarto names the men as Sampson, Gregory, and Abram, and the quarrel's linguistic pedantry creates a far more fraught scenario:

ABRAM
  Do you bite your thumbe at us, sir?
SAMP
  I do bite my thumbe, sir.
ABRA
  Do you bite your thumbe at us, sir?
SAMP
  Is the law of our side, if I say ay?
GREG
  No.
SAMP
  No, sir, I do not bite my thumbe at you, sir, but I bite
    my thumbe, sir.
GREG
  Do you quarrell sir?
ABRA
  Quarrell sir, no sir.[8]

This is where Gregory's linguistic pedantry becomes useful. Earlier on in the scene, his exchanges with Sampson appear to reveal a character who is either dense enough to take things literally ('we'll not carry coals.' 'No, for then we should be colliers' (1.1.1–2)) or over-exacting in the extreme ('I will take the wall of any man or maid of Montague's.' 'That shows thee a weak slave, for the weakest goes to the wall.' (1.1.10–13)). But as the scene progresses and the brawl brews, we see the necessity of such scrupulousness as Abraham keeps on asking, 'Do you bite your thumb at us, sir?' The repetition in the language creates a sense of the disdain reverberating between the characters, rendered more tense by the frequency of faux-polite words such as 'sir', and 'you' instead of 'thou', creating a pantomimic linguistic benefit of the doubt that thinly veils the disrespect lurking behind it. Until the sense of the gesture is ascertained, the men must remain gentle in word, if not in tone.

Such over-the-top reactions to the gesture, and the subsequent need for their deniability, emphasize how, in Renaissance England, gestures that undermined rank and status were often seen to be as insulting as a verbal obscenity.[9] This type of argument was common in Shakespeare's age, as we can see from Thomas Dekker's pamphlet *The Dead Tearme:* 'What swearing is there, what shouldering, what jostling, what jeering, what *byting of thumbs, to beget quarrels*!'[10] There were, in fact, a variety of gesticulatory ways to get on the wrong side of a Renaissance man: 'bearding, nose-tweaking, ear-boxing, gown-pulling, spitting and striking up heels' are just some of the colourful examples listed in Alexandra Shepard's book *The Meanings of Manhood in Early Modern England.*[11] There were even printed guidelines for engaging in such arguments. It is therefore not insignificant that Sampson's gesture is made in a public place, as actions such as these were supposed to occur 'on neutral territory to avoid any suspicion of advantage'.[12] According to Shepard, competitive masculinity and its inbuilt code of honour emerged as a lively and often unsettling feature of early modern society: 'violence was a vivid threat flamboyantly woven into the fabric of men's daily lives, often simply as the implicit threat suggested by bodily gestures and taunts, but nonetheless displayed as proof of strength and status in connection with a range of male identities.'[13] The opening scene of *Romeo and Juliet*, then, is very much in keeping with contemporary social mores of honour and status: Henry VII,

Henry VIII, and Elizabeth I all issued proclamations against public fighting,[14] but these measures were not enough to prevent civil disorder flaring up until the end of the century.[15] According to Lawrence Stone, 'street outbreaks persisted and the number of recorded duels and challenges jumped from five in the 1580s to nearly twenty in the 1590s.'[16] Charles Edelman correctly notes that such affrays performed on the popular stage would have been readily recognized as the sort an audience might see on the city streets,[17] and Murray J. Levith further observes that the characters at the opening of *Romeo and Juliet* act like London apprentices, with the brawl being reminiscent of a tradesmen battle.[18] Furthermore, there is a keen sense of such lower-class scuffles occurring because such people wished to imitate their betters[19]; perhaps Sampson and Gregory had seen one of Tybalt's previous swordfights and had been thrilled by the masculine bravado and street theatre that it entailed. In this way, Shakespeare presents a stark contrast between the expectation of 'two households, both alike in dignity' established in the prologue and the reality of what happens on the streets outside these houses; or, rather, he reveals both houses to be as bad as each other when it comes to incivility.

In her edition of the play, Jill L. Levenson notes that these exchanges parody the Renaissance duelling codes that underline the play as a whole:

> Samson, aware of legalities [...] does not acknowledge the object of his insult; he hesitates to make biting his thumb an official challenge [...] Abraham persists in attempting to confirm the insult, which would qualify as both a defiant challenge and an illegal act [...] Gregory sets the legal trap for Abraham, who neatly avoids it.[20]

By asking, 'do you quarrel, sir?' (1.1.50), Gregory is almost teasing Abraham; all three serving-men know that, although Abraham is clearly up for an argument, to answer 'yes' would demarcate the official beginning of a fight, which the

Montagues would have to take the blame for. This sense of fastidiousness both escalates the masculine tension and prevents outright violence from immediately occurring. The servants of the two houses are concerned with preserving honour in two seemingly contradictory ways: on the one hand, they want to prove their bravado, but on the other, they do not wish to be caught fighting in the street. It is almost a burlesque performance of masculinity, teetering between arrogance and timidity. The scene also parodies the action of gesticulation itself. The fact that the action can be misinterpreted reveals not only the shaky legal ground that the gesture's instigator stands on but also the gesture's lack of immediate clarity and consequent deniability, which is, of course, its power in such tense social situations. Indeed, John Walter's essay 'Gesturing at Authority' makes exactly this point: 'the performer of a gesture from which information is "given off" cannot be held fully responsible as to the intended meaning of the act and, if challenged, has some latitude to deny the message as wrongly received.'[21] Gestural theorist Adam Kendon also notes how insulting gestures often have a certain deniability about them in performance:

> in Germany there is a gesture in which the forefinger touches the side of the head and is rotated back and forth. It is used to mean 'he's crazy' and it is regarded as a grave insult. Its use has been the cause of fights and one may be prosecuted for performing it in public. A surreptitious version of it has appeared, however, in which the forefinger is pressed against the cheek. In this version the gesture can be performed in such a way that it could be mistaken for scratching the cheek or for pressing a tooth that was giving discomfort.[22]

This observation helps us make more sense of *Romeo and Juliet*'s opening scene, where immediately after the gesture, Sampson seeks to deny its intention to offend: 'No sir, I do not bite my thumb at you, sir, but I / bite my thumb, sir' (1.1.48–9).

This tension of pretend-politeness ('sir') reveals the capacity for an insulting gesture to be immediately translated into something seemingly nondescript.

While the *Oxford English Dictionary* is prone to listing Shakespeare as the instigator of now-common words and phrases, his inclusion of such an exchange in *Romeo and Juliet* is part of a far richer history of the usage of the thumb in gesture. And necessarily so: although Shakespeare might have some measure of responsibility for popularizing new turns of phrase, gesture cannot be immediately adapted in the same way as language. Hand signs develop and accumulate significance only very gradually through a culture's history, and while specific gestures indicating positive or negative attributes may fall in or out of fashion, the underlying implications behind them are inherently based on long-standing associations. Whether these complex gestural histories are known to those enacting them or not, they have remained in a cultural memory that spans lifetimes rather than years. Despite the fact that we no longer bite our thumbs to mark our contempt, the fact that early moderns did reveals some insightful relics of what kind of society they were a part of and which have otherwise been lost in the ephemerality of the moment.

Published in 1597, the appearance of 'to bite one's thumbs' in Shakespeare's first Quarto is preempted by two prior recorded instances in the *Oxford English Dictionary*: in J. Cranstoun's *Satirical Poems of the Time of the Reformation* in 1573 ('The Clerk was like to byte his thowmis') and in Thomas Lodge's *Wits Miserie* from 1596 ('giuing me the Fico with his thombe in his mouth').[23] The first recorded usage of 'to bring (a person) above the thumb' (in other words, to have someone under your control) was in 1464 in Paston's *Letters and Papers:* 'Thow thou can begyll the Dwk of Norfolk, and bryng hym abow[t] the thombe as thow lyst, I let the wet thow shalt not do me so.' Similarly, recorded usages of 'to hit one over the thumbs' (to punish or reprove sharply) begin in the sixteenth century. Beginning with Skelton's 'thwartyng ouer thom' in 1522, there is also a reference in *Hall's Union* from 1548, where it is used to chastise a woman: 'in the later ende of hys oracion, he a litle rebuked the lady Margaret and hyt her of... the thombes'.[24]

Because the thumb-bite is, to some degree, an archaic gesture by modern British standards, there is some debate over how exactly the movement was actually performed. Desmond Morris and his colleagues claim that perhaps the notion of thumb-biting as a gesture only extends to biting the thumbnail. Citing the seventeenth-century etiquette manual, *The Rules of Civility*, they posit:

> it would appear simply that 'to bite the thumb' is no more than a popular contraction of 'to bite the nail of your thumb', a fact often overlooked by Shakespearean actors, who tend to bite the whole of the thumb, rather than just flick the nail from behind the upper teeth.[25]

Yet Morris also equivocates by noting that the thumb-bite might be an augmented version of another obscene thumb-based gesture, the Spanish fig,

> which is generally assumed to be the same gesture. It has been interpreted as a variant form of fig-sign, with the thumb going to the mouth instead of between the fingers of the closed hand.[26]

The Spanish fig is a gesture which thrusts the thumb between the two first fingers of the same hand (for more on this gesture, see Chapter 2). It is possible that, with the hand in such a position, the thumb could then be placed in the mouth and 'bitten'. However, the 1899 Variorum edition of *Romeo and Juliet* decides to rule out this notion, scoffing that previous scholars are 'mistaken in supposing it identical with what is called *giving the fico*'.[27] G. Blakemore Evans' 1984 edition of *Romeo and Juliet* notes of the thumb-bite that '[t]here seems to have been some contemporary confusion between this phrase and "to give the fico (or fig)"'.[28] More recently, René Weis' 2012 Arden edition offers the idea that only the thumbnail is used. He cites Randle Cotgrave's 1611 *Dictionary of the French and English Tongues* to describe the gesture as 'putting the thumbnail into the mouth and with a jerk (from the upper teeth) make it to knack (that is pop)'.[29] Whether this gesture can be made audible or not will inevitably come down to performance conditions. When holding a Gesture Lab workshop in the Sam Wanamaker Playhouse at Shakespeare's Globe in August 2015, a group of actors and I staged *Romeo and Juliet*'s opening scene to observe the thumb-bite in action. Due to the intimate, indoor Jacobean theatre space and a hushed, attentive audience, we were able to *hear* the click of actor Dominic Brewer's thumbnail against his front teeth. It is unlikely that this would have been audible if performed outdoor on Shakespeare's Globe's main stage, the National Theatre's Olivier auditorium, or the Royal Shakespeare Company's main stage in Stratford-upon-Avon. However, the possibility of being able to hear the thumb-bite adds an extra element to its potential offence: even if the gesture is made at you when you aren't looking, the fact that you might be able to hear a 'tutting' sound is enough to alert you to the fact that an insult has been made.

Whichever way the thumb-bite is performed, the potency of the thumb as a social symbol dates back to ancient Rome, and its survival to the Renaissance (and arguably, to the present day) is a testament to its cultural significance. Its very linguistic roots are evocative of such a power dynamic: Isidore remarks that the thumb 'is called *pollex* because it holds sway (*polleat*) over the remaining [fingers] through its power and manly virtue'.[30] In his essay, 'Of thumbs', Montaigne traces the idea of a 'rule of thumb' as emerging from an ancient precedent:

> *Tacitus* reports, that amongst certain *Barbarian Kings*, their manner was, when they would make a firm Obligation, to joyn their hands close to one another, and

twist their Thumbs, and when by force of straining the Blood it appear'd in the ends, they lightly prick'd them with some sharp Instrument, and mutually suck'd them. *Physicians* say, that the *Thumbs* are the master Fingers of the Hand ... The *Romans* exempted from War all such as were maim'd in the Thumbs, as having no more sufficient strength to hold their Arms ... Some one, I have forgot who, having won a Naval Battel, cut off the Thumbs of all his vanquish'd Enemies, to render them incapable of fighting, and of handling the Oar ... And in *Lacedemonia, Pedagogues* chastiz'd their Scholars by biting their Thumbs.[31]

Montaigne makes it clear that there is a palpable connection between the thumb and a sense of power, particularly in his references to military might. Furthermore, his final claim that Lacedaemonian children were disciplined by having their thumbs bitten is verified by Plutarch, who refers to a 'punishement that aunswered crossely, or to litle purpose, was that his master byt him by the thumbe'.[32] Clearly, biting the most powerful digit of the hand was an effective way of asserting control and implying a hierarchy of power; and the fact that the mouth is not used for verbal chastisement, but for administering a nip to a wayward hand, creates a silent gesture of admonishment that, nevertheless, 'speaks volumes'.

The seventeenth-century gestural scholar John Bulwer also traces the history of the thumb, and he notes that 'if we see one BITE HIS THUMBE at us we soone infer he meanes us no good.'[33] Interestingly, he sees a connection between the movement of the thumb and the conveyance of an opinion. In his discussion of *collateraliter monstro* [I show both sides (of an issue)], he asserts that 'by diverse gestures of the thumb we signify the various motions of our mind'.[34] The *contemno* [I condemn] gesture he describes reveals how the thumb can express outright disdain in a manner that combines image with sound that, although far from linguistic, nevertheless conveys a significant sense of meaning: 'TO COMPRESS THE MIDDLE

FINGER WITH THE THUMB BY THEIR COMPLOSION PRODUCING A SOUND AND SO CASTING OUT OUR HAND is a gesture we use to signify our *contempt of unprofitable things* and to show, by gesture, how we *slight, contemn, insult,* and *undervalue* anything.'[35] By using the most powerful digit to suppress one of the lesser digits, the gesture symbolizes the symbolic crushing of an argument, idea, or individual. But the thumb is also used to convey positive opinion as well as negative: Bulwer's discussion of the *Approbo* [I approve] gesture describes it as 'the gesture of one *giving his voice or sufferage*, of one that *helpeth with his word at the time of election,* and of one showing his *assent* or *approbation* as Flavius Vopiscus writeth'[36] (this is essentially the same 'thumbs-up' gesture we still use today). And two thumbs were, and indeed, are, better than one, with the *Extollo* [I extol] sign of holding up both thumbs 'importing a *transcendency of praise*'.[37]

The prologue to *Romeo and Juliet* is one of the most famous openings in all of Shakespeare: 'Two households, both alike in dignity'; and yet our first meeting with these 'dignified' families, via their serving-men, involves an incredibly insulting gesture and a brawl. They are indeed 'both alike in dignity', in that they are both horribly rude to each other. Our introduction to the 'ancient grudge', as seen through the serving-men, enables a focus upon the production and replication of a tension, signified, in this case, by the thumb-bite. We never actually find out the primary cause of the feud; for all we know, it developed after a brawl between the two houses' serving-men, some of whom may have been fatally wounded and thus rendering the 'civil hands' of Montague and Capulet 'unclean' (prologue, 4). Such a hypothesis would also explain why it is only after the death of the 'star-crossed lovers' (prologue, 6) that the feud will end: while the lives of the serving-men are collateral damage, the deaths of Romeo and Juliet, as the son and daughter of Montague and Capulet, are too much to be tolerated. In other words, the animosity between the Montagues and Capulets does not merely travel in a top-down direction; it also rises up from the ranks of the non-elite to the elite that it serves.

Key to the vulgarity of the serving-men's insults is their role as lower-status citizens within the hierarchy of Verona. Such a tension reflects the dynamic between an elite, privileged ruling class, who make the rules of decorum, and a non-elite, lower class, who are marked out either by not following such rules or because they are not in a position to make such rules in the first place (note King Henry V to his bride-to-be: 'we are the makers of manners' (5.2.268–9)). Peter Burke comments that insulting acts in this period were 'a breach of the rules in one sense [but] in another sense followed rules or conventions as closely as a sonnet'.[38] Of course, shaming gestures, while breaking rules of etiquette, still adhere to the strictly coded associations of such insulting acts. In this sense, both perpetuation of etiquette and the breaching of it are two sides of the same coin: it is only in comparison with 'non-elite' characters that 'elite' characters can emerge.

Thumb-biting in plays is not limited to *Romeo and Juliet*, but it does not occur in many other surviving plays. What appears to be the only other dramatic example occurs in the anonymous *Dick of Devonshire*, where a character named Tiago exits biting his thumbs after being disarmed and tripped in a fight.[39] Lost for words, his resentment is externalized through a physical movement, which is referred to in the scene's stage direction: 'exit, biting his thumbs'. While in Shakespeare's play the thumb-biting instigates a fight, in *Dick of Devonshire* the gesture is performed when someone has lost a brawl, resorting to a gesture because his real actions have failed him. But perhaps the most important detail to note from this is that Tiago is not English, but Spanish: given that *Romeo and Juliet* is set in Verona, it seems that the thumb-bite is a gesture associated with use in continental Europe. This would explain why Sampson and Gregory need to explain the gesture's implication to its English audience ('which is disgrace to them if they bear it' (1.1.41)). It is unclear whether in *Romeo and Juliet* Shakespeare is confusing the gestures of

It is the Englishman against the foreigner (and one infatuated with foreign ways); the provincial against the metropolitan (or would-be sophisticate); the amateur against the pseudo-professional; the gentleman against the pretender or aspirant to high rank.[44]

Crucial to this is the interconnected relationship between otherness and familiarity. In his *Critique of Dialectical Reason*, Jean-Paul Sartre contends that 'I now comprehend the enemy *through myself* and myself *through the enemy*'.[45] Difference, or perhaps merely the ability to observe difference, occurs through comparison with something already familiar. What becomes unsettling about an apparent enemy, then, is their similarity to us: in attacking others, we attack what we seek to destroy within ourselves. As previously mentioned, Levith's argument links the servants' fight with the brawls which had already been occurring in London; while Shakespeare is not primarily using this scene to hold a mirror up to nature, he nevertheless draws attention to the threat of lower-class violence based on a code of masculine bravado, woven intricately into the everyday lives of his audience.

It is worth pausing here to reflect on how non-verbal communication can be associated with the non-elite. Although a variety of rhetorical handbooks detail the use of gesture in oratory, since antiquity hand signs have also been a means by which people uneducated in public speaking can get their point across. At least three surviving Roman documents cite a gesture known as *infestus pollex*, or, the hostile thumb.[46] This gesture appears to have been an action made by plebeians, since Quintilian notes that 'pointing out something with the thumb turned back I regard as accepted rather than really appropriate for an orator'.[47] For Quintilian, 'the hostility of the thumb in the upright position resides in its uninhibited erectness',[48] linking the crudeness of the digit with the vulgar masses as opposed to a refined elite. Given this, Sampson's thumb-biting – and Abram's reaction to it – begins to make more sense as a powerful gesture of insult. Noting an ongoing phallic association, Henk Driessen argues that out of the various ways to insult men, '[t]he most serious and powerful ones all involve gestured phallic obscenities'.[49] Bulwer describes an upright thumb protruding from a closed fist as 'a grave masculine action fit to advance the sense of *magnanimity*'.[50] This reveals how appropriate the gesture is after the scene's beginning, filled as it is with the threat of violence and phallic innuendo in the form of naked weapons and pretty pieces of flesh. Indeed, the play's opening scene moves swiftly between aggressive sexuality and masculine violence:

GREGORY

> To move is to stir, and to be valiant is to stand;
> therefore, if thou art moved, thou runn'st away.

SAMSON

> A dog of that house shall move me to stand. I will take the wall of any man or maid of Montague's.

GREGORY

> That shows thee a weak slave, for the weakest goes to the wall.

SAMSON

> 'Tis true, and therefore women, being the weaker vessels, are ever thrust to the wall; therefore I will push Montague's men from the wall and thrust his maids to the wall.

GREGORY

> The quarrel is between our masters and us their men.

SAMSON

> 'Tis all one. I will show myself a tyrant; when I have fought with the men, I will be civil with the maids, I will cut off their heads.

(1.1.8–22)

Here, the scene moves uncannily between potent male sexuality and the threat of gendered violence. Perhaps then, an erect thumb being bitten – implicitly linking sex with violence – was the same kind of affront to masculinity that the *infestus pollex* would have been. The thumb as a signifier of masculinity within the context of fighting and bravado also reveals how the *infestus pollex* is inextricably connected with the use of the thumb in the gladiatorial arena, where it was used to point contemptuously.[51] Despite various Hollywood portrayals of a 'thumbs down' gesture resulting in a gladiator being killed and a 'thumbs up' gesture in being spared, Gregory S. Aldrete argues that 'the ancient sources, while confirming that some gesture involving turning the thumbs was used, are vague concerning the precise nature of this gesture', and asserts the plausibility that the 'thumbs down' gesture, in this context, would have signalled the gladiator's life being spared.[52] Anthony Corbeill concurs with this assessment, arguing that 'the erect threat of an upraised thumb requests the deathblow'.[53] The image of an upright thumb can be seen to represent the triumph of manly might through the unimpeded extension of the most powerful digit. To bite it, therefore, is to undermine the most potent symbol of another's masculinity; performing this is an act of bravado which ultimately states that the gesticulator has the upper hand.

The distance between the composition of Shakespeare's play and a modern, post-twentieth-century audience means that the gesture takes on new elements in performance. When we start to look at film adaptations of the opening scene, we see how readily the pantomime of civility sits alongside the imminent threat of violence; in fact, Levith argues that the argument and fight are centred around 'the low comedy of physical action'.[54] Certainly, George Cukor's film production from 1936 adheres to this interpretation, although the film makes some substantial deviations from the original text. Cukor has the comic character of Peter, the servant to Juliet's nurse, instigate the thumb-biting and subsequent brawl. He initially makes the gesture while the two houses parade about the streets of Verona and is chastised by the nurse (to the delight of the Montagues). Once out of line, he walks past them again, making the same gesture; when questioned, he turns the gesture into a babyish thumb suck, again to the amusement of the other household:

the implication is that he is evidently not 'man enough' to develop the gesture into a more violent *action*.

In 1968, Franco Zeffirelli's film changed the gesture so that the thumb was not actually bitten at all: Sampson moves the thumb towards his mouth and then spits in the path of the Montagues. This interpolation attempts to combine something of the original gesture with an insulting movement that a 1960s audience would more easily recognize. While it succeeds in that the audience get a sense of the slight implied, the inclusion of spitting is certainly not suggested by Shakespeare's text or acknowledged in gestural history sources. However, when a film such as *West Side Story* is only *based* on the original text, physical movements can be updated with far greater license. The opening four minutes of the film contain no dialogue: instead, carefully choreographed movement is used to define the rivalry between the two gangs, the Jets and the Sharks. Finger clicking, basketball moves, dance, gesture, and facial expression are all interpolated to create a sense of wordless intimidation. In the original book of *West Side Story*, the Jets 'flick [Bernardo] off. He returns with other Sharks: they, too, are flicked off'.[55] The book also notes that '[t]he beginnings of warfare are mild at first: a boy being tripped up, or being sandbagged with a flour sack, or even being spit on – all with overly elaborate apologies'.[56] An actual fight between the gangs only erupts when Bernardo pierces A-rab's ear with his fingers,[57] to brand him with a stereotypical Puerto-Rican ear-piercing.

More fraught, however, is Baz Luhrmann's *Romeo+Juliet* (1996), where 'swords' are a make of gun, and the young men scream their lines at each other and then use mock-restraint to add on a demure 'sir' at the end. The whole scene feels almost cartoonishly immature, with the thumb-bite itself resembling a child pulling a face, which is more than enough to infuriate the previously sleek Capulets. The episode almost feels like a playground fight; except, of course, that these boys have guns. As the scene increases in danger, the tone is all the tenser for the serious ramifications emerging from such a childish slight. But as Judith Buchanan observes, it is a puerile fight that is intelligently done: the resulting shoot-out pastiches both Sergio Leone-style spaghetti Westerns 'and the stylish fight choreography of a John Woo film'.[58]

Luhrmann's is not the only production that includes contemporary allusions to create a useful shorthand for an audience who may not understand the ramifications of Elizabethan codes of conduct and insult. In Michael Bogdanov's staged production for the RSC in 1986–1987, a fight between Mercutio and Tybalt only escalated into genuine rage once Mercutio deliberately scratched Tybalt's Alfa Romeo.[59] A similar endeavour to help the viewer acknowledge the cause of the fight resulted in Franco Zeffirelli (1968) actively rewriting the actions of the scene: on his line, 'you lie', Abram actually walks away from the fight the Capulets are trying to instigate. When his foes hit the legs of an elderly man with a stick and run off laughing, it is then that Abram – a Montague, not a Capulet – cries, 'Draw, if you be men.' In this instance, it is not the insult of the gesture but the immaturity of the Capulets that angers the Montagues into participating in a brawl.

Of course, the thumb-bite is far from being the only pivotal scene involving hands in this play. As Farah Karim-Cooper points out, 'Shakespeare presents to us what it means to love at first *touch*.'[60] In 1.5, Romeo and Juliet's shared sonnet acclimatizes us to how Capulet and Montague hands may be used in acts of love rather than violence:

ROMEO
    If I profane with my unworthiest hand
    This holy shrine, the gentle sin is this:
    My lips, two blushing pilgrims ready stand
    To smooth that rough touch with a tender kiss.
JULIET
    Good pilgrim, you do wrong your hand too much,
    Which mannerly devotion shows in this,
    For saints have hands that pilgrims' hands do touch,
    And palm to palm is holy palmers' kiss.

(1.5.92–101)

Romeo's claim that his hand is 'unworthiest' and capable of 'rough touch' recalls the fisticuffs which occurred the last time two members of these rival households met. Here, the hands of Montague and Capulet meet each other, palm-to-palm in a lipless kiss, and while this is evidently a gesture of love rather than violence, the sexual overtones conveyed by the hands in the first scene remain in play. Karim-Cooper argues that

> [t]ouching a woman's palm was a far more intimate and erotic gesture than it is now understood to be. It was an expression of telling intimacy: the palm of the hand is… the place where the inner secrets of a life reside; it is also the part of the hand that has a very different texture to the dorsal or outer surface of the hand, being soft and sweaty or 'moist'.[61]

But while the shared sonnet is couched in the language of religious devotion, there is less innocence than we might expect from these pilgrims. Told to 'move not while my prayer's effect I take' (1.5.105), Juliet is very much the 'weaker vessel', as we saw women described by Samson in 1.1.15. The sheer intimacy of these two moist, warm hands touching shows that while the exchanges between the two houses, as in scene one, are civil in tone, raw sexuality in the form of masculine bravado is a key element of the atmosphere. Indeed, Romeo is being civil with this maid, but he will cut off her head, both in terms of taking her virginity and being ultimately responsible for her death.

Romeo and Juliet's opening scene encapsulates the essential motivations and actions which Romeo performs in the tragedy: fucking and killing. From the very beginning, his love (and lust) is 'death-marked' (prologue, 9). But the play's feud ends in one final action of touch between Capulet and Montague:

CAPULET
> O brother Montague, give me thy hand.
> This is my daughter's jointure, for no more
> Can I demand.
>
> (5.3.296–8)

This gesture of reconciliation, performed as a sombre conclusion to the play's whirlwind of violence, sex, and yet more violence, offers a moment between the two houses which calls for healing, reflection, and mutual respect. It serves as an open acknowledgement of joint responsibility, merging the symbolic blood on the parents' hands. The handshake is a world away from the play's opening scene: whereas the thumb-bite is performed with the possibility of deniability, the handshake accepts culpability and a shared social obligation. Toxic masculinity had previously shaped the men of this play into repeating a pattern of machismo and sexualized violence, but the conclusion shows us a world where despite society's potent pressure on male performance, redemption from these expectations is possible, albeit at a high cost.

2

Figging: Spanish Anxieties and *Ancient* Grudges in Pistol's *Henriad*

It's 2014, in no less apparently reverend a Shakespearean town than Stratford-upon-Avon, and the Royal Shakespeare Company are staging *2 Henry IV*. A bombastic soldier, rough round the edges and given to explosive bursts of braggadocio, exclaims the line 'When Pistol lies, do this, and fig me, like / The bragging Spaniard' (5.3.115–16). At this point, the part's actor, Anthony Byrne, enacts the pretence of roughly sodomizing himself with the pistol he is holding. The scene is vulgarly unambiguous: in the world of this production, to fig is to fuck.

However, John Bulwer describes the fig gesture as being somewhat different, referring to it as 'improbitatem objicio' (see Figure 2's gesture plate). Bulwer writes in *Chirologia*:

> TO LOCKE THE THUMBE BETWEENE THE NEXT TWO FINGERS, is an *ironicall* vulgarisme of the *Hand* used by Plebeians when they are contumeliously provoked thereunto, and see that they cannot prevaile by vieing words, their spleene appealing to their *Fingers* for aid, who thus armed for a dumbe *retort,* by this *taunting* gesture seem to say *avant*. This position of the *Fingers* with the Ancients

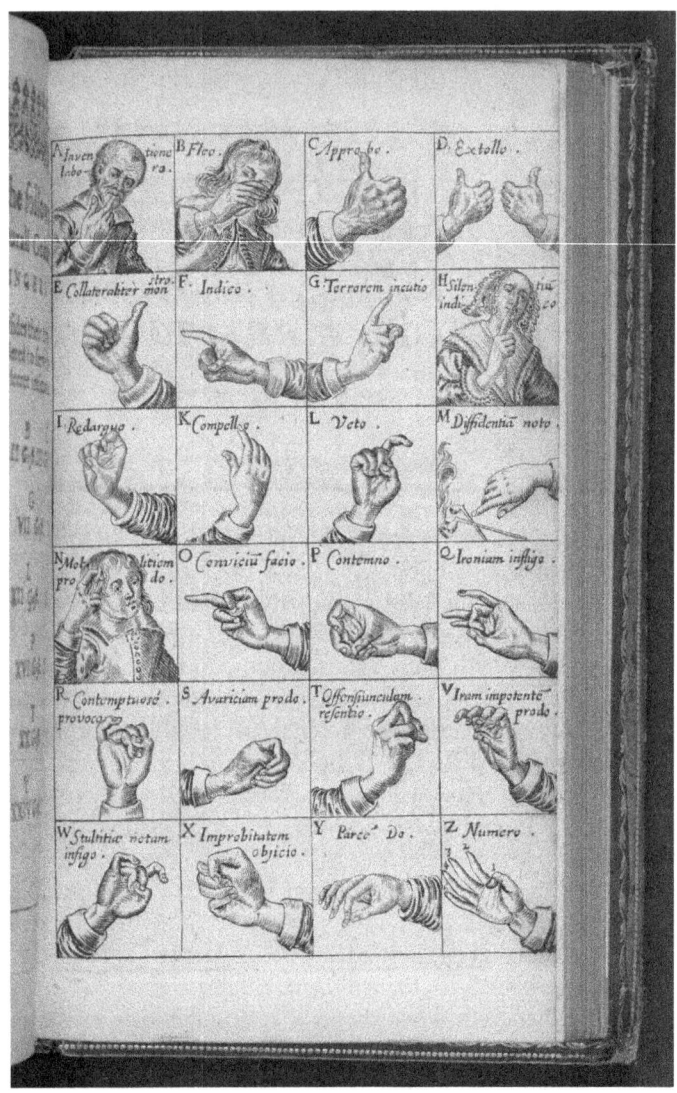

FIGURE 2 *Gesture plate, featuring 'improbitatem objicio' and 'Stultitiae notam infigo', from John Bulwer's* Chirologia *and* Chironomia, *1644, 189. © The British Library Board.*

was called *Higa,* and the moderne Spaniards by objecting the *Hand* formed to this *reproachfull* expression, imply as much as if they should say *paedicavi te,* as is usually their garb who *mock* little children.[1]

This seventeenth-century description of figging confirms the use of the gesture as being shaming or dismissive, and also links the gesture with the Spanish, who would use the fig as an apotropaic gesture to ward off the evil eye.[2] Clearly, it was an action rich in associations during the early modern period, so why was it amended in this 2014 performance?

It is sensible to assume that the gesture may have been changed because a 2014 audience would not necessarily know the reference or understand the action's meaning. However, in context, the line is fairly comprehensive; why then go to such trouble to not only amend the gesture but significantly amplify it into something far more overtly vulgar? If the reasoning behind this gestural revision was that a thumb gesture would be too small to be seen in the RSC's auditorium, then one wonders if that would have also been a problem for the scene's first performances. The original fig gesture would have been performed in an outdoor Elizabethan theatre containing at least as many people, if not more, than the RSC's capacity; the Globe is said to admit more than 3,000 people before it burned down in 1613. Admittedly, most performances would have had far fewer attendees, with the playhouse only at full capacity for special performances. Nevertheless, fluctuating audience figures do not amend the actual size and design of the playhouse. Modelled on the bear-baiting houses offering rival forms of entertainment, theatres such as the Globe had three levels of galleries in addition to standing room in the yard, with the Globe itself estimated to have covered nearly 2,500 square feet.[3] Given this, a gesture such as a Spanish fig, like the thumb-bite, would almost certainly not be clearly visible to all members of the audience. However, as I argued in the previous chapter, the possibility of *missing* such gestures was something that might add to their potential effect. The fact that such movements could be denied after their performance was all to the good, for it meant that should the gesture provoke a fight, the instigator of the gesture could claim that he had never made such a gesture in the first place and that he had been attacked without provocation.

The fig gesture is repeated by Pistol in *Henry V* ('The fig of Spain!' (3.6.58)), and it is evidently an action he reverts to at crucial moments. But why does this matter so much? It does so primarily because Pistol was a much more crucial character to the play's earliest audiences than he appears to be today. His name appears on the title page of the play's first quarto printing, which reads 'THE CRONICLE History of Henry the fift, With his battell fought at *Agin Court* in *France*. Togither with *Auntient Pistoll*'.[4] Perhaps with the dispatch of the popular Falstaff, whose death is revealed at the start of *Henry V*, Pistol was expected to fill the gap of a rambunctious, posturing figure, whose actions would serve as a foil to the better-born characters. It is also his graduation to becoming the husband of Mistress Quickly and to the role of the ensign (or *ancient*) within the English army which marks him out as noteworthy. The ensign was the lowest-ranking member of the officer class, with his role being that of the standard-bearer in battle. Essentially, this meant that he was the literal protector of his nation's visual identity in the face of the enemy. So when Pistol uses another kind of visual signifier – the Spanish fig gesture – its meaning becomes all the more charged. Are Pistol's signs all that they appear, or are there more troubling and subversive meanings behind them?

In this chapter, then, my exploration of *2 Henry IV* and *Henry V* interrogates the Spanish associations of the fig gesture, examining the wider ramifications such actions might have in evoking gendered humiliation and sexual violence. Such a fear would have been made all the more potent by the fact that an unmarried virgin queen was governing the country at a time when England was paranoid about impregnation and contamination by that feared foreign body: the Spanish Armada. This discussion will then lead to a consideration of the use of shaming gestures by the non-elite members of society, such as soldiers like Pistol: people who have little real political power, who can merely gesture towards the wider international tensions prevalent within their social worlds. Through this approach, I shall show how Shakespeare's plays depict not only the heads of state but the hands used to carry out their instructions. His inclusion of these gestures within his plays reveals an important concern about the operation and perpetuation of power in the hands of the ruling classes, performed at the expense of the soldiers and servants, who are coerced into propping up a system that actively limits their freedom.

Critics such as Nicholas Grene have argued that Pistol is the most 'straightforward' of the Eastcheap characters who go off to fight in France.[5] But this assessment should be problematized given that we seem to have collectively forgotten to consider how his gestures mark him out as having Spanish qualities, which become all the more troublesome in the context of the late 1590s. Let us turn to the scene in *Henry V* where Pistol makes the fig gesture at Fluellen, the Welsh captain. There are noteworthy differences between the first quarto text of 1600 and the Folio text of 1623, and I would argue that these are in keeping with the other emendations between the two texts. The quarto version is more explicitly vulgar:

Pist. [Pistol]
[715] Die and be damned, and figa for thy friendship.

Flew. [Fluellen]
[716] That is good.

Pist. [Pistol]
[717] The figge of *Spaine* within thy Iawe.

Flew. [Fluellen]
[718] That is very well.

Pist. [Pistol]
[719] I say the fig within thy bowels and thy durty maw.[6]

This version of the scene connects the fig gesture with the belief that Spaniards would poison their enemies using figs, given the obscene image of the fig being within the mouth, then being swallowed, and eventually ending up in the bowels. It may even reference the legend of Barbarossa, who in 1162 humiliated the defeated Milanese army by forcing the captives to pull figs out of the anus of a mule by their teeth. Perhaps the connotations of Barbarossa's punishment are also referenced in the opening lines of Ben Jonson's *The Alchemist*, where the ironically named Subtle argues with Face:

SUBTLE
   What to do? Lick figs out at my –
FACE
   Rogue, rogue, out of all your sleights.

(1.1.3–4)

This scene's beginning, rooted in a vulgar argument between two servants, echoes the tensions of the opening of *Romeo and Juliet* between other non-elite men, and these lines show a clear desire to fight for masculine control of a situation which lies beyond their grasp as lower-class characters. Perhaps then, the 'durty maw' in the quarto scene of *Henry V* is a reference to the idea of Fluellen biting the fig from the anus of a mule as punishment for what Pistol perceives to be his cowardice. However, the Folio version of the scene curtails any explicit scatological elements:

PIST [Pistol]
   Dye, and be dam'd, and Figo for thy friendship.
FLU [Fluellen]
   It is well.
PIST [Pistol]
   The Figge of Spaine.[7]

At first glance, it may seem odd that the first quarto, which expunges many elements in the play that would otherwise cause offence, should contain such a moment of obvious vulgarity. But, in fact, its appearance here actually reinforces the narrative of the first quarto. With the 1600 text cutting the choruses, references to Essex and Ireland, and collusions between the church and the crown, it attempts to cover its tracks from causing political offence. Why not, then, increase the obscene references to the feared Spanish and their unruly gestures in an attempt to display a greater sense of patriotism in the face of a barbarous Other?

At this time of national anxiety, the theatre was actively involved in shaping how power was received, and particularly its relationship to and engagement with the Other. Steven Mullaney observes of the two *Henry IV* plays that they

> reveal not a celebration of Tudor myths of power but rather a dramatic exploration of the ways in which that power was currently engaging residual, emergent, and otherwise strange cultures: bringing them under the scrutiny of its gaze, even actively rehearsing and participating in them, shaping its own rites of passage by passing *through* its cultural Others – incorporating certain aspects of the strange, making them familiar and absorbing them into the dominant culture, while radically rejecting or suppressing others.[8]

This awareness of Others within the English body politic, and its representation on the early modern stage, is also noted by Eric Griffin. His study, *English Renaissance Drama and the Specter of Spain*, argues that the literary boom of early modern England occurs at the same time as the country's conflict with Spain.[9] He argues that the citizens of the Elizabethan era were acutely aware of international tensions:

> [f]eeling the pressures of their historical moment, with its military conscriptions, refugee movements, dearth, and rumo[u]r, Elizabethans would have turned to the theat[re] not only for entertainment or relief but also to help them, as a community, to make sense of the times in which they lived, to interpret the challenges their world presented, and to understand the nature of the enemies they faced. In the process,

the Elizabethan theat[re] played a substantial role in conveying to the English a sense of who 'the Spaniard' was, in convincing them of his designs on their nation, and in inculcating Black Legend assumptions as representing historical truth.[10]

Such responses to the Other can be viewed within Elizabethan England's response to outside threats. The English not only replicate the fig gesture upon the popular stage but, in 1591 and 1592, a tract entitled *A Fig for the Spaniard* was published and sponsored by Elizabeth's government, turning the gesture of their enemy against them, and appropriating a piece of Spanish culture out of fear that the Armada may invade their own nation.[11] Containing the 'lively portra[ying of] the damnable deeds, miserable murders, and monstrous massacres of the cursed Spaniard', the text both highlights and perpetuates the 'stranger crisis' of the late sixteenth century, at the precise moment when Shakespeare emerges as a playwright.[12] Other depictions of the Spanish in this period, such as Edward Daunce's *A Brief Discourse of the Spanish State* (1590), describe 'The naturall Spaniard, being ... mixed with the Gothes and Vandals, [and is] given to theevery and drunkenness'.[13] Shakespeare's creation, then, of Pistol as a thief and a drunk, prone to fig gestures and bursts of bombast, aligns him with contemporary racial profiling of the Spanish character, and the triumphant scene where Fluellen forces Pistol to eat a welsh leek can be seen to represent the desire for the British to get their own back upon an outsider more prone to giving his enemies figs to chew on. To build on my quotation of Sartre from Chapter 1 ('I now comprehend the enemy through myself and myself through the enemy'), Pistol's place within the English army becomes complicated by his gestural tics. For all his bravado (or, perhaps even because of it), his choice of gesture marks him out as a particularly troubling presence.

To be sure, Pistol's linguistic choices as well as his gestures also mark him out for scrutiny. It may not be coincidental that the word 'foutre' is used by both the ensign and Katherine, the French princess, despite their obvious disparity in social status. Pistol's outburst 'A foutre for the world and worldlings base!' (*2H4*, 5.3.96) appears a few lines before he mentions being figged 'like / the bragging Spaniard' (*2H4*, 5.3.115–16), and the word comes up again in *Henry V* during Katherine's English lesson:

KATHERINE
Ainsi dis-je, d'elbow – de nick, *et* de sin.
  Comment appelez-vous le pied et la robe?
ALICE
De foot, *madame*, et de coun.
KATHERINE
De foot, *et* de coun? *O Seigneur Dieu, ils sont les mots de son mauvais, corruptible, gros, et impudique, et non pour les dames d'honneur d'user.*

(3.4.44–9)

Katherine's confusion between 'foot' and '*foutre*', and the bawdy use of the French word punning on 'fuck', connects her with Pistol; both of them can be seen to be tainted by foreign elements. While such foreignness is to be expected of Katherine, it is damning in a character fighting on the side of the English. The '*foutre*', when spoken by a character or deployed through a gesture, such as a fig, is a tic or a clue that the character in question has something that marks him or her out as potentially non-English, or at the very least, on the wrong side of national trustworthiness.[14] The irony, of course, is that 'foutre' can and *is* mistaken for the English word 'foot'; in this sense, attempts at the construction of national identity and difference go both ways. These thumb gestures, then, can be seen as a shorthand for characters whose foreignness we must keep a wary eye on. Such gestures are incorporated by Shakespeare into the performance to signal something particular about their enactors; they become a signifier for a more barbarous way of living in the same way that wearing a crown operates as being the theatrical signifier for a king.

In Renaissance drama, a fig is often evoked at a moment of tension during a scene. Richard Barnfield's *A New Tragicall Comedie of Apius and Virginia* (published in 1575) includes the line 'A Fygge for his vncourtesie, / That seekes to shun good company'; George Wapull's *The Tyde Taryeth No Man* (published 1576) features 'Tush a figge for him, let him doe what he can'; Christopher Marlowe's *Edward II* (pub. 1594) has the King say 'then a Fig for all my vnckles frienship'; and Robert Wilson's *The Three Ladies of London* (published 1584) uses the dismissive 'Tush a figge for honestie'. Other examples linking the fig specifically with Spain include Thomas Dekker's 1607 *The Famous History of Sir Thomas Wyatt* ('a figge for the Spaniards'), Thomas Heywood's 1636 *A Challenge for Beautie* ('And so a Figge for Spaine'), James Shirley's *The Maid's Revenge* from 1639 ('I care not a Spanish fig what you count me'), and two different plays by John Webster: *The White Devil* in 1622 ('I doe looke now for a Spanish fig') and *The Duchess of Malfi* in 1623 ('a spanish figge for the imputation'). There is also a mention of a fig in *Arden of Faversham* (1592), where Will, a murderer and former soldier, says '"Preserved" – a fig!' (9.144). The Newgate Calendar refers to him as 'Black Will' and details his love of sack and sugar, further confirming this fig-user as someone who, like Pistol, might frequent similar locations to the Eastcheap tavern. Further intriguing fig references can be found in another Shakespeare play, *Othello*, when Iago refers to the notion of virtue as a fig (1.3.320); I will return to this point at this chapter's conclusion.

A 'fig' is invoked at a less tense, although still laddish, occasion in *2 Henry VI*, when Horner toasts his serving man, saying 'a fig for Peter' (2.3.67). Horner, like Pistol, also has a military connection: he is an armourer. The word's usage is therefore consistent with characters presenting bombastic bravado in a military context, where the body and its gestures are a particularly pertinent site for the presentation and examination of masculinity. For instance, we may also consider Armado the Spanish braggart in *Love's Labour's Lost*, who comments on Moth that '[h]e is not quantity enough for that Worthy's thumb' (5.1.122–3). While not referring to a gesture *per se*, Armado's use of the thumb to signify that someone is small and ineffective is in keeping with the fig gesture's use as a means of insulting someone's manhood. Such a culture of performative masculinity in the military cultivates the

FIGURE 3 *Jan Sanders Van Hemessen,* Die Verspottung Christi, *painting, 1544. Credit: Bavarian State Painting Collections. Photo courtesy of Wikimedia under Creative Commons Attribution-Share Alike 4.0 International (https://creativecommons.org/licenses/by-sa/4.0/deed.en).*

need to live up to certain gendered expectations in terms of bravado and the maintenance of honour; failure to meet these expectations creates loss of honour and the need for rebuking or teasing. This results in the production of internal shame: a feeling that one has failed to live up to the required standards of society's expectations.

Other examples connecting fig gestures with a sense of shame derive from biblical sources. Various Renaissance artists depict figs being performed during the mocking of Christ. In Figure 3, the Dutch painter Jan Sanders Van Hemessen (*c*.1504–1575) presents us with people performing gestures towards Christ as he prepares to be crucified, with two children in the bottom right-hand corner also keen to join in with the abuse. One of these children is performing the fig gesture, while others leer at Christ with their tongues, teeth, and hands. The painting offers us a profound sense of the claustrophobia of the shaming process, with Christ surrounded on all sides by mocking and jeering. Christ is crossing his left arm over his body as if to protect himself from the influx of humiliation, and he averts his eyes from the men crowding him; to look directly into the faces of his tormentors might be too emotionally painful, but such a gaze also implies a level of appropriate humility.

Flemish artist Frans Franken II (*c*.1581–1642) created similar scenes. In this oil on copper image (Figure 4), a man carrying a cap with a feather holds up a fig gesture in front of Christ, who gazes away from the offending action. The other figures around the gesticulating man provide reactions to both Jesus and the gesture itself. A larger man to the left of the gesticulator is pointing towards the insult aimed at Christ, and a man to the left of him points towards Christ. In this example, Christ once again refuses to meet the eyes of the crowd; but unlike in Hemessen's painting, here Christ is looking up towards Heaven as if literally willing himself to rise above such earthly degradation. Of course, as the son of God, he is already elevated by his divine status; so while these paintings are useful to us in providing visual examples of figging and shaming, they do not replicate the social dynamic

FIGURE 4 *Frans Franken II,* The Mocking of Christ, *oil on copper, c.1581–1642. Credit: Private Collection Photo © Christie's Images/ Bridgeman Images.*

between Pistol and his companions. But Franken's artwork draws attention not only to the shamed Christ but also to the shameful actions of the mob surrounding him. While Christ's body is alabaster white, with a halo around his head as he looks up to heaven, the viewer's eye is nevertheless drawn down the diagonal line of a raised arm, belonging to a man in the bottom right of the picture. This individual is learning upon Christ's pedestal, in a stance reminiscent of a groundling leaning upon an amphitheatre's scaffold. There is a real sense of drama in this picture, particularly in the fact that if this is a performance – with Christ as leading man – it is going badly.

The origin of the fig's association with shame can be traced back to the biblical Fall of Man. Before eating the fruit of the tree of knowledge, Adam and Eve 'were both naked, the man and his wife, and they were not ashamed' (Genesis 2.25).[15] After tasting of the fruit,

> the eyes of them both were opened, and they knew that they were naked, and they sewed fig tree leaves together, and made themselves breeches.
>
> Afterward they heard the voice of the Lord God walking in the garden in the cool of the day, and the man and his wife hid themselves from the presence of the Lord God among the trees of the garden.
>
> But the Lord God called to the man, and said unto him, Where art thou?
>
> Who said, I heard thy voice in the garden and was afraid: because I was naked, therefore I hid myself.
>
> (Genesis 3.7–10)

As we see from this passage, Adam and Eve literally use the leaves of a fig tree to cover up the parts of their bodies associated with shamefulness. This is depicted in an oil on canvas painting by Pol de Limbourg (Figure 5), which shows the Fall and Expulsion from Eden. In it, we see the naked and unaware Adam and Eve picking and tasting the fruit, before departing the picture on the right-hand side, disgraced, and with fig leaves covering their genitalia. Kenneth Clark's study on the nude figure in art cites this particular painting as an example of how, post-Fall, the human body 'ceased to be the mirror of divine perfection and became an object of humiliation and shame'.[16] Writing from a philosophical

FIGURE 5 *Limbourg brothers, 'The fall and the expulsion from Paradise', from* Très Riches Heures du Duc de Berry, *vellum, 1415–1416. Credit: Condé Museum. Courtesy of Wikimedia (https://commons.wikimedia.org/wiki/File:Limbourg_brothers_-_The_Fall_ and_the_Expulsion_from_Paradise_-_WGA13035.jpg).*

perspective, J. David Velleman also considers the expulsion from Eden as the moment when genitals became humiliating body parts: '[t]he genitals became shameful, I suggest, when they became private ... our creation myth traces the origin of shame to the nakedness of our first ancestors'.[17] As I discussed in Chapter 1, the thumb's erectness resulted in the belief in the digit's inherent vulgarity. This is a connotation which can also be carried over into the thumb's deployment in the fig gesture, although it is also thought that the fig can be said to resemble the female pudenda (which derives from the Latin, meaning 'thing to be ashamed of'). The fig, then, not only resembles human genitalia but also recalls the fig leaves used to cover humanity's first experience of shame.

There are also specific references to the fig gesture from another religious story, although one written during the Renaissance period itself. Dante's *The Divine Comedy* features a character called Vanni Fucci, whom we meet in Cantos 24 and 25 of the *Inferno*. There is a special place in Hell reserved for Fucci, who spent his life as a thief, and admits to stealing holy objects from the chapel of an Italian cathedral. Yet down in the Inferno, he remains defiant, and at the start of Canto 25, he makes a familiar gesture:

> As his words ended, so the robber threw
> Both hands and both their figs up and he roared:
> 'Take that, God, for they are aimed at you.'[18]

William Blake even depicts this episode in his series of watercolour illustrations of Dante's epic poem (Figure 6). However, the connection between Dante and Shakespeare extends further. Not only is Fucci similar to Pistol in his gestures and sense of defiance, but both are involved with looting places of religious worship. When Pistol makes his fig at Captain Fluellen in *Henry V* ('The fig of Spain!' (3.6.58)), it is because the Captain refuses to pardon his friend Bardolph, who has apparently stolen a pax from a French church. Similarly, in the Canto preceding Fucci's figs, the Italian confesses that

> I'm here in this great depth because I stole
> The goodly furnishings of the sacristy,
> And others falsely bore the blame on their soul[.][19]

FIGURE 6 *William Blake,* Vanni Fucci 'Making Figs' against God *(1824–1827), illustration for* The Divine Comedy *by Dante Alighieri (Inferno XXV, 1-15), pen and ink and watercolour over pencil and traces of black chalk, with sponging, 52.7 × 37.2 cm (sheet) (National Gallery of Victoria, Melbourne, Felton Bequest, 1920 (1005– 1003)).*

Even Pistol's name is a connection with Fucci, who hails from the town of Pistoia, where pistols were originally manufactured. These uncanny links not only reveal Shakespeare's clear knowledge of Fucci's story in *The Divine Comedy*: it has the potential to cast 3.6 of *Henry V* in a whole new light. Bardolph may well have been innocent of the crime in question, with Pistol – the real thief – intervening out of guilt lest his friend be punished unfairly. Read in this way, Pistol's use of the fig gesture reveals more about his own shame, with the insulting action resulting from the knowledge that he cannot save his friend without telling the truth and condemning himself. The fig, then, becomes simultaneously a symbol of aggression and cowardice, both self-preserving and self-loathing. In 3.6, the fig gesture represents Pistol's distinct lack of action to intervene and save his friend's life by admitting his own shame.

Also crucial to the dramatic efficacy of Pistol's gestural altercation is the class tension between him and the person

FIGURE 7 *View of the Sistine Chapel ceiling painted by Michelangelo di Lodovico Buonarroti Simoni (1475–1564). Photo by: Universal History Archive/UIG via Getty Images.*

he is arguing with, Captain Fluellen. Earlier on in the scene, Pistol speaks to his superior with due reverence: 'Captain, I thee beseech to do me favours. / The Duke of Exeter doth love thee well' (3.6.20–1). However, the flattery has no effect on Fluellen, who rejects Pistol's plea. As an inferior soldier, there is nothing more Pistol can do in this situation: the vexation consequently comes out in the form of a vulgar gestural insult. Such frustration is similarly vented in a small detail of a fresco painting in the Sistine chapel, featured among Michelangelo's 'irreverent putti'. Figure 7 shows the image of the prophet Zechariah being taunted by two young boys who make a fig gesture behind his back; however, Michelangelo modelled his Zechariah on Pope Julius, a man disliked for his unkindness.[20] It seems that Michelangelo had been treated poorly by Julius, whose 'authoritarian brusqueness' humiliated the artist on a daily basis.[21] In the fresco, Michelangelo does not get the last word as such, but at least he gets this visual taunt: a rebuking gesture performed simultaneously behind Julius' back and in plain sight on the chapel ceiling.

The symbolism of social hierarchy can even be found within the digits of the hand itself. In his book *The Hand: A Philosophical Inquiry into Human Being,* Raymond Tallis urges that the thumb's freedom of movement in comparison with the fingers gives it powerful sway over the rest of the hand:

> The thumb can be moved in many more directions than the other fingers, so that he can speak to them all, and they can all speak to him, but they cannot speak to each other. If, then, the thumb is the ring-master, it is because he is the only digit able to relate to all the others and, what is more, in an asymmetrical fashion. Tip-to-tip contact with the other digits seems reciprocal; but when it is a question of side-to-side, the thumb seems to be the toucher, controlling the pressure, and the other finger the touched.[22]

As well as presenting an anthropological argument for the social significance of thumbs, the language Tallis uses, deliberately or not, underlines the prior arguments for the specific power that gesture literally embodies. Firstly, he refers to the thumb as 'he', rather than 'it', reinforcing a gender hierarchy; and secondly, he describes the fingers as 'speaking' to each other, even though their very curiosity lies in their literal dumbness. Furthermore, if the thumb is the master of the hand, 'biting' it or crushing it between fingers as a fig is a symbol of overthrowing a higher authority, which is precisely what Pistol wishes to achieve in this scene. Since he cannot, the gesture serves as a metaphor for what he desires to happen.

But social tensions are replicated on a far larger scale, and this is why Pistol needs a voice (or a hand): because so many others in his position (or even worse) do not. National identity is the subject of Benedict Anderson's *Imagined Communities: Reflections on the Origin and Spread of Nationalism*. In it, he describes a nation as 'an imagined political community',[23] explaining that

> it is imagined as a *community*, because, regardless of the actual inequality and exploitation that may prevail in each, the nation is always conceived as a deep, horizontal comradeship. Ultimately it is this fraternity that makes it possible, over the last two centuries, for so many millions of people, not so much to kill, as willingly to die for such limited imaginings.[24]

I would argue that such processes extend back further than two centuries – in fact, all the way back to the early modern period. The act of dying for one's country upholds an exploitative elite. In this sense, perhaps military desertion is not cowardice, but political astuteness performed by those not so readily taken in by nationalist rhetoric. Soldiers such as Pistol may end up stealing from churches, but the greater crime may well have been committed by the kings themselves who established a society in which the lower classes need to steal in order to survive. Henry espouses the rhetoric of comradeship:

We few, we happy few, we band of brothers.
For he today that sheds his blood with me
Shall be my brother; be he ne'er so vile,
This day shall gentle his condition.

(4.3.60–3)

But such solidarity is an illusion deployed to urge soldiers on to battle. When Henry knows the day is won, and reads the list of the dead, he skips over the identities of the men he only recently 'gentled':

Edward the Duke of York; the Earl of Suffolk;
Sir Richard Keighley; Davy Gam, esquire;
None else of name, and of all other men
But five-and-twenty.

(4.8.104–7, my emphasis)

The fatalities may have been relatively low, but the names of the gentlemen are still deemed more important than the lives of working-class soldiers. For this reason, it is all the more crucial that we observe their insulting gestures as acts of frustration performed within a society that constantly denies them what is promised.

By 1599 – around the time when *Henry V* was written and performed – the war with Spain had been ongoing for twenty years, with heavy expenditure causing widespread frustration over the unpopular rise in taxation.[25] At this point, the Privy Council was divided over the next move, with Elizabeth wanting to play the other European powers off against each other and Essex arguing for a direct attack on Spain as outlined in a pamphlet he published in 1598.[26] Yet Robin Headlam Wells provides a crucial perspective of the military class of the period:

For the common soldier the reward of victory would no doubt have been much like that of Pistol: no honours and titles, but a life of begging and stealing … Little wonder that those unfortunate enough to be conscripted to fight England's foreign wars expressed their resentment by desertion and mutiny.[27]

This sense of unease is epitomized by how, by the end of *Henry V*, Pistol is the only member of the old Eastcheap crew who survives. While the French enemy has been resoundingly defeated at Agincourt (although, of course, the final chorus ominously questions how long such a peace will last), the more insidious threat of Pistol and his Spanish qualities remains in the Elizabethan consciousness.

The invasion of France and the marriage to Katherine by Henry V are dramatized by Shakespeare because it is precisely what the English people Shakespeare presents onstage fears the Spanish will do to them. At the height of political, military, and national uncertainty, it is little wonder Shakespeare turned to other parallel moments in English history. Claire McEachern writes that 'in early modern England, state power was largely concentrated in – or at least symbolically configured by – a person'.[28] However, by the late 1590s, the rule of Elizabeth I was causing consternation among both court and country weary of an elderly female ruler. Katherine Eggert's assessment of *Henry V* as 'the play that most commemorates the approaching end of a Tudor queen'[29] is an analysis which acknowledges the complex and even contradictory notions of fear, impatience, frustration, and pre-emptive nostalgia that accompanied the final years of the Elizabethan era. With this in mind, the bawdiness prevalent in much of the history plays composed in this period should be read with an edge of impatient aggression hidden by the outward appearance of their humour and cheekiness.

E. A. M. Colman's study of the use of bawdy in Shakespeare's works notes that such language occurs far more frequently in *2 Henry IV* than in *1 Henry IV*.[30] Part of this statistic can be accounted for by the introduction of the character of Pistol and what his language symbolizes in terms of sexual violence tied up in military bravado. Howard and Rackin's description of the

Eastcheap tavern as 'a feminized, theatrical space'[31] makes all the more sense when we consider Pistol's boisterous and crude invasion of it, a comparison which holds up as Pistol moves into the action of *Henry V* by marrying Nell Quickly, invading the land of France, and taking on the effeminized French nobility. Colman goes on to argue that bawdy 'plays a much less important role in *Henry V* than in either part of *Henry IV*, and on the whole it is less firmly integrated thematically with the political material',[32] but here I seek to differ. *Henry V* is in fact where the bawdy and the political become aligned; the fig that Pistol proffers has gone from being comical-sexual in *2 Henry IV* to threatening and serious in *Henry V*, just at the same time as Hal's sexual prowess develops from learning and joking with bawds (tasted before tossed aside and consumed among capons and sac) to making a marriage that aligns the sexual with the political, preparing to invade her body shortly after invading her country. *Henry V* is where Hal's laddish habits in Eastcheap become foreign policy in France, with the women there for the taking and useful merely in terms of their roles as political and sexual commodities. And Pistol's tonal shift between *2 Henry IV* and *Henry V* – even while using the same gesture – reflects this yet further. In these plays, the sexual is nearly always aligned with the political: inevitably, it comes back to the question of who ends up getting fucked, and by whom.

Howard and Rackin's reading of Henry's wedding is especially adept in revealing this thematic link: 'Katherine is preparing to be occupied, although her occupation will be called marriage'.[33] But the most striking use of female chastity as an exchangeable commodity is in Henry's threat to destroy the 'fresh fair virgins' and 'pure maidens' by 'hot and forcing violation' if the town of Harfleur will not yield to his army (3.3.14, 20–1). Harfleur, of course, has no choice but to submit to Henry; the gates of the town are opened and penetrated rather than the bodies of the maidens, but the imagery is clear: power, when it comes to invasion, is equated with sexual dominance. Coppélia Kahn's reading of masculine identity continues this analogy, concluding that male violence against women via sexuality is the dominant mode of power until Henry begins wooing Katherine.[34] However, once we consider the implications of the ageing Virgin Queen Elizabeth, this reading can be extended further into the political marriage itself. Given the frustration with a now-infertile, unmarriageable queen and the precarious stance of Tudor power, it is possible to read *Henry V* as a play that above all emphasizes misogynistic impatience. By 1599, Elizabeth I may well have been seen as a frigid old woman, who fended off romantic advances in her younger days, leaving England vulnerable to attack and unable to fend off potential Spanish invaders to the body politic. It is this misogyny that lies behind the repeated use of the fig or the thumb-bite gesture in plays such as Pistol's half of the *Henriad*. As with many sexual comments uttered by boisterous men, what starts out as 'just a joke' can often escalate to threats or outright gendered violence.

Before this chapter is concluded, it is worth noting not only that Shakespeare features an ensign character in another of his plays but that this character refers to virtue as 'a fig'. That jealousy in the theme of *Othello* is self-evident, but such jealousy begins in the mind of Iago, rather than Othello, and it is this covetousness which aligns the fig gesture with the evil eye. The fig gesture was used to ward off the evil eye, which would cause harm to whomever its gaze fell on.[35] It was thought that those drawing the envy of others – through beauty, in the case of Desdemona, or status and valour, in the case of Othello – would attract the evil eye's attention and therefore bring them harm.[36] *Othello*'s key theme of jealousy is brought into even sharper distinction when we view the play not only through the lens of an evil eye but through the fig gesture that was used to ward off such wickedness, particularly when we note the number of references to eyes, sight, vision, and 'ocular proof' that the play contains. The fig references also provide a deeper meaning to the references to poison gnawing at Othello from the inside, and even Othello announcing his intention to poison Desdemona, with Iago then advising that he not use poison, but strangle her instead. Poison would have been a wiser move as it would be less traceable back to its source (as Iago must have known: Spaniards were alleged to use poisoned figs to kill off their enemies). Iago's coercion of Othello into suffocating Desdemona thus has two strategic advantages: it removes the element of poison that Iago may be associated with, and puts the agency of her death quite literally back into Othello's hands and away from his own. Jan Kott's reading that 'Iago is not satisfied with devising the tragedy; he wants to play it through, distribute all the parts and act in it himself' therefore seems all the more credible when read alongside the literary conventions of the braggart, the political and social fear of the Spanish, and the military status that Iago shares with Pistol.[37] Both Iago and Pistol are actors and ancients, keen to take control of the narrative and use it to serve their own ends at the expense of the officer class.

Antony Byrne may have performed a different gesture when he played Pistol in 2 *Henry IV*, but he captured the essence of what it meant to a twenty-first-century audience, not all of whom could have bridged the gap between the 1590s and 2014 with the knowledge of what a Spanish fig implied. Thumb gestures in this period are inherently associated with vulgarity and a plebeian mode of expression unsuited to the elite. The ongoing animosity between Elizabethan England and Spain is epitomized in such gestures: it captures the sexual imagery of military bravado, the frustration of being ruled by a female monarch, and the fear of miscegenation implied by a Spanish invasion that may have already happened without England really noticing, given the appearance of Pistol within Henry V's army. Of course, the power to do anything about all of these concerns is out of reach from the non-elite. Such physical insults from this non-elite class become symbols of the agency they wish was metaphorically within their grasp. The elite, however, have no use for such frustrated movements: they have no need to gesture towards a desire for power when it is already in their hands.

3

Spitting at Richard: Taming the Beast in *Richard III*

Spitting is a performed act of defiance that is wordless, yet oral. When aimed at someone during the Renaissance period, it becomes a literal crossing of the line separating accepted bodily gestures from the grotesque, resulting in a physical violation that is still recognized today. Yet even though the spitter is the one to cross this boundary, the shame falls on the person who has been spat upon: the victim is marked out by the contempt of a contemporary who voids disgust from their very guts. In her essay on spitting images, Michèle H. Richman asserts that 'there is little to equal the humiliating effect of receiving such a blow [as spitting] to the sanctity of the human face'.[1] Understandably, then, spitting – alongside actions such as nose-tweaking and ear-boxing – frequently caused defamation suits in early modern England.[2] For instance, John Cooper of Sussex is recorded as humiliating a sidesman of his parish, 'calling him rogue and rascall, knave, villayne and divell, and in a beastly manner [did] spitt in his face'.[3] As there is no appropriate response to the indignity of being spat upon, those insulted are reduced to an object. The performance of spitting, therefore, helps to mark the territory of reproach within early modern society and indicate not only a way in which compunction was communicated but the reasons why such compunction was felt and inflicted.

The next two chapters examine the ways in which Shakespeare stages the expectoration of certain undesirable characters from society. This chapter reads the scene where Richard of Gloucester is openly spat at by Lady Anne; the following chapter takes *The Merchant of Venice*'s Shylock as its subject, a man who is berated and spat upon 'many a time and oft' (1.3.102–8). An exploration of these plays shows the relevance of gestural shaming by exploring how early modern bodies are a microcosmic version of the wider body politic, where rejected entities are purged from its system. These next two chapters, then, are companion pieces to Chapters 1 and 2. They consider plays Shakespeare wrote during the late Elizabethan period, when fear of invasion by the Spanish had been long prevalent. While Chapters 1 and 2 explored the idea of vulgarly phallic gestures as embodied metaphors for the feared invasion of the English body politic, the following two chapters analyse the idea of gestures which epitomize the embodied metaphor of purging the body politic of such undesirable peoples. In *Richard III*, we see how the action of spitting upon Richard reflects society's rejection of his disabled body; in *The Merchant of Venice*, we see how the resentment towards the Jewish moneylender is epitomized through people spitting at him in the street.

My reading of these plays and their references to spitting is based around Janet Adelman's phrase 'boundary panic',[4] which Rachel Trubowitz also employs in her essay '"But Blood Whitened": Nursing Mothers and Others in Early Modern Britain'.[5] While these works look at the notion of boundary panic in a gendered sense, we must further examine how spitting is an act that induces feminization in the victim. Given the affiliations between the open mouth, feminine indiscretion, and spitting as a taming act, we shall see how spitting on someone necessarily feminizes that person as a body that is marked out as unclean, uncivilized, and in need of chastisement. To come into contact with such a body evokes 'boundary panic', which I would define as a fear – irrational or otherwise – of social, bodily, or otherwise literal boundaries being crossed. This definition allows us to consider the tensions and the prejudices in the plays of Shakespeare, as well as the issues and concerns of the age in which they were written. Spitting, then, operates as a gesture which inflicts shame: as an act of non-verbal communication, its performance carries social currency, marking disgust and conveying dissent.

In the second scene of *Richard III*, Lady Anne is utterly confirmed in her opinion of the knavish Duke of Gloucester; while he insists on the sincerity of his love for her, she parries his every argument:

RICHARD
  It is a quarrel most unnatural
  To be revenged on him that loveth thee.
ANNE
   It is a quarrel just and reasonable
   To be revenged on him that killed my husband.

(1.2.139–42)

This back and forth continues, with the exchanges becoming of increasing brevity:

RICHARD
  He that bereft thee, lady, of thy husband,
  Did it to help thee to a better husband.
ANNE
   His better doth not breathe upon the earth.
RICHARD
  He lives that loves thee better than he could […]
ANNE
   Where is he?
RICHARD
   Here

(1.2.141–7)

At this point, Anne realizes that rhetorical tropes will only take her so far, so she gives up on stichomythia altogether and spits at the man who killed her husband:

RICHARD
　Why dost thou spit at me?
ANNE
　Would it were mortal poison, for thy sake.
RICHARD
　Never came poison from so sweet a place.
ANNE
　Never hung poison on a fouler toad.
　Out of my sight, thou dost infect mine eyes.
RICHARD
　Thine eyes, sweet lady, have infected mine.
ANNE
　Would they were basilisks, to strike thee dead.
(1.2.153–9)

She equates King Henry's murderer with a foul toad given his slimy advances towards her, but she is also content to present herself as a poison-spitting snake in order to condemn him; she is happy to lower herself if it means spurning him. Indeed, Edward Topsell's *The Historie of Serpents* tells us that '[b]y the Serpent in Holy-writ, are many obseruatiue significations; and first, that the deuill himselfe, which is *Malus deus mali mundi,* an euill God of an euill world, should be termed and expressed by a Serpent'.[6] But then, by becoming serpent-like, Anne unwittingly aligns herself with the original tempter in the garden of Eden, as if proving Richard's point that it was *her* who enticed *him*. Topsell even tells his readers that the enmity between snake and man is expressed in the qualities contained by both species' saliva:

　And the truth heereof is to be seene at this day, for by a kind of secret instinct, and naturall motion, a man abhorreth the sight of a Serpent, & a serpent the sight of a man. And as by the tongue of the serpent, was wrought mans confusion, so by the spettle of a mans tongue, is wrought a serpents astonishment [...]

The first manifestation in nature, of mans discord with serpents, is their venom; for as in a serpent there is a venome which poysoneth a man: so in a man, there is the venom of his spittle, which poysoneth a serpent. For if the fasting spittle of a man, fall into the iawes of a serpent, he certainly dieth thereof.[7]

Yet it is worth considering how spitting, when done in the sincere belief that it wards off evil, is a sympathetic act when the audience is on side. Despite Richard's admirable Machiavellianism, the audience certainly feel pity for Anne when she is propositioned.

Despite spitting upon Richard, Anne ends up having no choice but to accept a ring from him. Many critics have worked hard to justify this resolution, with Denzell S. Smith arguing, 'What could better exemplify Richard's audacious self-confidence than to have him woo this particular woman at this particular time?'[8] Michael Torrey suggests that she leaves the situation 'both charmed and temporarily free of the revulsion toward Richard that she formerly felt';[9] however, there is a wider scope for performative interpretation here. In the first instance, such a reading does not give enough credit to Anne herself. With her husband dead and her power and influence minimal, spitting at Richard is a remarkably bold move, as even though Richard offers her his sword to kill him with, realistically, she is unable to wield it. It is not necessarily that she is won over by Richard, but she cannot kill him for four reasons. The first is practical: the stage direction '*She falls the sword*' (1.2.186) implies that she may be physically incapable of using what is most likely a hefty, weighty medieval sword. The second is political: Even if she were able to wield it, what would happen to her after killing the new king's brother? The third reason is ethical: If she is personally responsible for Richard's death, how could she maintain the moral high-ground? The fourth and final reason is social: What other choice does she have, as a widowed woman whose husband and father were affiliated with the losing side of the most recent battle in the Wars of the Roses? There are many casualties of war, and many spoils; Anne becomes both as Richard claims her for his bride. She may say that she accepts him 'With all my heart, and much it joys me too / To see you are become so penitent' (1.2.222–3), but these lines may be as emotionally void as her act of letting fall the sword. By this point, she is acting out a role she has no choice but to play.

Sympathy for Anne, the spitter, rather than Richard, the spittee, emerges from the fact that the attention Anne receives is not merely unwanted but also comes from someone whom early modern society has marked out as monstrous; in his own words, Richard is 'Cheated of feature by dissembling Nature, / Deformed, unfinished' (1.1.19–20). The fact that Richard is marked out as physically different is read by Renaissance culture as being 'a portent of divine wrath, as a symbol of political upheaval'.[10] Ian Frederick Moulton points out that a broadside from 1568 called 'The forme and shape of a monstrous Child, / born at Maydstone in Kent' has the subtitle 'A warnyng to England', and he notes that 'the broadside reads each deformity of a male infant's body as representing a specific corruption of the English nation'.[11] Ewan Fernie also outlines the role of physiognomy in Richard's shamelessness as a villain, writing that 'he looks vicious, so he will be vicious; he is physically warped and bent, so he rejects straightness and makes, in J. P. Brockbank's phrase, "deformity license depravity"'.[12] Disability scholars such as David T. Mitchell and Sharon L. Snyder even argue that Richard's physical appearance 'underline[s] his own metaphysical unfitness to govern'.[13] Yet Torrey takes issue with such readings, arguing for a more ambiguous approach. Despite his outward appearance, Richard frequently manages to deceive:

> On the one hand, the visible signs of evil on Richard's body make his metaphysical status available for all to see; on

the other hand, in deceiving others Richard shows that his deformity sometimes fails to signify his evil to them.[14]

Torrey's analysis of Richard reveals the malleability of deformity, as something that gives him the opportunity to 'refashion' himself 'into a sign of anything but the inward truth'.[15] The ambivalence of the connection between Richard's deformity and his immorality is felt particularly strongly in the spitting scene. It is not that Anne is unaware of his evil nature; rather, it is the fact that she is all *too* aware of it, but is trapped by social circumstance into accepting his proposal. This is what prompts both sympathy for her and astonishment at Richard's audacity. Upon Richard's intrusion to the scene, the body of Henry VI begins to bleed afresh, indicating Richard's own guilt:

ANNE
    Blush, blush, thou lump of foul deformity,
    For 'tis thy presence that exhales this blood
    From cold and empty veins where no blood dwells.
    Thy deeds, inhuman and unnatural,
    Provokes this deluge most unnatural.

(1.2.57–61)

While scholars such as Derek Dunne have argued for the equivocation of blushing as a symbol of veracity on the early modern stage,[16] here Anne is calling for blood to rush to Richard's cheeks in order to replicate the blood he spilled in battle. The freshly oozing blood, like the spittle soon to be projected, marks out Richard as a transgressor.

The performative potential in 1.2 is crucial to how audiences come to view Richard in various productions; in fact, the credibility of Richard's later successes hinge on the audacity of this very scene. Antony Sher portrayed Richard for the RSC in 1984 using crutches onstage to scuttle unnervingly across the boards. Of the first night, he wrote: 'The Lady Anne scene goes well. Just before her spit, on the spur of the moment, I slide one of the crutches under her skirt and between her legs ... it shocks both of us as well as the audience, creating a rather wonderful moment'.[17] We see here the decision to use deformity as a tool of power: by using the props of his disability as a way into Anne's petticoat, Sher creates a dramatic moment of genuine boldness precisely because it thwarted the audience's expectations as to how disabled people behave. By purposefully acting out against this ignorant assumption, Sher's portrayal became a performance born out of warped frustration. In the RSC's 2007 production of *Richard III* at The Courtyard, the scene became charged with an uncomfortable eroticism. Having been spat at in the face by Anne (Hannah Barrie), Richard (Jonathan Slinger) touched his saliva-covered chin and seductively licked her essence off his fingers. At the 1977 Stratford, Ontario Festival, Brian Bedford's portrayal of Richard crossed similarly murky boundaries: after Anne 'shocked herself' by spitting upon him, he not only used her fingers to wipe her spittle from his face but he also licked her fingers clean.[18] A similar performance occurred when Alan Bates played Richard in John Hirsch's 1967 production at the Canadian Stratford Festival: he wiped 'Anne's spittle from his face and offer[ed] it back to her again on his deformed hand'.[19] There appears to be a performative trope here, wherein once Anne has crossed an accepted social boundary by spitting on Richard, Richard himself must go further in transgressing what is acceptable. The grotesque regurgitation of saliva by Anne is trumped by Richard's ingestion of her bodily fluid; of course, this is not indicated by the original play text, which merely has Richard respond, 'Why dost thou spit at me? [...] Never came poison from so sweet a place' (1.2.147; 149). Despite Anne's best intentions, he is still not repulsed, *but she still is*. The performance practices of this scene, and the additions they make, give us an indication of how we appropriate Richard as a villain, from bogeyman of the Tudor myth to a libidinous transgressor, both of whom society is keen to ward off.

Richard III and, as we shall see, *The Merchant of Venice* are not the only plays where Shakespeare makes something of spitting. Unlike the key plays of this chapter and the next, the examples which follow rarely deploy the act of spitting itself in performance. However, they remain a useful insight into the action's associations. Earlier comedies, such as *Comedy of Errors* and *The Taming of the Shrew*, include spitting references that evoke a potentially crude, patriarchal gender politics. *Taming* features a moment during Bianca and Lucentio's music lesson where one of the instruments is out of tune, and Lucentio suggests, 'Spit in the hole, man, and tune again' (3.1.39). While this line could be played innocently, it also contains sexual possibilities, given the use of 'spit' as an early modern euphemism for 'to penetrate sexually'. In *Comedy of Errors*, Adriana confronts Antipholus of Syracuse, thinking he is her husband, by exclaiming, 'Wouldst thou not spit at me, and spurn at me[?]' (2.2.133) when telling him, 'My blood is mingled with the crime of lust' (2.2.140), implying that if she is guilty of sin, she should be marked out by the act of spitting. By the middle of Shakespeare's career, the comedy *As You Like It* has Rosalind (admittedly, in disguise as Ganymede) advise Orlando that in order to cure lovesickness, she would adopt contradictory behaviour: 'then entertain him, then forswear him; now weep for him, then spit at him' (3.2.398–400). Another example of spitting as a defiant act by a female character can be found in *Measure for Measure*, Shakespeare's early Jacobean comedy, when we hear that Pompey has accused Elbow's wife of depravity: 'but as she spit in his face, so she defied him' (2.1.82–3). References to spitting also occur in Shakespeare's other history plays. As we see in *1 Henry IV*, Falstaff tells Hal that 'if I tell thee a lie, spit in my face, call me horse' (2.4.186–7). These comments from Falstaff link the idea of untrustworthiness with being less than human, necessitating the punishment of spitting, but all of these examples show how spitting is deployed as a taming or corrective act.

Spitting references also evoke tension in *Richard II*. When Bullingbrook challenges Mowbray, Mowbray responds, 'I do defy him, and I spit at him' (1.1.60). Bullingbrook counters this insult by appropriating a similar image in his rebut, and although the spitting he mentions is figurative rather than physical, it conveys the strength of his feeling and the sense of humiliation he intends to cast upon his rival:

> ere my tongue
> Shall wound mine honour with such a feeble wrong,
> Or sound so base a parle, my teeth shall tear
> The slavish motive of recanting fear,
> And spit it bleeding in his high disgrace,
> Where shame doth harbour, even in Mowbray's face.
> (1.1.191–6)

As in 1.2, we see a (somewhat more oblique) reference to the act of blushing. Mowbray's face is where 'shame doth harbour', and even if he is not blushing, the implication is that he soon will be when Bullingbrook's bloodied tongue hits him (either because Bullingbrook's blood will stain his rival's cheek or because the action itself is so humiliating it will invoke actual blushing). A similar sense of spitting and defiance carries an extra insult in *Timon of Athens*, when Timon says to Apemantus, 'Would thou wert clean enough to spit upon!' (4.3.358). The line is doubly shaming: not only does Timon want to spit on him but he fears that to do so would risk contagion. Finally, in Shakespeare's late play, *Cymbeline*, Posthumous berates himself for falsely accusing Imogen of infidelity with the line '[s]pit, and throw stones, cast mire upon me' (5.5.259). This line bears a similarity to Isaiah 50.6, which includes the words 'I gave my back to the smiters, and my cheeks to the nippers: I hid not my face from shame and spitting'. In both examples, we see the idea of inner shame being purged by the inflicted performance of a physical, externalized shaming act such as spitting.

Spitting is a culturally codified act within the Renaissance period. Brett Greatley-Hirsch notes that spitting is often referred to in early modern literature, and argues that:

> [a]ttitudes toward spit and spitting, like any other bodily fluid and function, offer important insights into early modern

notions of propriety and social order, as well as changing perceptions of the body and its materiality, its relationships to affect and cognition, its role in enculturation, and its connections to the physical world.[20]

Attitudes to spittle have certainly altered over time, as is evident through reading texts such as conduct manuals. Antoine de Courtin observes in his *Nouveau traite de civilité* that '[f]ormerly [...] it was permitted to spit on the ground before people of rank, and was sufficient to put one's foot on the sputum'.[21] Less savoury is an example cited by Montaigne in his essay 'Of Custom': 'There are others, who when the King spitteth, the most favoured Ladie in his court stretched forth her hand; and in another countrey, where the noblest about him, stoupe to the ground to gather his ordure in some fine linnen cloth'.[22] In 1578, Walter Darrell's behavioural manual about the conduct of servingmen was published, telling us that 'it is an ill sight, to lill out ye tounge'.[23] Presumably spitting, then, would be even more frowned upon. Similarly, Mateo Alemán's 1623 text *The Rogue* describes lilling out the tongue as being an 'Idiotlike' posture that makes men 'take the degree of fooles'.[24] Alemán was a servingman, and it is noteworthy that both his text and Darrell's handbook insist that poking out the tongue is something that even working-class citizens should avoid. Yet there were also some positive connotations of spittle as a fluid, if not of spitting as an act. Greatley-Hirsch reminds us that the 1601 translation of Pliny's *Natural History* by Philemon Holland includes a chapter on 'the properties of a mans spittle', laying claim to the bodily fluid's potential to be used as an aid 'to relieve stiffness, to avert witchcraft, and to increase the efficacy of medicine and charms'.[25] For instance, in John Webster's *The Duchess of Malfi*, we hear Bosola teasing an old lady for keeping Jews' spittle in her make-up cabinet (2.1.39–40), corroborating Pliny's use of it as a form of bodily aid in medicine and other forms of bodily enhancement such as cosmetics. Spit's potential healing qualities are noted alongside the apotropaic effect of warding off supernatural threats; both of these properties should be read alongside the act of spitting as a way of marking out an individual as socially unacceptable. While this may seem contradictory – how can spittle have both positive and negative connotations simultaneously? – the two are inextricably linked. Spittle's favourable or unfavourable aspects depend entirely on perspective: for those using the fluid to ward off someone unwanted, spittle clearly has helpful properties, but the effects are obviously negative for the person being fended off.

Another Renaissance writer who espoused opinions on spitting etiquette was Erasmus, who noted that spitting near another person was liable to nauseate anyone who had the misfortune to witness such a thing.[26] In fact, he offers the following advice on the conduct of spitting in public in his manual, *De Civilitate Morum Puerilium*:

> Whan thou spittest turne thy face aside, to th'intent thou spit vpon no man. If thou haue caste anye ordure or filthinesse vpon the ground, thou must trede it out with thy fote as I haue saide already, to the ende that it trouble no mans heart nor stomake. If it be not lawfull for to turne thee, receiue and gather thy spittle into thy handkercher.[27]

These restrictions of good manners and conduct were a powerful social bind in the early modern period, especially when dealing with the tongue and the mouth in connection with acts such as spitting. Erasmus further chastises anyone who pokes out their tongue in scorn, saying that '[h]e mocketh some manne that draweth out his tonge at him'.[28] While tongue-poking is meant to be an act which mocks others, the performance can result in you being the source of mockery yourself. However, Erasmus also wrote *Lingua*, a fascinating and often entertaining tract on the use and misuse of language, which can even be said to poke its tongue out at his critics. At the time of writing, Erasmus was having to defend himself against various forms of misrepresentation and slander, and it is this context which explains 'the brooding dominance of *calumnia* at the centre of the *Lingua*, and the bitterness of his allusions to both mendicant friars and established theologians'.[29] His experiences with the malice of others led him to the sincere belief that '[i]t is really a worse fate to be mocked than loathed ... For a man reaches the peak of misfortune when he is so afflicted that he deserves no kindness or compassion, but suffers mockery into the bargain'.[30] This point of view is reflected in some of *Lingua*'s most colourful passages, which emphasize the almost bestial nature of the tongue and the potential vulgarity of orality:

> Nature covered the eyes with nothing but a frail membrane, suited only for sleep, but buried the tongue virtually in a dungeon, and bound it by many bonds – above, near the back of the palate, again on either side at the opening of the throat, and finally with cables stretching down into the chest-cavity. It is tied underneath to the lower jaw right up to the rampart of the teeth. [...] Nature sets in its path the double rampart and barrier of the thirty-two teeth. [...] Nature also set in its path the double doors of the lips, to show, I suppose, that we have a valuable treasure in the tongue, since she has hidden it away so thoroughly, but also showing the great danger of using it carelessly or out of season; hence although it is held down by many cables, she has enclosed it within a double palisade, to prevent that unbridled licence which is not a matter of uttering words, but of blurting out whatever comes into one's head.[31]

This context around the mouth as a site of danger and transgression furthers the concept of spitting as a shocking act, with the mouth deployed as a weapon against an unfavourable person or their opinions. Our tongues are like monsters hidden deep within a dark dungeon, restrained by ropes lest it wriggle free and cause civil unrest. It is a member whose power we rightly fear; if we know what is good for us, we should bridle it within the body and not let an idle tongue sneak out from the doors that enclose our mouth, the lips. Politeness – by not spitting, or simply by not saying something untoward – can only be maintained by control over the mouth, that potentially monstrous orifice whose damp depths should remain respectfully hidden, unless we need to lash out at someone who truly deserves it.

The idea of sputum being a person's essence, and one capable of being used to aim at someone as a weapon against the imposition of unfavourable notions or characters, is favoured by the ethnographer Marcel Griaule. He argues that '[s]aliva is deposited soul; spit is soul in movement'.[32] Other modern sociologists, such as Norbert Elias, also expand upon spitting and its cultural associations. Elias is keen to remind us that although spit was analysed for medical diagnoses, spit was not seen as a carrier of the germs themselves until the nineteenth century.[33] Of course, the sticky physicality of spittle still had the power to cause disgust: as a personal essence, saliva should be kept within the confines of the body producing it and, if expelled, should be done so discreetly. It is no wonder then that reactions to the act of spitting are inextricably linked to the idea of what Elias calls 'the civilizing process'. In his book of the same name, he reveals how the progress of civilization is in part down to how, previously, external influences would reprehend us for actions such as spitting, but that these are, over time, commandeered by the development of a person's sense of social responsibility: 'prohibited tendencies (e.g., the tendency to spit) partly disappeared from consciousness under the pressure of this internal restraint or, as it may also be called, the pressure from the "superego" and the "habit of foresight"'.[34] This internalization of shame and guilt as part of the civilizing process is reflected by Renaissance notions of bodily boundaries. While the classical body is imagined as almost hermetically sealed off from the outside world, the grotesque body is seen as being 'in process, constantly transgressing its limits and open to the universe'.[35]

Mikhail Bakhtin's analysis of the grotesque body enables us to imagine how spitting at someone engenders shame by crossing bodily thresholds that ought to be sealed off from the outside world. In *Rabelais and His World*, Bakhtin contends that 'the theme of mockery and abuse is almost entirely bodily and grotesque'.[36] Of course, throughout *Richard III*, the Duke of Gloucester is himself marked out for his bodily difference:

> I, that am curtailed of this fair proportion,
> Cheated of feature by dissembling Nature,
> Deformed, unfinished, sent before my time
> Into this breathing world, scarce half made up.
>
> (1.1.18–21)

Richard's 'unfinished' body identifies him as a grotesque figure within the early modern period, and although the play's production history rarely sticks to one specific way of displaying his disabled form, the text offers us a glimpse of a body which does not meet society's expectations, transgressing the body's 'usual' boundaries. Such conceptions align Richard with Bakhtinian notions of corporeal transgression, and go some way to explicating why such bodies were spat upon. For Bakhtin, the mouth along with the anus are the open boundaries of grotesque imagery and ribaldry, as these are the orifices from which things can 'detach themselves from the body and lead an independent life'.[37] These 'newly conceived bodies'[38] – such as spittle – are in direct violation of the notion of the civilized body as having sealed boundaries where the 'signs of its inner life' are removed from view. Carla Mazzio agrees with this troubling quality of the mouth, and in her essay 'Sins of the Tongue in Early Modern England', she equates the tongue with a disturbing Otherness borne out of its changeable locus, as it is able to move in and out of the body and into the space of another.[39] Spitting surpasses even this, actually leaving the mouth and consequently breaking the boundaries of both body and civility. Bakhtin gives us a colourful insight into how the transgression of social boundaries evokes a sense of chaos:

> The grotesque body is not separated from the rest of the world. It is not a closed, completed unit; it is unfinished, outgrows itself, transgresses its own limits [...] This means that the emphasis is on the apertures or the convexities, or

on various ramifications and offshoots: the *open mouth,* the genital organs, the breasts, the phallus, the potbelly, the nose. (my emphasis)[40]

Spitting constitutes a grotesque act. The mouth is an orifice that gapes open, capable of ingesting and spewing, both a doorway for nourishment and a potential emetic exit from our bodies. When spit detaches itself from the confines of the mouth, it becomes a new, foreign, and unwanted body. It becomes all too apt a metaphor for those human bodies figured as outsiders such as Richard, who infect or contaminate the body politic, and whom early modern culture is keen to expectorate. In the act of spitting upon them, they are marked out as different, and therefore dangerous.

This action of spitting repulses us because spitting itself is a physical manifestation of repugnance: when somebody spits, it is quite literally an act of repellence, regurgitating personal essence to avoid the assimilation of something unwanted. This corresponds to Julia Kristeva's discussion of abjection in *Powers of Horror*:

> Loathing an item of food, a piece of filth, waste, or dung ... 'I', do not assimilate it, 'I' expel it. But since the food is not an 'other' for 'me', who am only in their desire, I expel *myself*, I spit *myself* out, I abject *myself* within the same motion through which 'I' claim to establish *myself*.[41]

The idea of spitting or vomiting as an action which protects the person doing it aligns with the notion of Anne spitting at Richard as he makes his unwanted sexual advances to her. Kristeva's equation of disgust with the desire to spit at the person/thing evoking such repugnance also observes how such an act is rooted in not only rejection but the denial of *assimilation*. The spittle comes to represent the rejected person, purged from the body of society having emerged from within its boundaries.

Discussing the distinctions between bodily behavioural codes, social status, and power, Peter Stallybrass asserts that '[t]o examine the body's formation is to trace the connections between politeness and politics. But because these connections are never simply given, the body can itself become a site of conflict'.[42] The increased use of handkerchiefs, separate cutlery, and eating bowls in the Renaissance period 'emphasized the borders of a closed individuality at the same time as it separated off the social elite from the "vulgar"'.[43] This observation reveals how Renaissance concerns about social purity are predicated on the desire for bodily purity; therefore, to spit upon another is to mark the person out as a contaminated body, unworthy of society. This notion concurs with Michel Foucault's assessment of the ceremonies of public punishment, where

> it [is] the task of the guilty man to bear openly his condemnation and the truth of the crime that he ha[s] committed, [making the guilty man] herald of his own condemnation [...] the condemned man published his crime and the justice that had been meted out to him by bearing them physically on his body.[44]

Spit is one such mark of shame, and one that heralds distinct possibilities about the nature of saliva as a fluid and its effects on personal identity, and how the act of spitting implies a discourse of disgust and refutation of character. Foucault's observations also extend to the idea of a transgressor within society's rules being a monstrous figure: 'he is worse than an enemy, for it is from within society that he delivers his blows – he is nothing less than a traitor, a "monster"'.[45] Anne often refers to Richard's lack of civility – early on in 1.2 she tells him 'Villain, thou knowst nor law of God nor man. / No beast so fierce but knows some touch of pity' (1.2.70–1) – and she also relegates him to the level of beasts, further calling him a hedgehog and a toad (1.2104; 150). The violation of being spat upon is inextricably linked to a step backwards in humanity's civilizing process. The insulted person essentially becomes seen as a non-human object who can have little or no response to the spitting, thus losing their sense of autonomy; although the spitter is seen as uncivil, the person spat at is tarnished by the same brush (or, should I say, the same saliva). Despite this, Richard manages to overcome this insult and marry the woman who spits upon him, but he is, of course, still ultimately expectorated from the body politic by the play's conclusion, just as society expects.

Civilization is essentially defined in opposition to our more bestial instincts. One noticeable way in Richard is treated is that he is often described by other characters as animalistic in some way, often as a dog. Richard, 'the hell-hound that doth hunt as all to death' (4.4.48), is able to use his doglike position to his advantage, fashioning selves of loyalty or savageness depending on what he needs to gain from any given situation. Throughout Richard III, we hear warnings about Richard's wolfishness, from the image that 'he could gnaw a crust at two hours old ... this would have been a biting jest' (2.4.28–30), to being called 'dog' by Queen Margaret (1.3.215). Shakespeare was also not the first to describe Richard III in such terms. Historical tracts keen to demonize Richard in order to perpetuate the Tudor Myth also feature canine descriptions. For instance, Edward Hall's 1548 *The Union of the Two Noble and Illustre Families of Lancastre and Yorke* emphasizes Richard's doglike jaws and bestial voraciousness: 'when he strode musing he would byte and chaw besely his nether lippe, as who sayd, that his fyerce nature in his cruell body alwaies chafed, sturred and was ever unquiete'.[46] Additionally, Peter Stallybrass and Allon White note the House of York's symbolic associations with the boar as being particularly indicative of Richard's place within early modern culture: pigs, like dogs, are partly domesticated, fed on scraps, and live on the margins between beasts and society.[47] By aligning Richard with such creatures, it communicates the desire that he be placed apart from civilized company, allowed to exist merely on the sidelines of domestic experience rather than assimilated properly into human society.

Crucially, dogs were spat at in order to be tamed, as is apparent in Thomas Middleton and Thomas Dekker's *The Roaring Girl*, when it is indicated that Gallipot 'spits in the dog's mouth' (2.1.383). This action was a way of showing affection to dogs, as noted in Richard Overton's *A New Bull-Bayting*, when a dog is praised in the following way: 'I never saw a Dogge do better; he has brought away a piece of his Nose; well done Towzer; Spit in his mouth, and stroak him on the back.'[48] Although the footnote in Simon Barker and Hilary Hinds' edition of *The Roaring Girl* presumes that Tiltyard is 'calling and whistling for the dog'[49] when he says, 'Where's his water-dog? Puh – pist – hur – hur – pist' (2.1.378), it is plausible that the words could be a transcription of the sound of spitting. A few lines later, Master Gallipot replies to his mistress, saying, 'Faith that's well – hum – pist pist', followed by the stage direction to spit in the dog's mouth. Given that Middleton's introductory epistle to the 1611 quarto version of the play addresses 'comic play *readers*'[50] (my emphasis) rather than audiences, perhaps Dekker and Middleton are deliberately drawing attention to the physicality of the spitting act, with the 'pist' evoking the sound of saliva being spat out forcibly between the lips, and the 'hums' and 'hurs' as the hocking up of sputum from the lungs. Dekker and Middleton are using the onomatopoeia in these lines to help the reader to hear as well as visualize the uncouth performance of spitting. In this way, spitting upon Richard places him in the same social category as dogs that are rewarded or punished for their behaviour and are spat upon to tame their beastly ways. It should come as no surprise to recall the fact that Richard's death is announced thus: 'the bloody dog is dead' (5.5.2); unable to be tamed, he is ultimately rejected and destroyed by the society from which he emerged.

Taming is necessarily a 'feminizing' act in this period: it is a process which seeks to remove personal agency and replace it with 'masculine' control. Given Richard's shaming by Anne, and this chapter's analysis of bodily difference, it is useful to consider Ellen Samuels' discussion of the equations between gender and the abled body:

> Western thought has historically claimed, not a difference, but a correspondence between disability and femininity ... [Hence] the de-masculinization of disabled men, who are then lumped together with women, children, and the elderly in the realm of abject and dependent bodies.[51]

But, if anything, Richard is an over-'masculinized' figure by the standards of the early modern period; indeed, critics such as Ian Frederick Moulton argue that Richard's masculinity is unruly and uncontrollable due to his ability to 'destroy and corrupt but not create'.[52] Although there is 'effeminized disorder' in the *Henry VI* plays, Moulton's analysis is that the portrayal of Richard's disabled body, rather than a feminization, actually represents an over-masculinized response to the House of Lancaster's troubled reign.[53] Anne's taming act of spitting and, ultimately, Richard's defeat by Richmond are acts intended to feminize this dangerous masculinity. Lynda E. Boose notes that early modern society's 'underlying model of "the publick Peace" is inseparable from and constituted by the reinforcement of gender difference'.[54] Indeed, the fact that the ailing King Edward is described effeminately ('sickly, weak and melancholy')[55] reveals how Richard's masculinity is an overcompensation for Edward's – and indeed, Henry VI's – 'feminine' qualities. In this sense, the body politic must be maintained in a manner similar to the balancing of humours, with any excess purged for the good of the larger body. Spitting, in this context, becomes a taming act intended to neutralize Richard's unruly body – and its unruly masculinity – for the overall good of a well-balanced body politic.[56] With *Richard III* being composed during the reign of Elizabeth I, and introducing her own grandfather as the hero figure who saves England from the doglike Richard, an early modern audience is comforted by the play's conclusion and implicit endorsement of the current status quo. Living under a female ruler, who despite the best efforts of the Spanish had managed to keep out invasion (in itself, a potent 'boundary panic'), the creation of Richard III's grotesque, hyper-masculinized body –

only for it to be rejected and defeated – is a satisfying narrative for the play's original audiences to consume. By spitting on and defeating the last Plantagenet tyrant, the body politic of Elizabethan England is purged, and the over-masculinized chaos of Richard is replaced by someone who will come to symbolize its antithesis: the measured and virtuous Virgin Queen.

4

Spitting at Shylock: Shameful Conversion in *The Merchant of Venice*

Spitting embodies, evokes, and perpetuates feelings of disgust felt for bodies considered Other in the early modern period. As we saw in the previous chapter, it is an act that is performed in order to mark out someone *perceived* as different as *physically* or even *morally* different: the taming act of spitting uses the fluid identities of saliva to label the person spat upon as marginalized from society; or someone who, the spitter feels, ought to be.

What makes spitting in *The Merchant of Venice* such an intriguing case is how the actors playing Shylock have talked about their own isolation from the rest of the cast, as if the enactment of the drama spills over into reality. Patrick Stewart took the role in 1963, 1978, and 2011, and claims that 'one thing that has been the same in every experience is that somehow, in the company of actors, you find yourself being treated as an outsider: I've never been teased and made fun of more than I have on those occasions. People gang up on you when you play Shylock'.[1] Desmond Barrit, who played Shylock in 2003, agrees with Stewart. He recalls, 'Such is the nature of the piece that, when we started rehearsing, I felt outside of everything. I felt that I was being alienated by the rest of the cast, that I wasn't being included in social activities'.[2] Anthony Sher remembers how he 'had an awful lot of other actors' saliva in my beard, and when it's your own beard you really want to shampoo it all off'.[3]

Perhaps one of the reasons why playing the role of Shylock has this effect on the performers is that they cannot help but be physically affected by the enactment of hatred upon their person. When I saw Patrick Stewart perform the role for the RSC at Stratford in 2011, the audience audibly gasped as the broken Shylock, following the announcement that he must convert to Christianity, was spat upon by the actor playing Gratiano. It was genuinely shocking because, although the hocking up of phlegm was being staged for the plot, the saliva falling on this esteemed Shakespearean actor was real. In that moment, the audience seemed to feel sympathy for two people at once: Shylock and Stewart. It is a harsh reminder that the performance of spitting cannot be faked: the enactment of spitting in drama necessitates its reality.

In the mid-sixteenth century, having been accused of heresy and imprisoned, the Archdeacon of Winchester John Philpot spat upon a fellow Protestant who dared to defend the old heresy of Arianism. Philpot was burned at the stake for his beliefs in 1555, but before this, he wrote his *Apologie of Iohan Philpot Written for Spitting upon an Arrian, with an Inuectiue against the Arrians (the Very Natural Chyldren of Antichrist) with an Admonition to All That Be Faythfull in Christ, to Beware of Them, and of Other Late Sprong Heresies, as of the Most Enemies of the Gospell*. Published posthumously in 1556, Philpot uses his tract to apologize in the sixteenth-century sense of the word, namely, to *justify* his decision to spit on someone rather than to express regret for doing so and explain the many ways in which the Arian got what was coming to him.[4] Some rather choice extracts from the text serve to illustrate his convictions:

> Who hauyng any spitte in his body, may not thinke it wel bestowed vpon suche wicked blasphemours of God

and his worde? *I* woulde I had a fountayne of spitle to spatle on them, I woulde my spittle myght be of so great vertue against them, as the wordes of S. Paule was against Bariesu[.][5]

Philpot is unequivocal that his act of spitting is as effective and as virtuous a defence of his beliefs as language would be. Philpot describes the Arian as 'arrogaunt, ignoraunt and obstinatlye blinded'[6] and focuses less on why he spat on him, asking instead why more of his Christian brethren did not follow his example, recalling that Moses was praised for assaulting an Egyptian for his contrary religious beliefs.[7] One of the more chilling justifications of his actions is that God himself condones his aggressive zeal, saying, 'God loueth not luke warme souidiars, in ye batel of fayth, but suche as be earnest and violent, shall inherite his kyngdome'.[8] His act of spitting is his own attempt at a violently crude baptism, an enforced bid at conversion with the Archdeacon marking out the Arian as having sinful thoughts by hawking water from his righteous mouth in an act of spiritual cleansing.

In this chapter, it is my contention that the spitting on Shylock in *The Merchant of Venice* is intimately connected with his eventual conversion to Christianity. From the first moment we learn of Shylock being spat upon in the play's third scene, the moneylender's eventual conversion is foreshadowed by Antonio's line '[t]he Hebrew will turn Christian, he grows kind' (1.3.171). *The Merchant of Venice* reveals how the biblical narrative of religious persecution has been reversed: since the Jews spat upon Jesus, the Christians must now spit upon the Jews. It is a grotesque inversion of a grotesque image. For Shylock, the enforced conversion is far worse than being spat upon, but they share similar traits. Both acts mark him out as 'herald of his own condemnation':[9] in being 'cleansed' of his Jewishness, he is tarnished by Christianity, his identity forever tainted by the water of his enemies that cannot be washed away. The boundary panic experienced by the Venetians over his Jewish identity is perfectly matched by the boundary panic of Shylock being spat upon, with the latter becoming an embodied social metaphor of the former.

Shylock's adversaries perform the act of spitting on a 'misbeliever' to mark him out as physically, as well as spiritually, distinct. Shylock's speech in 1.3 contains some of the most poignant evidence of how he is shamed within Venetian society:

> Signior Antonio, many a time and oft
> In the Rialto you have rated me
> About my moneys and my usances.
> Still have I borne it with a patient shrug,
> For sufferance is the badge of all our tribe.
> You call me misbeliever, cut-throat dog,
> And spit upon my Jewish gaberdine,
> And all for use of that which is mine own.
> Well, then, it now appears you need my help.
> Go to, then, you come to me, and you say,
> 'Shylock, we would have moneys.' You say so.
> You, that did void your rheum upon my beard
> And foot me as your spurn a stranger cur
> Over your threshold, moneys is your suit.
> What should I say to you? Should I not say,
> 'Hath a dog money? Is it possible
> A cur can lend three thousand ducats?' Or
> Shall I bend low and in a bondman's key,
> With bated breath and whispering humbleness,
> Say this: 'Fair sir, you spat on me Wednesday last,
> You spurned me such a day; another time,
> You called me dog: and, for these courtesies,
> I'll lend you thus much moneys.'
>
> (1.3.102–24)

In the space of twenty lines, Shylock refers three separate times to being spat on; in particular, his 'Jewish gaberdine', a marker of religious difference, is singled out as an object for shame. We should note that Antonio's action of spitting at Shylock's beard may well be related to the beard's status as a symbol of traditional masculinity, which Antonio wishes to negate through spitting in order to 'feminize' him and neutralize any agency he might possess. As in Christopher Marlowe's earlier play, *The Jew of Malta*, Jews are referred to as aliens in *The Merchant of Venice*, as we see when Portia is passing sentence upon him ('If it be proved against an alien / That by direct or indirect attempts / He seek the life of any citizen [...]' (4.1.345–7)). This sense of the foreign, unknown Other is coupled with the fear of contamination from such a body. In fact, Lancelot speaks his grief at being Shylock's servant, calling his master 'a very Jew' (2.2.86) and saying, 'I am a Jew if I serve the Jew any longer' (2.2.91–2). The implication here is that Jewishness is contagious and can spread to others if one spends too much time in their company. Indeed, Gobbo goes on to say that Lancelot 'hath a great infection' (2.2.103) from serving Shylock; the Jew must be spat out of the body politic before he contaminates the state of Venice yet further.

The persecution of the Jews was an ancient phenomenon which was still affecting Europe in the early modern period. In 1492, around 50,000 Jews were given an ultimatum of either leaving Castile and Aragon or converting to Christianity (the latter is, of course, Shylock's ultimate fate).[10] John Hale's *The Civilization of Europe in the Renaissance* emphasizes the inconsistent treatment of Jewish minorities in the fifteenth and sixteenth centuries: 'Jews were expelled from Naples in 1501 and allowed back in 1509, from Genoa in 1516, only to return the following year. They were driven from Florence in 1494, allowed back in 1513, banished again in 1527 and readmitted in 1531'.[11] As a consequence, the status of Jews within European society was regularly in flux, leaving them at the mercy of changing legislation and lacking a distinct homeland. Martin Luther called for the banishment of Jews, labelling them a 'disgusting vermin', and these pestilent associations were rooted in their denial of Jesus Christ's divinity.[12] As Aaron Kitch points out, Marlowe's Maltese Jew, Barabas, shares his name with the murderer freed by

Pilate, which resulted in the condemnation of Christ and consequently the scapegoating of Barabas as a Jew,[13] an allusion which was surely one of Marlowe's considerations in naming his eponymous character.

Within Venice itself, the Jews were subject to a variety of ostracizing treatments. According to W. D. Howells, they were

> obliged to wear a badge of yellow color upon the breast, to distinguish them from the Christians, and later a yellow cap, then a red hat, and then a hat of oil-cloth. They could not acquire houses or lands in Venice [...] They were assigned a dwelling place in the vilest and unhealthiest part of the city, and their quarter was called Ghetto, from the Hebrew *nghedah*, a congregation. They were obliged to pay their landlords a third more rent than Christians paid; the ghetto was walled in, and its gates were kept by Christian guards, who every day opened them at dawn and closed them at dark, and who were paid by the Jews.[14]

Physically marked out as different through the wearing of specified garments and given no alternative but to live separately from the other citizens, the Venetian authorities were responding to a keen sense of 'boundary panic'. In England, the social treatment of Jews was less harsh. James Shapiro insists that 'while Jews were not fully tolerated or granted citizenship in early modern England, they were never subject to violent attacks, forced to convert, penned up in ghettos, or burned in inquisitorial fires, as they were elsewhere in Europe'.[15] Furthermore, Shapiro sets out to disprove J. R. Green's belief that 'from the time of Edward to that of Cromwell no Jew touched English ground'.[16] He cites a wide range of contemporary documents, including the testimony of Pedro de Santa Cruz, a prisoner of war who was repatriated to Madrid in 1588 following a ten-month detention in London. In the surviving material, Pedro de Santa Cruz testifies that there were many Jewish Marranos in the city, claiming that it 'is public and notorious that in their own homes they live as such observing their Jewish rites; but publicly they attend Lutheran Churches, and listen to the sermons, and take the bread and wine'.[17]

There remained significant social tension regarding foreigners within English society, perhaps due to suspicion of those who ostensibly attended the required churches in public but worshipped differently in private. While there were no specific violent attacks on Jews living in London, there were riots attacking the city's 'aliens' in the sixteenth century, which may well have included anti-Jewish sentiment. In the May Day riots of 1517, London's immigrants were 'brutally attacked', and in Spring 1551, there was both a formal complaint made against the aliens to the Lord Mayor and an attempt to attack foreigners which was prevented by the city authorities.[18] Gillian Woods also notes that dramatists such as Shakespeare 'seem to capitalize on the tensions of 1590s London [which] reached a peak in 1593 with the publishing of libels threatening violence against strangers'.[19] An example of this was the Apprentice riot in Tower Hill on 29 June 1595, where 'the poor tradesmen made a riot upon the strangers in Southwark, and other parts of the City of London'. During this violent outburst,

> a crowd of a thousand or so stoned the city officers who tried to pacify them [...] What disturbed the rioters of 1595 so much about the aliens they attacked was that these strangers were 'seen as forming an inward-looking society of their own deliberately cutting themselves off from their hosts'.[20]

This behaviour from the Londoners seems at first contradictory: they are frustrated that there are aliens in their city at all, but further angered by the fact that they keep to themselves. However, this tension is not contradictory but remains entirely part of a city's suspicion of its immigrants: that they are parasites who enjoy the benefits of the city, but who are not seen to give anything back in return. Woods further argues that '[a]nti-alien sentiments ran high at periods of economic crisis',[21] and as John Hale notes, this led society's marginal Jews to be blamed when trouble arose, such as 'when wars went wrong or when food shortages pushed prices sky-high; these were times when preachers called for vengeance upon the crucifiers'.[22] The Jews' betrayal of Jesus Christ would remain a primary reason for their apparent untrustworthiness in the eyes of the Christians, and being Jewish was evidently seen as a synonym for being deceitful, as we see in *1 Henry IV* when Falstaff attempts to convince Hal and Poins of his honesty by saying 'or I am a Jew else, an 'Ebrew Jew' (2.4.173).

The idea that Jews such as Shylock may be inherently untrustworthy is further highlighted through canine imagery in *The Jew of Malta*. In one of Barabas' numerous asides to the audience, he sneers that '[w]e Jews can fawn like spaniels when we please, / And when we grin, we bite' (2.3.20–1). This moment capitalizes on his inhumane, bestial qualities, as someone who lives on the margins of society rather than being fully assimilated into it. Barabas further tells us that in order to show he knows his place, he must '[h]eave up my shoulders when they call me dog' (2.3.24). In this latter example, he uses the exact same image that Shylock will go on to use in *The Merchant of Venice* when describing his ill-treatment at the hands of men like Antonio: he bears it all 'with a patient shrug' (1.3.105), even when called a 'cut-throat dog' (1.3.107). Yet this linguistic echo nonetheless allows Shakespeare to play with the meaning of these lines. Barabas' speech implies that his Jewish nature allows him to dissemble and play the part of a lowly social outcast while at the same time cynically exploiting the possibilities that such a marginal position offers up. While Marlowe presents the outsider Jew as having malicious agency precisely because of his alien status, Shakespeare indicates that Shylock is only allowed to be what society labels him. The three separate references to dogs within his lengthy speech in 1.3 ('[y]ou call me misbeliever, cut-throat dog' (1.3.107), 'Hath a dog money?' (1.3.117), and '[y]ou called me dog' (1.3.123)) evoke how Shylock has been worn down gradually to the level of a subservient beast. Even the language describing Shylock as bending 'low', having 'bated breath' and a sense of 'humbleness' hints at the idea of an obedient dog begging to be treated kindly, having been tamed by a strict master (1.3.119–20).

While Barabas dies screaming '[d]amned Christian dogs' (5.5.85), Shylock is only allowed to stay alive provided that he himself becomes a Christian dog. As Brett Greatley-Hirsch observes, 'if Shylock is figured as a dog, then Antonio symbolically adopts the role of dog-trainer', and as we saw in Chapter 3, spitting was a method used to placate dogs and communicate their lower status within the pack.[23] The function of dogs in social metaphor is, according to Bruce Boehrer, threefold: 'as intimate friend or companion', 'the identification of dogs with slaves and other abjected individuals', and 'the association of dogs with predatory outsiders'.[24] As Greatley-Hirsch notes, Jews fall under the latter two categories.[25] But the process of dehumanizing people to the level of beasts is not without inherent danger. Shylock's lines '[t]hou call'dst me dog before thou hadst a cause, / But since I am a dog, beware my fangs' (3.3.6–7) hint at the monstrosity that society can create when it shames its members. Indeed, Shylock even says that he '[e]ngaged my friend to his mere enemy, / To feed my means' (3.2.261–362). These ideas of wolfish biting and cannibalism recall the 'biting' usury and penury that Jewish moneylending was said to cause. Combined with Antonio's very literal fear of having Shylock take his flesh, we discover not just a boundary panic at Jews crossing social lines but the fear of Jews consuming and destroying Christians and of the Christians themselves being digested and assimilated into a Jewish body. Perhaps it is sinisterly apt that Shylock greets Antonio with the phrase 'Rest you fair, good signor! / Your worship was the last man in our mouths' (1.3.51–2). In Shylock's final scene, we hear his desires described as 'wolfish, bloody, starved, and ravenous': a dog who is clearly ready to turn on his master (4.1.138).

Yet, recent scholarship by Emma Smith interrogates our assumptions about Shylock's racial identity and its signifiers.

She argues that when the history of Jewish characters upon the early modern stage is fully considered, there is very little to 'support the assumption that Elizabethan audiences were primed to expect a wicked stereotype, or even that such a stereotype can be traced'.[26] Marlowe's Barabas, as Jewish stage villain, is an outlier, and other 'Jewish characters in drama before *The Merchant of Venice* are rare and sufficiently diverse' to revoke the notion that there might be particular physical stereotypes, such as red hair or large noses.[27] In fact, James Robertes entered the copy of a new book listed as 'the Marchaunt of Venyce or otherwise called the Iewe of Venyce',[28] and the interchangeable title reveals an intriguing degree of exchange between two of the play's central characters, wrestling each other for prominence in the Stationers' Register in much the same manner as their dramatized battle of wills. Such interchangeability also recalls Portia's question: 'Which is the merchant here, and which the Jew?' (4.1.170). There is little way of knowing whether or not William Shakespeare ever seriously considered naming his play 'The Jew of Venice'. However, it is with some certainty that his play can be read in part as a response to Marlowe's popular *The Jew of Malta*, which had its first recorded performance in 1592. It is therefore plausible that 'The Jew of Venice' as potential title for *The Merchant of Venice* is a colloquial association between Marlowe's classic drama and Shakespeare's. Throughout the play's history, from performance to print culture, we see the play's uneasy variance between Shylock and Antonio as to which of them gets ownership of the story. But, more than that, it means that Shylock must be spat upon and be marked out as physically different from the Venetians in order to avoid such confusion. As a response to *The Jew of Malta*, *The Merchant of Venice* capitalizes on the Jewish-villain trope, which Marlowe introduced to the stage in order to further explore the social expectations of Jewishness.

In Marlowe's play, Katherine marks Barabas out as a distinctly Other body: 'Converse not with him, he is cast off from heaven' (2.3.160). Yet this sense of spiritual bankruptcy is compounded by how early modern culture applied categories of difference to the Jewish body by perpetuating spurious beliefs about their hygiene.²⁹ Given the medieval and early modern notion that bad odours spread disease, it is easy to imagine city authorities segregating Jewish aliens for this purpose, aligning morality with practicality, which naturally led to the further perpetuation and normalization of the myth. In fact, Jonathan Gil Harris reminds us that Jewish bodies are often linked with grotesquely faecal images³⁰ and recalls how Barabas reappears from the Maltese sewers and is thus styled as 'cultural excrement'.³¹ And yet, despite this threat of contamination, they could not be further controlled: if they were killed to control their numbers and encroachment 'their bodies might contaminate the air'.³²

Crucially, fears about the Jewish body's odours and strangeness were predicated on the widely held early modern belief that male Jews menstruated. Thomas Calvert's *The Blessed Jew of Marocco* or *A Blackamoor Made White* relates the myth that Jewish men were divinely punished for their sins against God's son by being subjected to '*cursu menstruo sanguinis*, with a very frequent Bloud-fluxe'. In a mistaken bid to cast off this curse, 'they every yeare get the blood of some Christian Childe, whom they murder; whereas if they had understood aright, this *sanguine Christiano*, was Christs blood that they should get, which in the Sacrament we receive, to the healing and saving of sinners, so many of us as are turned to Christ, we are presently healed of our Father's curse'.³³ The myth of this bodily punishment might have influenced and perpetuated the belief that Jews were thought to give off a repugnant odour, referred to by Harris as *foetar judaicus*.³⁴ Menstrual blood was defined by Leviticus as a foul secretion, and it was thought that those who menstruated had the potential to infect others with their touch.³⁵ Katz concludes that 'the location of male Jews in an indeterminate middle gender zone could be very unsettling in a mental culture that tended to see things very much in terms of binary oppositions'.³⁶ Rachel Trubowitz persuasively argues for the acknowledgement that the leaking of menstrual blood from a male Jewish body places Jews in close proximity to wet-nurses as a 'female' threat to social and familial stability – a perception strengthened by anti-Semitic attitudes towards circumcision ... Such leakage was also perceived as both symptom of and explanation for what was thought to be Jews' insatiable thirst for Christian blood.[37]

Shylock is spat on because he is already considered feminized and because this notion must be further perpetuated. It is easy for an audience to forget that Jessica's mother is absent from the drama; so too is Abigail's mother and Barabas' wife in Marlowe's play. It is possible, though, that the feminization of Barabas and Shylock's racial identities means that, for the Venetians and Maltese (and possibly an Elizabethan audience), the mother-figure is present in the male Jewish body. Both women and Jews were marked out by the supposed vulnerability of their bodies and were defined in opposition to the masculinized, 'completed', and unleaky corporal form. Gail Kern Paster's influential book *The Body Embarrassed* describes how Renaissance medical texts, iconography, and oral culture inscribe

women as leaky vessels by isolating one element of the female body's material expressiveness – its production of fluids – as excessive, hence either disturbing or shameful. It also characteristically links this liquid expressiveness to excessive verbal fluency. In both formations, the issue is women's bodily self-control or, more precisely, the representation of a particular kind of uncontrol as a function of gender.[38]

Indeed, some of the characters in *The Merchant of Venice* wish for Shylock's speech to be controlled too. Lancelot says of Shylock, 'Give him a halter!' (2.2.99), linking him with a typically feminine need to be orally restrained. In the words of Boose, 'shame is already a gendered piece of cultural capital', and her article on the restraining of women deemed 'scolds' underwrites the early modern fashion for silencing voices that question the community's *status quo*.³⁹ Boose's exploration of women being forced to wear bridles restraining the mouth and tongue, then, has further ramifications for Shylock: Gratiano answers, 'A halter gratis – nothing else, for God's sake' when the court ask what mercy should be shown to Shylock (4.1.375). But there is an even more sinister meaning here, with a halter also being another word for a hangman's noose. Execution, of course, is the ultimate punishment; God forbid that Shylock should speak, or spit, back.

Trubowitz also notes the belief in Jewish violence, as alluded to in Calvert's text. It was believed that Jewish gangs pursued 'blood-libels', whereby they would abduct and kill a Gentile child and drink purifying Christian blood from its veins in order to stop the believed menstruation of Jewish men.⁴⁰ This appears to be a horrifying inversion of the Puritan imagery of ministers as nourishing mothers, from which churchgoers could 'sucke in religion'.⁴¹ The Jews are seen as the antithesis of this image, parasitically sucking out Christian goodness. The inverted images we are presented with here not only reveal the antithetical cultural associations of Christians and Jews but also that these cultural associations are deliberately constructed in direct opposition to each other. This adds to our gendered reading of Shylock's motives and enhances our reading of what I earlier referred to as his 'wolfish' desire for a pound of Christian flesh. It is another way in which he is an Other on the wrong side of society's boundaries, who must be purged from the Elizabethan body politic. It is conceivable, then, that Shylock's desire for Antonio's pound of flesh is to gain the Christian blood that will rid him off his menses. It was also believed that baptism would stop the 'courses' in Jewish men,⁴² and perhaps Antonio's request that Shylock 'presently become a Christian' (4.1.383) can be read as an example of mercy from a Christian man very nearly crucified by the Jew. More often than not, Shylock's acceptance line of 'I am content' (4.1.389) is performed with heavy resignation,⁴³ but given this reading, perhaps there is some potential for interpretation in the opposite direction. However, it is unlikely that such an interpretation could be made reasonably clear to an audience, and besides, it still forces Shylock to convert against his will despite his strong religious beliefs.

Yet such religious tension ironically aligns Shylock with Jesus himself. The shaming of Jesus is undoubtedly the most noteworthy cultural incident of spitting that would have been known in Renaissance society. The Gospel of Mark says of Christ's fate at the hands of the Jews: 'And they shall mock him, and scourge him, and spit upon him, and kill him: but the third day he shall rise again' (Mark: 10:34). A sermon published in 1619 'On the Foole and His Sport' given by the preacher Thomas Adams contends that Christ was spat at on the way to his crucifixion 'to purge away our uncleannesse'.[44] Evidently, such physical scorning is part of the prophesied death for God's son, and his taking on of mankind's sins and shame; it is as if the mocks, scourges, and spits literally become part of humanity's burdens as borne by Christ.

Visual representations of Jesus being spat upon often occur in the 'ecco homo' tradition, which depicts the buffeting of Christ. While Bruce Smith argues that in early modern visual culture, 'the spitting is turned into a thrusting out of tongues', there are at least three examples where the spittle itself is visible.[45] Figure 8 shows Meister von Messkirch's blindfolded, barefoot Jesus, with a slight halo around his head, being spat at by two men: on the left, a man who grabs Christ's head to prevent him turning away as he spits, and on the right, a kneeling man who sticks his fingers down his throat in order to retch up an impressive projectile of spittle. We see a similar depiction in Johann Koerbecke's *Marienfelder Altar* (*Mocking of Christ*) (Figure 9). Again, those intimidating Jesus move close to his face in order to spit at him (note the man depicted to the immediate right of Jesus). In these examples, we see depictions of Jews spitting upon Christ as a crucial part of his pre-crucifixion shaming ritual. The images depict Christ being shamed, but the sympathy is very much focused on him precisely *because* we know the rest of the Christian story,

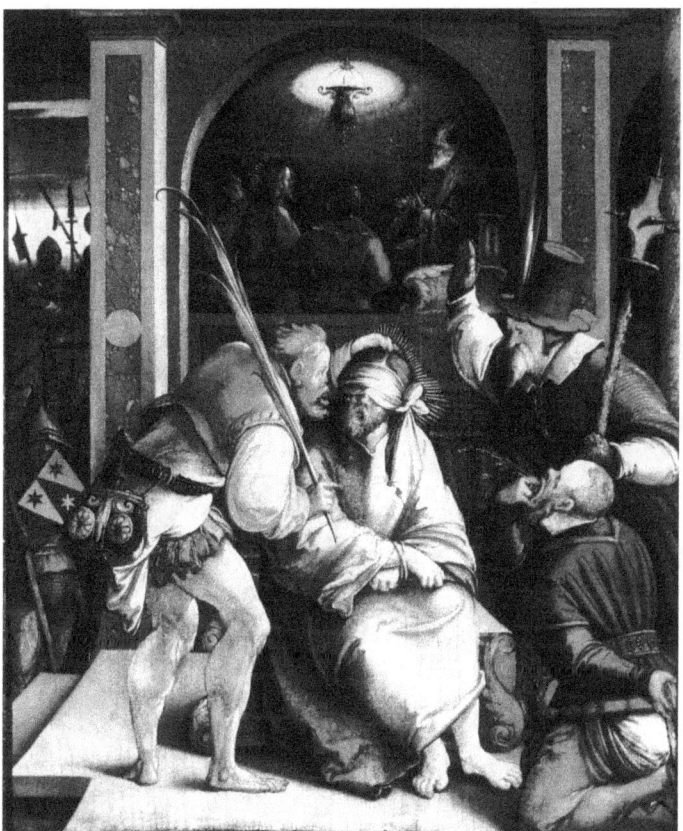

FIGURE 8 *Meister von Messkirch,* Verspottung Christi (Mocking of Christ), *tempera and oil on wood, c.1535–1538. Courtesy of Wikimedia (https://commons.wikimedia.org/wiki/File:Verspottung_Christi.jpg).*

and that those spitting at him will go on to be proved wrong as Christ proves his divinity by rising again. These visual representations suggest that it is those spitting who should be ashamed of themselves, even as they engage in the shaming of another. In this way, we see how spitting upon someone

FIGURE 9 *Johann Koerbecke,* Mairenfelder Altar, linker Flügel außen unten rechts: Verspottung (Mocking of Christ), *painting (tempera on panel), 1457. Courtesy of Wikimedia (https://commons.wikimedia.org/wiki/File:Johann_Koerbecke_Verspottung.jpg)*

can create empathy for them due to the cruelness of the degradation, creating in *The Merchant of Venice* a sympathy for Shylock which is not extended to Barabas in *The Jew of Malta*.

The Christian association of water with transformation lends the act of spitting a further intriguing connotation. Thomas Adams' 'Sermon upon the Passion' equates spitting and expiating our sins upon Christ with the purging rites of baptism and the embracing of the Holy Spirit by the soul. He writes of Christ that '[h]is face was besmeared with spittle, because we had spit impudent blasphemies against heauen ... Hee would be polluted with their spettle, that hee might wash us'.[46] There is a certain fluidity between the hawking of the spittle and the waters of baptism, as if they are part of an exchange of identities where an unholy liquid is swapped with a holy one, thus transforming a sinful soul into one that is blessed. Consequently, baptism is seen as a symbol of the passion of Christ, as implied by Romans 6.3:

Know ye not, that all we which have been baptized into Jesus Christ, have been baptized into his death?

The Passion and the rites of baptism are therefore ritually linked in the Christian cycle of death and rebirth, with the sins of the world, represented by the shameful blasphemies spat upon Christ, being cleansed by the holy water of sanctification. While Shylock has been spat upon by Antonio before, it is the baptismal act of conversion which proves to be the most shameful water forced into the Jew's face. The earlier incidents of spitting humiliated Shylock because of his spiritual *difference*; his conversion humiliates him into submission to a religious *similarity* with the Christians he despises.

Little wonder, then, that during the play we see so much evidence of Shylock's insularity within the Venetian community. Wishing to keep his family away from the rest of society on the night of the Christian revels, he says:

> What, are there masques? Hear you me, Jessica,
> Lock up my doors, and when you hear the drum
> And the vile squealing of the wry-necked fife,
> Clamber not you up to the casements then
> Nor thrust your head into the public street
> To gaze upon Christian fools with varnished faces;
> But stop my house's ears – I mean my casements –
> Let not the sound of shallow foppery enter
> My sober house.
>
> (2.5.27–35)

The enjambment between the lines marks his urgent concern that his boundaries will be crossed; in fact, he is already imagining such transgressions taking place. He fears that the Christian partying will penetrate his house, or, to be frank, his daughter. He even seems to confuse the two at one point, accidentally personifying the house ('but stop my house's ears') and equating his property with his daughter. He struggles to protect both from Christian influences and fails in this endeavour by the play's conclusion. Two scenes earlier, Shylock's daughter Jessica complains that '[o]ur house is hell' (2.3.2) and wishes to escape the Jewish domestic boundaries that contain and restrict her. 'Becom[ing] a Christian and [Lorenzo's] loving wife' (2.3.20) is her way of breaching these boundaries and facing a future where she can be a wife of a Christian rather than a daughter of a Jew, and it is worth speculating which of these two things are more important to her. She bemoans:

> Alack, what heinous sin is it in me
> To be ashamed to be my father's child!
> But though I am a daughter to his blood
> I am not to his manners.
>
> (2.3.15–18)

While many teenage daughters are likely to find their fathers embarrassing, the social context of ghettoized living has presumably encouraged feelings of shame within herself at her own identity, and her decision to marry Lorenzo is a sad choice to eliminate what is Jewish within herself.

The Merchant of Venice is set within a society marked by boundary panic in many senses, and not just in a way that impacts upon the Jewish community. The economy is predicated on foreign exchange, and the merchant Antonio's high risk trade investments are described thus by Shylock:

> he hath an argosy bound to Tripolis, another to the Indies; I understand moreover upon the Rialto he hath a third at Mexico, a fourth for England, and other ventures he hath squandered abroad. But ships are but boards, sailors but men; there be land rats, and water rats, water thieves and land thieves – I mean pirates – and then there is the peril of waters, winds and rocks.
>
> (1.3.15–21)

There is a very real possibility that the vessels carrying wealth will be dashed upon the shore of a strange land, and indeed that is exactly what happens to Antonio's investments: not one vessel escapes 'the dreadful touch / Of merchant-marring rocks' (3.2.269–70). As Antonio quite literally loses everything on the boundary of a foreign shore, it is easy to see the tension inherent in mercantile exchange. Despite the potential profits, there is an undeniable risk of trading with Others in the Elizabethan period.

Of course, this is not the only example of trading in the play. Portia's casket game has been established by her father in an attempt to ensure that she is matched with someone who apparently deserves her. Given her own lack of power in this situation, Portia also feels a kind of boundary panic. At the close of 1.2, she exclaims, 'Come, Nerissa; sirrah, go before: / Whiles we shut the gate upon one wooer, another knocks at the door' (1.2.109–10). She is bombarded on all sides by potential suitors, none of whom are to her liking, and she wishes herself to be shut away from them. Notably, the only man she likes is fellow Venetian Bassanio and finds fault with the foreign men who seek to win her heart (or at least, the right casket). When Portia enters the scene in 2.7, it is with a character that the Folio names 'Morocco', conflating his identity with his race in a manner that cannot help but be compared with Shylock often being named simply as 'Jew'. After the Prince of Morocco selects the wrong casket, Portia's relief is clear: 'A gentle riddance! Draw the curtains, go. / Let all of his complexion choose me so' (2.7.78–9). Foreign trade within the Venetian economy is one thing, but Portia is relieved not to cross racial boundaries in her marriage.

In Venice, and other early modern European countries (England included), trade was becoming increasingly dependent upon foreign investment and exchange. The boundary panic of the Venetians, like those of Elizabethan Londoners, may then also be tied up in a fear of impending reliance on strangers and aliens. While panic about them is often voiced in imagery redolent of carnivorous sub-human dogs who will literally bleed them dry, or as spiritually corrupt would-be betrayers, such fears are deeply rooted in the creeping dependence that the Venetians – and the English – have on such 'strangers'. Antonio's choice to spit upon Shylock evidences such resentment: even though he spits at a man he conceives of as being a devil-like creature, he knows that turning to him for a loan is his only way of helping out his much-loved friend Bassanio. Shylock's feminized body, believed to be leaky, strange, and odorous, gives the Venetians a more easily expressible reason for hating the Jews in their city on an everyday level, but given the conclusion of the trial scene in *The Merchant of Venice*, the persecution of his person is ultimately bound up in the culmination of all these elements: how his religion represents him as 'other' to the Christians.

With Jewish characters such as Shylock and Barabas, we see how the fears of increased contact with the Other in a burgeoning mercantile age leads to the experience of our own inadequacies, and consequently the need to perform social acts of overcompensation by enacting gestures that perpetuate the agency we fear is being lost. *The Merchant of Venice* reminds us that we are a society who crave villains as much as we need heroes: we are manipulating the immediate past to suit our own ends, and constructing enemies in order to define our own selves. We may spit out these undesirables, but it does not change the fact that they originated from our own deficiencies, and therein lies their shame, rooted within our own. This tension reveals the shamefulness of spitting: the emotion, and, indeed, the saliva, are our own disgust projected onto others.

5

Horning: Fragile Masculinity in *Othello*

FIGURE 10 *From the title page of* The Resolution of the Women of London to the Parliament, *woodcut, 1642.* © *The British Library Board.*

The above image (Figure 10) is from a political tract entitled *The Resolution of the Women of London to the Parliament, Wherein They Declare Their Hot Zeale in Sending Their Husbands to the Warres, in Defence of King and Parliament*. Published in London in 1642 on the brink of the English Civil War, the text implores 'let our husbands fight, they are mad-brain'd enough, they can fight with their poore wives, let them try now if they can fight with their enemies'.[1] The wives of such men have much to gain in this scenario: 'then will we in our husbands absence, live as merrily as may be, drinke, feast, and walk abroad; and if we have a minde to it, keep and maintaine a friend, that upon occasion may doe us a pleasure'.[2] The woodcut has clearly been re-appropriated from a previous usage. The 'go to the wars' speech bubble has been inserted in such a way as to take away the detail at the edge of the wife's face, meaning that, although this tract was published in 1642, the image, given its re-used state, must have an earlier provenance. What is more, this well-used image captures a sense of a particularly potent anxiety: the fear that while a man risks life and limb for king and country, a woman will use her newfound freedom to entertain extramarital lovers.

This particular fear is signalled in the woodcut by the use of the horns sitting on the husband's head. The signifier of horns growing out of a man's forehead – seemingly able to grow through hats or other headgear, as we see here – acts as a visual indicator that the man is a victim of cuckoldry. Due to the horns' placement on top of the head, the man wearing them is unable to see them himself and unwillingly becomes a site of mockery to everyone else. This is one of the most painful things about cuckoldry: that everyone knows about your shame before you do yourself. It is not merely that your wife has been unfaithful; it is that you were the last to know, and that your friends, family, and colleagues were all able to see what you could not. Such is Othello's fear; however, it is a misplaced one, conjured into his mind by the malevolent Iago.

While the idea that a cuckold unknowingly wears horns on his head is figurative rather than literal, the use of the *cornutu* gesture to symbolize such shame was real indeed. Consisting of the index and little finger being raised (to represent the horns) with the thumb tucking the middle and ring fingers into the palm of the hand, it was a gesture widely known in the Renaissance as a way of slandering a man and undermining his honour and masculinity. The idea of seeing horns upon the head of a cuckolded man translates his body into a site where shame can easily be read; this is further alluded to in the above woodcut as the horned man is also holding a horn book: a study primer sealed with a clear sheet of horn. Such primers were often used to learn alphabets or prayers, which led to an association of the material of horn with reading. Reading horns upon a human body, then, creates a particularly potent idea of *body language*, where the physical appearance or actions of a person can be endowed with deeper meaning if one only knows how to read it correctly. While Othello is not *actually* cuckolded, the *fear* that he is undermines his status, sanity, and makes him vulnerable to the shaming process to the extent that he commits murder and eventual suicide, aiming to destroy his shame by killing his wife and himself, thus erasing the language of shame he fears is written on their bodies for all to see.

Othello gives us a drama driven by what we would now call 'fragile masculinity': the paradoxical notion that while men are traditionally attributed with qualities such as strength, any questioning of a man's worth results in hypersensitivity. This inevitably reveals that 'masculinity' and 'femininity' are constructed presentations shaped by cultural expectation rather than innate identities. Bruce R. Smith writes how notions of masculinity seem to be precarious within Shakespeare's work, and how these notions differ from being born biologically male. Using David Gilmore's work on concepts of cultural masculinity, Smith argues that to be masculine is 'something that must be worked toward and maintained' and is not inherent to any*body* in particular.[3] For this reason, masculinity is constantly in flux. Therefore, manhood is what Gilmore describes as 'a restricted status', one in which 'there are always men who fail the test'.[4] Military men, such as Othello and also Macbeth, are perhaps especially vulnerable to ideals of masculinity. As Smith notes, Macbeth's masculinity 'is constantly on the line':[5] Macbeth claims, 'I dare do all that may become a man, / Who dares do more, is none' (1.7.46–7), yet his wife still questions him, asking, 'Are you a man?' (3.4.55). Indeed, such is Lady Macbeth's desire for her husband to maintain his status as a stoic, resolute soldier, that she wishes to be of a similar nature herself, calling to be unsexed and drained of the nourishing breast milk which proclaims her a woman (1.5.40–8). Instead of a creator, a role traditionally associated with the feminine capacity to reproduce, she wishes to be a destroyer, a soldier bent on death. Like Macbeth, Othello also resolves to protect his status within Renaissance modes of masculinity; in fact, he does this from the play's opening scenes: 'My parts, my title and my perfect soul / Shall manifest me rightly' (1.2.30–1). But it is Iago who taunts his masculinity to the point of madness: 'Are you a man? have you a soul or sense?' (3.3.377). In Othello's case, seeking a stable form of masculinity in the face of marital infidelity turns him from military general to 'repugnant barbarian',[6] epitomizing a precarious masculinity undermined by the fear of failing to live up to certain social expectations of manhood.

This chapter focuses on the instability of signifiers themselves; the very act of interrogating these gestural images and the meaning they convey is precisely what gives them potency in these plays. As Paul Menzer puts it, 'For an art that depends on the derivable meanings of external habits, the unreliability of "indicators or symptoms" of distress or grief or joy or fear constitutes a genuine crisis'.[7] Othello never once sees someone making the cuckold's horns at him, but his *belief* that it might be happening is enough to drive him to insecurity in his masculinity and ultimately his mad revenge. Such actions, from their ephemeral moment of performance, remain alive and present when remembered or reimagined. It is this notion of past shame being relived and mocked through imagined gestural moments that lead to the insanity and ultimate tragedy of *Othello*.

In his late Elizabethan comedy, *A Midsummer Night's Dream*, Shakespeare gives us his multifaceted take on the dramatic imagination through his staging of mechanicals-turned-actors and a fairy kingdom capable of playing out the political tensions of Athens itself. As the final act begins, the newly wedded Theseus, responding to his now-wife, Hippolyta, ponders the workings of imaginary forces:

> *Lovers and madmen have such seething brains,*
> *Such shaping fantasies*, that apprehend
> More than cool reason ever comprehends.
> *The lunatic, the lover, and the poet*
> *Are of imagination all compact.*
> *One sees more devils than vast hell can hold:*
> *That is the madman.* The lover, all as frantic,
> Sees Helen's beauty in a brow of Egypt.
> The poet's eye, in a fine frenzy rolling,
> Doth glance from heaven to Earth, from Earth to heaven,
> *And as imagination bodies forth*
> *The forms of things unknown, the poet's pen*
> *Turns them to shapes and gives to airy nothing*
> *A local habitation and a name.*
>
> (5.1.4–18, my emphasis)

Here, we read how an 'airy nothing' can, with the use of imagination, be conjured into 'such shaping fantasies'. Interestingly, Theseus uses 'bodies' as a verb ('imagination bodies forth'), emphasizing how reading body language gives the imagination over to flights of fancy. Imagination is itself an act of creation, staged within the scaffold of the mind itself, and Theseus is able to see its potential dangers. Over time, the forces of imagination become a darker presence in Shakespeare's work. Writing *Othello* only a few years later, the imagination's ability to create fantasies becomes more monstrous, and, curiously, in the final scene, Desdemona tells

Othello, 'you're fatal then / When your eyes roll so' (5.2.37–8), recalling Theseus' line in *Midsummer* 'The poet's eye, in a fine frenzy rolling'. Theseus is talking of 'the lunatic, the lover, and the poet' in this speech: Othello goes on to become all three, speaking some of the play's most beautiful verse just before he murders his wife in a mad act of wounded love.

While there are comic monstrosities such as Bottom in *Midsummer*, *Othello* gives rise to monsters of the mind, where the hero believes 'a horned man's a monster, and a beast' (4.1.62). Unlike *Midsummer*, this is no dream, but a waking nightmare. These acts of creation, once unleashed, cannot be stopped, and the images that are created in Othello's mind become so potent precisely because they are fantasies which reshape themselves with every new piece of information into something yet more hideous. What is even more disturbing for an audience is how Iago himself tells Othello 'oft my jealousy / Shapes faults that are not' (3.3.150–1), the horrifying irony being that Iago is telling the truth of his own failings. But like the horns Othello fears are on his head, the audience sees the wool being pulled over his eyes. It is just as the Moor fears: he really is the last to know what is actually going on in terms of Iago's deceptions. Othello is destroyed not by an infidelity that never happens, but by the contagious fragile masculinity which spreads to him from Iago.

Othello's search for the 'ocular proof' (3.3.363) of his wife's infidelity culminates in an obsessive reading of her gestures with Cassio. Given that we cannot ever truly know the internal thoughts of someone else, it is tempting to try and read gesture or bodily performance as evidence of genuine emotion. John Lidgate's *The life and death of Hector* is a text which gives us insight into the relationship between inner emotional turmoil and its presentation as outward gesture. Here, we see two different descriptions, the first presenting a contented man, and the second presenting one who is angry:

> But when a man a smiling face doth make,
> With outward show of loue, and speaketh kind,

> They do his words and all his gestures take
> To be th'effects of his interior mind [...]
> So much his mind from him was alienate,
> That t'yeeld himselfe by no meanes then he might,
> And at his heart he was so passionate,
> Which boyled with such ranchor and dispight,
> That all that him beheld would iudge him mad,
> So strange a looke and gesture then he had.[8]

Of course, the first description needs to be problematized given how an outward appearance of happiness does not necessarily mean it is reflected in a person's own mind; in fact, it is this issue which makes the potential for reading gestures as proof of any sincere emotion a difficult one.[9] As I have written elsewhere, 'Gestures are performed actions: they are not necessarily evidence of certain emotions being felt, but they reflect the *desire* for there to be evidence'.[10] Reading the performance of certain emotions at face value is not always wise, particularly if Iago is involved, whose moniker 'honest' is specifically designed to draw attention to this discrepancy in his character.

Othello's mission is to capture the 'ocular proof' of his wife's betrayal, but instead the play reveals to us how what we see can be manipulated. In fact, the role of vision within early modern culture was being inherently questioned at this time. Stuart Clark argues persuasively that, during this period, 'European visual culture experienced not so much the rationalization as the de-rationalization of sight'.[11] Developing John Berger's belief that 'the relationship between what we see and what we know is never settled', Clark writes that such a relationship is constantly unfettered in the Renaissance, stating that '[i]n one context after another, vision came to be characterized by uncertainty and unreliability, such that access to visual reality could no longer be normally guaranteed. It is as though European intellectuals lost their optic nerve'.[12] Such concerns about the reliability of vision as a means of comprehending reality become especially dangerous in tragedies such as

Othello. Claire McEachern notes that Shakespeare does not actually feature any cuckolds in his plays, and yet the fear that a character may become one is one of his most repeated tropes.[13] Observing that cuckoldry is dramatic irony personified, she writes that

> [t]he dread of cuckoldry is a dread of becoming visible, the observed of all observers, of having your inmost domestic business revealed to the world. Thus a cuckold is emasculated, not merely by having his place taken by another, but in being rendered vulnerable to representation. The cuckold, who has failed to see his wife's behaviour, becomes a sign for others to see.[14]

For a man like Othello, who has worked against prejudice to ascend to a high military rank, the thought of becoming an unwilling spectacle and a site of ridicule spells disaster. But if the revelation of infidelity results in emasculation, then what is also revealed is the inherent fragility of masculinity itself. The act of revelation displays the act of carefully constructed masculinity, which, once deconstructed, it is forever undermined and cannot be viewed in the same way. This is the fear of the cuckold: that he loses ownership over the way others see him.

Returning to the gesture of cuckoldry itself – the *cornutu* – we may unpack more layers of meaning. Bulwer's *Chirologia and Chironomia* refers to the action as '*stultitiae notam in figo*', and he describes it as 'present[ing] the index and eare-finger wagging, with the thumb applied to the temples' (see Figure 2, and the gesture marked 'W').[15] He writes of it as an action

> used in our nimble fingered times to call one Cuckold, & to present the badge of Cuckoldry, *that mentall and imaginary horn*; seeming to cry, O man of happy note, whom fortune meaning highly to promote, hath stucke on thy fore-head the earnest-penny of succeeding good lucke; all which upbraiding tearmes many understand by this gesture only of the Fingers; for in this sense *the common use hath made*

it the known signall of disparagement, so naturally apt are the Fingers to speake scoffes ... your broad verball jest is nothing neare so piquant as these foule habits of reproach by gesture, which broch men as it were with a spit, and having once entred into the quicke like shafts with barbed heads a long time gaule with a sticking mischiefe: and to this feat of mockery the Fingers have been proclive to fashion out contempt, provoked forward by a naturall dicacity.[16]

Contemporary comic actors of Shakespeare's time are recorded to have used such gestures to mock certain audience members, much to the amusement of the other playgoers. Richard Tarlton, when pointed at by an audience member sitting in the gallery, gave a return gesture by holding up two fingers. The spectator 'asked him why he made hornes at him', and Tarlton responded that his fingers 'are tipt with nailes, which are like hornes, and I must make a shew of that which you are sure of'. Allegedly, this altercation continued at some length until the audience member, embarrassed, left the theatre, 'plucking his hat ouer his eyes' as he did so.[17] Another cuckolding jest is recorded in Anthony Copley's *Wits, Fittes and Fancies* (1595), and it gives us a rather tongue-in-cheek twist on the notion of 'ocular proof' being used to discern whether a wife is faithful or not:

An honest man that had but one eie and a quean to his wife, entring vpon the sudden into his bed chamber by night, a knaue chanced to be then a bed with her, who hearing her husbands voice, shifted him suddenlie behind the doore, and thus she said vnto her Goodman: What husband, is't you euen welcome my good husband: I hope in God my dreame is come to passe: I was euen now adream'd that you could see with either of your eyes, in so much as I waked for joy, and I hope to find it true: And with that she arose from out her bed, & comming toward him: Good husband (she said) let me lay my finger on your seeing eie, and then tell me whether you discerne anie thing with the other:

He answered: No, not anie thing. In this mean time she beckened to the Adulterer to be gone: who straight slipped from behind the doore downe the staires, and so scap'd quite away.[18]

This tale may well be apocryphal, but at its heart is a message about the power a cunning woman can have over her husband, where her lust for adultery is matched by her shrewdness in covering up the liaison. The story is undeniably amusing, which only goes to make the fear of cuckoldry more horrifying: no man wants to be made a laughing stock by his wife.

Traditionally, the legend behind the cuckold relates to ornithology, with the cuckoo being a creature that places its eggs in another bird's nest so that they might be raised by a different parent. W. Carew Hazlitt's *Dictionary of Faiths and Folklore* posits that the cuckolded husband, 'timid and incapable of protecting his honour, like that bird, is called by its name, and thus converted into an object of contempt and of derision'.[19] But there are a plethora of further associations with the horn gesture, one of which involves the practise of hunting. Emperor Andronicus would hang up the stag horns he had acquired to 'denote at once the manners of the city, the lasciviousness of the wives he had debauched, and the size of the animals he had made his prey, and that from hence the sarcasm spread abroad that the husband of an adulterous wife bare horns'.[20]

The manhood of a soldier is seen as an especially important status, and this is particularly pertinent in our analysis of Othello's jealousy. Carew Hazlitt also observes how the wearing of horns occurred during the Crusades, when they were used to distinguish between various national armies.[21] Furthermore, it is said that the emblem of horns became the sign of a cuckolded soldier, given his absence from home for several years. However, this symbol was not considered a laughing matter by everyone, as Carew Hazlitt advises: 'woe be to the man in those days that should have made a joke of the Holy War; which indeed, inconsideration of the expense of blood and treasure attending it, was a very serious affair'.[22] '[T]o put up horns against a neighbour's house' carried as much legal weight as that of a written libel in Spain and that it was also against the law in Venice, where even the son of a Doge was punished for committing this offence in the fourteenth century.[23] That Renaissance Venice should be a place where the allegation of cuckoldry is especially sensitive should heighten our sense of the gravity of Othello's tragedy; that the soldier who dupes him, Iago, has a Spanish name and also believes himself to be cuckolded, doubly so.

The fear of the cuckold's horns, and the prioritizing of 'ocular proof' in *Othello*, is emphasized by Jan Kott's comment that the play is 'a tragedy of gestures'.[24] In fact, it is a play about the tragic consequences of misreading such signs. Misjudging or mistiming gestures can happen at any time; it even occurred during King Christian of Denmark's visit to England in 1606. While staying at a county house in Theobalds with King James and his party,

> Christian, thinking he was being funny, made the cuckold's horns at the aged Charles Howard, earl of Nottingham, the Lord Admiral of England who was the legendary victor over the Armada and who had recently married a young wife, Margaret Stuart, a distant cousin of King James. Violent protests by defenders of the lady's virtue and the earl's honor followed this boorish act. The lady herself was so deeply wounded that she continued to protest the insult to her honor through diplomatic channels for years. The shamed Danes promised to control their drinking and showed their delicacy by putting silver chains on the thumbs of anyone who imbibed too much and then nailing the chains to a post.[25]

It is especially noteworthy that the king of Denmark made the gesture at the expense of the lord admiral, who was instrumental in defeating the Armada; such insinuations recall Carew Hazlitt's observation that military men are often cuckolded because of their extended time away from home. Of course, Charles Howard had only recently married his young wife, but the honour and standing of such a man, not to mention the age difference between the two of them ('for I am declined / Into the vale of years – yet that's not much' (*Othello*, 3.3.269–70)) was evidently more than enough to arouse his latent fears.

Shakespeare's treatment of cuckoldry in his wider work ranges from the comic, to the tragic, to the plain ambivalent. In comedies such as *The Merry Wives of Windsor*, attempts at cuckoldry seem like a competitive sport: on occasion, characters are unable to talk about anything else, or indeed speak a different word: '[f]ie, fie, fie! Cuckold, cuckold, / cuckold!' (2.2.296–7). One of the most noteworthy elements to this comedy is that it is the women, Mistress Ford and Mistress Page, who have the last laugh at the expense of Falstaff as well as their suspicious husbands. Once again, we see how it is the usurping of male power by wily women which makes the trick particularly effective. While *Much Ado about Nothing* shares its comic genre with *Merry Wives*, its treatment of the women accused of infidelity is far darker. The play's opening scene treats cuckoldry with a humorous touch, although the obsession over it among the male characters (who have just returned from military service) is clear. Benedick, for one, declares:

> The savage bull may, but if ever the sensible
> Benedick bear it, pluck off the bull's horns and set
> Them in my forehead; and let me be vilely painted, and
> in such great letters as they write 'Here is good horse
> to hire', let them signify under my sign, 'Here you may
> see Benedick, the married man.'
>
> (1.1.244–9)

Claudio then comments that Benedick is 'horn-mad' (1.1.251), but of course he is the one who will falsely believe his bride, Hero, to be unfaithful to him; a mistake which has nearly tragic consequences. The tragicomedy of Shakespeare's late play, *Cymbeline*, deploys the accusation of cuckoldry to similar effect. Posthumus Leonatus is tricked by Iachimo into believing that his wife, Imogen, has cuckolded him. Iachimo bears a curious similarity to Iago not merely in name but by his obsession in 'proving' the infidelity of an innocent woman; if anything, Iachimo is a better candidate than Iago for the famous moniker of 'motiveless malignity' ascribed by Samuel Taylor Coleridge. Asking for 'some corporal sign' as proof of the infidelity (2.4.119), Iachimo produces Imogen's ring, which he stole from her finger as she lay sleeping and, to further convince Posthumus of Imogen's lust, tells him of a mole under her breast of 'most delicate lodging' (2.4.134–6). This detail is enough proof for Posthumus, who replies to Iachimo:

> If you will swear you have not done't you lie,
> And I will kill thee if thou dost deny
> Thou'st made me cuckold.
>
> (2.4.144–6)

Cymbeline still manages to reunite the lovers eventually, saving the lovers from the tragic fate of Othello and Desdemona. A more prosaic reference to cuckoldry occurs in Shakespeare and Fletcher's *Henry VIII*, with the Porter's Man saying,

> but if I spare any
> That had a head to hit, either young or old,
> He or she, cuckold or cuckold-maker,
> Let me ne'er hope to see a chine again [.]
>
> (5.3.21–4)

The play ends with the christening of the future Queen Elizabeth, and perhaps it is for the best that Shakespeare and Fletcher did not include the accusations of Anne Boleyn's infidelity and subsequent beheading. Despite favour for the reign of Elizabeth, it is hard to imagine spectators watching the action of *Henry VIII* without recalling that the union between Henry and Anne would not stay happy for long. An ambivalent approach to infidelity is also seen in *All's Well That Ends Well*, when the Clown uses a syllogism to arrive at a conclusion which seems to welcome cuckoldry:

> if I be his cuckold, he's my drudge. He that comforts my wife is the cherisher of my flesh and blood; he that cherishes my flesh and blood is my friend; ergo, he that kisses my wife is my friend.
>
> (1.3.43–6)

However, a play like *Troilus and Cressida* is predicated on an infidelity, given that it depicts the Trojan war (caused by Helen leaving her Greek husband Menelaus for the Trojan Paris). In 5.8, the two rivals fight, with Thersites providing a running commentary:

> The cuckold and the cuckold-maker are at it. Now bull! Now dog! 'Loo, Paris, 'loo! Now, my double-horned Spartan! 'Loo, Paris, 'loo! – The bull has the game. Ware horns, ho!
>
> (5.8.1–4)

Thersites refers to Menelaus as the bull, given his cuckold's horns, and Paris as the dog. Dogs were used to bait bulls in the bull-baiting contests that took place close to the Globe and Rose theatres; similarly, the two soldiers are pitted against each other in an engrossing battle, turning these men into beasts.

Othello provides us with a place where everyday gestures and actions are scrutinized, with incorrect meanings all too often ascribed to them. Iago is often the person to put different misreadings into people's minds, such as when he sees Cassio being friendly with Desdemona:

IAGO
> Didst thou not see her paddle with the palm of his hand? Didst not mark that?

RODERIGO
   Yes, that I did, but that was but courtesy.
IAGO
   Lechery, by this hand: an index and obscure prologue
   to the history of lust and foul thoughts.
                                                        (2.1.251–6)

Although Roderigo offers an innocent explanation, Iago quickly refutes such an interpretation of the gesture. His repeated questions ('Didst thou ... Didst not ... ?') are the first step in unbalancing the certainty of the action's meaning. Interestingly, Iago then makes a pun: 'Lechery, by this hand', by which he swears on his own hand that the gesture of Cassio's hand upon Desdemona's is a mark of inconstancy. The irony, of course, is that it is Iago himself (and his hand too, symbolizing his disruptive agency), who is the dishonest soldier. Iago refers to Cassio and Desdemona's actions as 'an index and obscure prologue to the history of lust and foul thoughts', and here we see Iago's own version of palm reading: using the language of the hand as an index to 'discover' (or rather, create) unsavoury business. The fact that this index is 'obscure' is all to his advantage: that the hand is capable of being read with multiple possible interpretations ensures that meaning remains unstable, with both truth and lies unable to be proved, allowing suspicion of signs and their meanings to spread. Iago pushes this technique further in 4.1, when he advises Othello to watch Cassio's actions:

IAGO
   Do but encave yourself
   And mark the fleers, the gibes and notable scorns
   That dwell in every region of his face;
   For I will make him tell the tale anew
   Where, how, how oft, how long ago, and when
   He hath and is again to cope your wife.
   I say, but mark his gesture, marry, patience,
   Or I shall say you're all in all in spleen
   And nothing of a man.
                                                        (4.1.82–90)

'Mark his gesture' is Iago's way of giving Othello the 'ocular proof' that he desires. It is notable too that Iago tells Othello, 'Or I shall say you're all in all in spleen / And nothing of a man.' This charge against Othello's masculinity – that by being 'in spleen', he is being inconstant and therefore putting his supposedly Stoic manhood in question – is precisely the kind of fluctuation in meaning which Iago seeks to manipulate via his exploitation of gender politics and social expectations. When Cassio begins to tell Iago of his mistress, Bianca, his story is inevitably misread by Othello:

CASSIO
> She was here even now, she haunts me in every place. I was the other day talking on the sea-bank with certain Venetians, and thither comes the bauble and, by this hand, falls me thus about my neck –

OTHELLO
> Crying 'O dear Cassio!' as it were: his gesture imports it.

CASSIO
> So hangs and lolls and weeps upon me, so shakes and pulls me! Ha, ha, ha!

OTHELLO
> Now he tells how she plucked him to my chamber.
> (4.1.132–41)

A particular cruelty of this scene is that Cassio is acting out Bianca's gestures: 'by this hand, falls me thus about my neck'. The deictic 'thus' implies that he mimics her movement, and in doing so Othello believes Cassio is re-enacting a scene of lust with Desdemona: 'his gesture imports it'. Next, Othello begins to construe ideas of his own, imagining that Cassio shows how Desdemona 'plucked him to my chamber'. Once the initial suspicion has been planted in his head, his mind begins to fill in the gaps prompted by the ambiguity of Cassio's gestures.

One of the reasons why gesture and deportment, even when their meanings are misconstrued, can seem so persuasive, is that bodily actions frequently *can* reveal genuine inner emotions.

Desdemona is one of the few characters in the play who sees gestures for what they are, reading her husband in his turmoil:

DESDEMONA
>Alas, why gnaw you so your nether lip?
>Some bloody passion shakes your very frame,
>These are portents: but yet, I hope, I hope
>They do not point on me.
>
>(5.2.43–6)

She sees his eye rolls and lip bites as 'portents': an especially ominous reading which is all too perceptive, given her ensuing fate. Furthermore, her hope that such signs 'do not point' on her is an unfortunate recollection of the exposing and piercing nature of public shame itself, the very humiliation Othello fears he is facing. This gripping concern is all the worse because Othello is already imagining how horrendous the situation will be when others judge him for being made a cuckold: the shame he feels is the internalized fear of public disapproval. Of course, it is this kind of imagination that sets off Iago's revenge against Othello in the first place:

IAGO
>As I confess it is my nature's plague
>To spy into abuses, and oft my jealousy
>Shapes faults that are not
>
>(3.3.149–51)

Iago concedes that he lets his imagination get the better of him, misconstruing signs into worst-case scenarios, particularly given his belief that his own wife, Emilia, has made him a cuckold too, and with none other than Othello himself. Iago's revenge against these imagined slights is to bring Othello down to his level:

IAGO
>As he shall smile, Othello shall go mad.
>And his unbookish jealousy must construe

> Poor Cassio's smiles, gestures and light behaviour
> Quite in the wrong.
>
> (4.1.101–4)

Iago's imagination, fuelled by his fragile masculinity, is his curse, and one which he passes onto Othello, who believes 'that [Desdemona] with Cassio hath the act of shame / A thousand times committed' (5.2.209–10). The only place such an act has been committed, of course, is in his own mind.

The use of horn imagery becomes a kind of mascot for Othello's worries, and his belief that 'On horror's head horrors accumulate' (3.3.373) is all too reminiscent of the fact that horror breeds horror when the imagination is left to its own devices. Othello uses the shared social knowledge of horn imagery to test Desdemona's knowledge of her apparent crime:

DESDEMONA
  Why do you speak so faintly?
  Are you not well?
OTHELLO
  I have a pain upon my forehead, here.
DESDEMONA
  Faith, that's with watching, 'twill away again.

(3.3.287–9)

Othello's passive-aggressive comment about the pain upon his forehead alludes to the common myth of a cuckolded man growing horns upon his head, with the deictic 'here' implying that he strokes his head, almost as if he expects to find such horns himself. It is a gesture which implies another gesture: that of the *cornutu* Bulwer describes, whereby a man is mocked by hands making the sign of the horns. It is ironic that Desdemona explains her husband's pain by saying, 'that's with watching'. While in Desdemona's own meaning, her comment refers to Othello's sleeplessness, it unexpectedly reveals the truth of the matter: Othello's pain has come about because he has scrutinized – watched – too closely and come to the wrong conclusions.

The use of horn imagery is a technique also exploited by Iago at the beginning of Act Four:

IAGO
  How is it, general? Have you not hurt your head?
OTHELLO
  Dost thou mock me?
IAGO   I mock you? No, by heaven!
  Would you would bear your fortune like a man?
OTHELLO
  A horned man's a monster and a beast.

(4.1.59–64)

Iago's jibe has the desired affect, putting the image of horns into Othello's mind once more, and then further questioning his masculinity by asking, 'Would you would bear your fortune like a man?' However, the idea of bearing a fortune, or indeed a burden or a load, is more likely the job of an ass: the horned beast, which Othello fears he is turning into. Ewan Fernie writes that 'the central figure in *Othello* is that of the human person as beast'.[26] Indeed, travel accounts from the period are all too prone to associate racial difference with a less-than-human mode of existence. In particular, some texts describe men 'furnisht with such members as are after a sort burthensome unto them'.[27] Again, we read the language of the loaded animal: just as a cuckold must carry the burden of his horns, travellers from the period depict racial difference in terms that are both sexual and bestial. *Othello*'s representation of masculinity, therefore, intersects with the fear of becoming a beast, or becoming less than human, if designated 'less than a man' through the act of cuckoldry.

Othello's pain at this transformation is evident in 4.2:

OTHELLO   Had it pleased heaven
  To try me with affliction, had they rained
  All kinds of sores and shames on my bare head,
  Steeped me in poverty to the very lips,

> Given to captivity me and my utmost hopes,
> I should have found in some place of my soul
> A drop of patience; but, alas, to make me
> The fixed figure for the time of scorn
> To point his slow and moving finger at!
>
> (4.2.48–56)

There is a sense that in the moment of public humiliation, time slows down. 'The fixed figure', unable to escape the gaze of society and its jeers, is at the mercy of those who will laugh and point at him, but such fingers, although they move, are 'slow': the concentrated mockery entraps Othello in an eternal present of shame. Perhaps this is why he is fixated on 'ocular proof' as evidence for his wife's infidelity: his fear is that he will himself become the 'ocular proof' of a cuckolded soldier, with horns upon his head and the cruel laughter of the crowd:

> Villain, be sure thou prove my love a whore,
> Be sure of it, give me the ocular proof.
>
> (3.3.362–3)

The horror of shame is bound up in the horror of looking conspicuous, which is all the more ironic given the play's domination by what Karen Newman describes as 'a scopic economy which privileges sight'.[28] It is a further irony that Othello is so adamant to demand proof of that which would make him a figure of shame. This confusion reigns because of his tendency to take what he sees at face value and to take an image for the truth. Edward Washington notes that '[w]hen Othello contemplates the sleeping Desdemona, with genuine ardor he murmurs words of Petrarchan praise and love'.[29] In this moment, Othello privileges the image of love and beauty rather than the reality of it. This disconnect between the signifier and the signified needs to be read in a gendered sense: it epitomizes the denial of female agency inherent in such blazonic imagery, which is all about the control of a woman's body being trapped in a static moment. This Petrarchan obsession with how women appear to others, anatomized and fixed upon the lines of a page – or in the idealized mind of a lover – is a further reflection of fragile masculinity. But it is a fear that goes in both directions: just as men wish to control the appearance of their wives, in case anything untoward is read in their bodies or gestures, men too fear they will be read in a negative light.

Images of the horn carry with it their own associations with the visible, with McEachern pointing out how 'horn was known for its light-bearing and light-shedding properties; polished, it served as material for windows and lanterns (lant-horns) as well as hornbooks'.[30] Horns, therefore, were inextricably linked with the act of seeing.[31] On this point, it should also be noted that there is no definite textual evidence of the *cornutu* gesture actually being made at any point in *Othello*; that is to say, there is no performance cue for the movement as there is with the thumb-bite in *Romeo and Juliet* or Anne's spitting upon Richard III. Yet the very fact that the cuckold gesture may not actually appear is precisely my point about Othello's fears. The gesture of horns, and the imagery that goes along with it, is rooted in a shared social knowledge of such signs. Originally, Cuckold's Haven had been a literal place, and yet as Douglas Bruster notes, 'by 1623, London had so assimilated the myth into its literary vocabulary that actual, physical testament – the pole with its animal horns – became unnecessary'.[32] In a sense, this notion can also be applied to whether or not we see the horn gesture: even if it is not explicitly performed, its implication is there, which in the mind of a suspicious man is more than enough to arouse fear. This idea of a phantom gesture, which may or may not appear, can also be controlled by performative gaps in the text. Some actors may choose to deploy the *cornutu* gesture, taking the script's language about horns as a cue, but some may not. If such gestures *are* performed, the actor playing Othello himself will not see their performance onstage; therefore even if the other actors are *not* making horns, Othello may well think it is happening.

As a military leader, Othello is fully aware of the importance of appearances, and it is in his role as the ensign (or ancient) that Iago can take full advantage of this, as, to quote Fernie, '[i]t is the ancient's job to guard his general from infamy and shame'.[33] It is crucial that we recall our discussion of the Spanish fig gesture from Chapter 1 here, especially as Iago shares the same military status of ensign with Pistol. Iago, like Pistol, also uses the spanish fig to show when he thinks something is unworthy of him (such as virtue (1.3.320)), and Barbara Everett's reading of *Othello* as having key Spanish influences becomes crucial in this context. Everett's observations that Iago is the Spanish version of James, that Shakespeare carefully reiterates the use of Spanish names such as Iago and Roderigo in the first scene, and that St James, or Santiago Matamoros ('the moor-killer'), was the patron saint of Spain reveal that the immediate tensions of *Othello* would have been far more obvious 400 years ago than they are today.[34] It is also posited by Everett that the stock character of the braggart soldier is introduced into the play only to be questioned: an audience may expect a Moorish captain to be a braggart, but our expectations are subverted by his noble qualities.[35] In Italian comedy, such a braggart 'is often the deceived husband [who] is also most characteristically a new national type: the *Spanish* soldier of fortune';[36] and this plot is exactly the kind of drama that Iago wishes to fashion in the life of Othello by convincing him that his wife is unfaithful. And yet, of course, it is Iago who is the Spanish braggart ensign, wielding his figs and desperate to prove himself, and indeed it is he who first believes that he is cuckolded ('it is thought abroad that 'twixt my sheets / He's done my office' (1.3.386–7)).

Iago's motivation in this case is rooted in the notion that a woman, by committing adultery, is taking on a more traditionally masculine role. Feeling less than a man, he wants to inflict the same shameful emotion upon the man he believes slept with his wife. Juliet Dusinberre writes on how the unfaithful wife 'forces on her husband the passivity of the cuckold [...] Imagining himself wronged, Othello feels his identity as a man of action dissolve'.³⁷ In this sense, Othello's very idea of who he is – man, soldier, husband – becomes negated. Masculinity itself is at the mercy of the threat of cuckoldry. Jyotsna Singh, in analysing narratives of sexuality, is keen to emphasize how the fragility of masculinity is seen through the emotion of jealousy. She writes of 'the fear that wives can turn into whores or, put another way, that wives and whores are indistinguishable'.³⁸ Of course, this concern is not merely jealousy; it is, as Singh acknowledges, '[t]he fear and horror of female sexuality that permeate Renaissance discourses about women',³⁹ or, in other words, basic misogyny. Early modern Europe saw the 'release of bile and wild humour' to tease men in particularly unfavourable contexts.⁴⁰ Hale notes that

> [t]he remarriage of a widower, the marriage of a man to a much younger woman, notorious instances of cuckoldry [...] nagging or scolding: all were used as an excuse to make an uproar outside the victim's house, with gangs of youths shouting ribald comment, banging saucepans, ringing bells and blowing horns in a cacophony of insult.⁴¹

Such an incident actually takes place in the opening scene of *Othello*, when Iago and Roderigo assault Brabantio's house with news of his daughter's relationship:

RODERIGO
   What ho! Brabantio, Signior Brabantio, ho!
IAGO
   Awake, what ho, Brabantio! Thieves, thieves, thieves!
   Look to your house, your daughter, and your bags!
   Thieves, thieves! [...]
   Zounds, sir, you're robbed, for shame put on your gown!
   Your heart is burst, you have lost half your soul,
   Even now, very now, an old black ram
   Is tupping your white ewe! Arise, arise,
   Awake the snorting citizens with the bell

> Or else the devil will make a grandsire of you!
> Arise I say!
>
> (1.1.77–80; 85–91)

Such discourse adopts the male gaze as the default setting for viewing women and in doing so 'constructs the fantasy of their infidelity'.[42] Crucially, Singh argues that

> in the fantasy of dishonour brought to life by Iago, Othello's masculine hono[u]r can only be 'saved' by marking Desdemona, as the representative of all woman, as a 'whore'.[43]

This strategy recalls a Foucauldian line of thought, wherein society must mark out the transgressor for their crimes; here, however, the state is replaced by the dominant mode of patriarchy, but the two operate on strikingly similar terms. Such modes of power are also recalled by Madelon Gohlke, who writes that '[i]t is those who perceive themselves to be powerless who may be incited to the acts of greatest violence'.[44] This observation may be particularly true of soldiers, forced by the necessities of violence that war facilitates.

While I would not say that the patriarchy in this period – or at present, any other – in general thinks of itself as powerless, it is the fear that they might *become* powerless which motivates the gendered acts of violence against the women who serve as a threat to their dominance either implicitly or overtly; because for those used to privilege, equality – or even mutual respect – appears like oppression. The irony is that such apparent oppression is what results in men feeling vulnerable, and therefore, 'effeminized'. The fears of such an emasculating process perpetuate both this unhelpful binary between vulnerability as being 'feminine', in addition to the discourses which equate masculinity with honour, strength, and agency of action. Such binaries may win privileges for patriarchy, but it is also a Pyrrhic victory: by aligning masculinity with such values, it means that their own gender is just as capable of deconstruction as the idea that women are vain, inconstant, and must be taught to be socially passive. This feedback loop of gender identity and its reception by others is deafening, but the patriarchy's only response is to shout louder, perpetuating hypocritical double standards yet further. It is not only to the cost of male pride, however. As Margaret Atwood has pointed out, men feel threatened by women because they are 'afraid women will laugh at them'; women feel threatened by men because they are 'afraid of being killed'.[45] In essence, *Othello* is not a play about a great man's tragic fall. It is a play about masculinity being so fragile that it shatters; a furious avalanche of self-pity and wounded pride which buries the rest of society along with it.

6

Handwashing: Feminine Shame in *Macbeth*

The thought of regicide is never far away in Shakespeare's tragedies, but it is only in *Macbeth* that we see the disturbing aftermath of shame, anxiety, and trauma played out by those responsible for the death of a king. Sleepwalking in the dead of night, Lady Macbeth is gripped by the fear that the blood of Duncan's murder remains on her hands. Accordingly, this chapter focuses on Lady Macbeth's hands after the murder of King Duncan, exploring the cultural associations of her gestures of handwashing alongside the ramifications of staging her somnambulant shame. *Macbeth* is described by Alison P. Hobgood as '[a] play about fear and consumed by fear',[1] and she discusses the emotion of fear-sickness, a feeling not dissimilar to shame. Fear-sickness is an early modern malady not wholly dissimilar from modern conceptions of paranoia, and Hopgood argues that it 'was responsible for a host of maladies as it degenerated an individual's psychological and physiological states'.[2] This chapter does not just focus on individualized fear, however, but extends this feeling to the newly established Jacobean state.

Othello marks the start of Shakespeare's tragic period, post-dating the pattern of comedies and history plays in the late 1590s, and *Macbeth* only continues this trend into a darker period of his drama. That these plays are written just as Elizabeth I is dying, with James I becoming King in 1603, reflects this growing sense of national uncertainty. The gestures contained within these plays, fuelled by insecurity and paranoia, are symptomatic of far wider social and political tensions. While poetic works such as Edmund Spenser's *The Faerie Queene* (which I will return to shortly) ostensibly flatter Elizabeth's status as sovereign during her reign while simultaneously undermining the visual culture of symbolic power that she perpetuated, plays such as *Macbeth* explore the masculinity of military men just at the time when a man takes the throne for the first time in fifty years: a man also determined to make peace with England's long-term enemy, Spain. Within the drama of *Macbeth* is an exploration of a fearful cultural moment over the advent of a new, male sovereign, and the insecurity it created within the English body politic.

For Stuart Clark, problematizing the sense of sight in the early modern period reveals how 'debates about the reliability of vision [is] itself a political issue'.[3] I would argue that this contention is rarely truer than at the beginning of a new monarch's reign, bringing with it a fresh political regime and a necessity for the state to maintain and convey a sense of absolute authority in the midst of potentially radical changes. King James VI of Scotland became King James I of England in 1603. His ascendency to the English throne naturally made use of theatrical spectacle, but he had always been interested in the workings of theatre. He was a lover of plays, and when an English theatre company visited Edinburgh in 1593 and again in 1599, he patronized their endeavours to the sum of £333 6s. 8d. on both occasions, also granting them a license to perform in public despite Puritan protests, and £40 'to by timber for ye preparatioun of ane hous to thair pastyme'.[4] James' rise to power in England gave him an opportunity to extend his understanding of theatrical performance to an international level: in August 1604, the entertainment the king gave to the Constable of Castile at Whitehall was described as 'royal theatre'. Given James' wish to bring about peace with Spain and to underscore such a détente through public oath and ceremony, Kinney is right to observe that, for James, 'policy and principle [were] performative'.[5]

However, despite this overt sense of confidence, James was also aware of the use of performance to overcompensate for what were actually political insecurities; after all, the power of the stage is 'the power of fiction', where individuals may 'view themselves as actors in their own lives, as artificial and artfully manipulated constructions'.[6] Mullaney argues that James understood the inherent precariousness of performing an identity. Rather than being able to turn such performativity into an advantage, the sense of cultural self-awareness could in fact lead to increased paranoia over how appearances were being viewed in reality.[7] If we read James' advice to his son on public relations, we see such concerns about the vulnerability of (re)presentation, with James writing how 'a King is as one set on a skaffold, whose smallest actions and gestures al the people gazingly doe behold'.[8] While at first reading, this observation might convey an almighty sense of authority, such authority actually becomes inverted upon the realization that the power lies not with the monarch, but with the people whose eyes are upon him: eyes capable of interpreting his actions in any number of unintended directions. The power of spectacle, then, is double-edged: when gestures are scrutinized, they are not done so in the knowledge of the intentions behind them, but through the projections of the audience viewing the actions.

James had different political priorities to his predecessor and preferred to think of himself as a peacemaker. He attempted to restructure the violent fabric of everyday life by requesting an end to carrying 'Gunnes and traiterous Pistolets', in addition to asking that men cease to wear armour underneath their garments as an act of self-defence.[9] Furthermore, he wanted an end to international hostilities, and one of James' first actions as the new king of England was to cease war with Spain. The Treaty of London, signed in August 1604, signalled this peace. Unfortunately, this action was an unpopular move in the eyes of the English people. Anti-Spanish and especially anti-

Catholic tensions continued in England for the next twenty years: James' openly Catholic queen and the suggestion of a Spanish marriage for his heir were more than enough to cause consternation, but the Gunpowder Plot of 1605 brought levels of national paranoia to fever-pitch.

It is vital, then, that we consider these events when reading plays such as *Othello* (1603) and *Macbeth* (1606). While James was a pacifist, these two plays, produced just as he takes the English throne, have at their centre military figures. Of course, these plays are both tragedies, and perhaps they reveal the need for peace and stability. But the plays also gave contemporary audiences stories of military men to audiences still hungry for war and deeply suspicious about a détente with the Spanish. As we saw in the previous chapter, *Othello* is a play concerning the Machiavellian dealings of a character with a suspiciously Spanish name, the signifiers of masculinity and military honour, and how the 'ocular proof' of performed actions are not what they seem. The Scottish play also contains troubling tropes for the new Jacobean period.

Macbeth dramatizes the 'Stuart Myth', establishing James' divine right as king as well as legitimizing Scottish history and its new assimilation into the English monarchy, and is one of only two Shakespeare plays (the other being *Henry VIII*) which were specifically designed for Stuart performance.[10] Consequently, the play is littered with references likely to appeal to James. For instance, in the scene where Lady Macbeth washes her hands in her sleep, she is observed by the figure of a Doctor. Ever one for a generous self-serving metaphor, James described himself as a physician as part of his rhetoric in declaring his ability to be England's sovereign. As part of an address he gave in 1604, he declared, 'It is the King's part (as the proper Phisician of his Politicke-bodie) to purge it of all those diseases, by Medicines meete for the same'.[11] He would also style himself as the nation's 'loving nourish-father', with the implication that, as patriarch, he was similar to a male mother.[12] These anecdotes give us two points of entry into *Macbeth* 5.1. First, we can see how James' idea of sovereignty – of being the body politic's physician – is reflected in the role of the Doctor who observes Lady Macbeth's behaviour and diagnoses that '[f]oul whisperings are abroad. Unnatural deeds / Do breed unnatural troubles' (5.1.71–2). We can also note a reference to the ritual of 'the King's touch' in 4.3, when the Doctor tells Malcolm:

> there are a crew of wretched souls
> That stay his cure. Their malady convinces
> The great assay of art, but at his touch,
> Such sanctity hath haven given his hand,
> They presently amend.
>
> (4.3.141–5)

From the reign of Edward the Confessor, it was believed that a king's hands had healing powers. James revived this tradition, which was said to cure scrofula, or 'the King's Evil'. Second, James' description of himself as a 'loving nourish-father' confuses the gender binary of feminine care over a nation perpetuated by Elizabeth I, a radical 'unsexing' also akin to Lady Macbeth's desire that her milk be taken for gall (1.5.48).

Lady Macbeth seems ultimately unable to negate the qualities associated with her gender, despite her wish that 'no compunctious visitings of nature / Shake my fell purpose' (1.5.45–6). As Callaghan notes,

> Lady Macbeth becomes troubled with feminine remorse, guilt, and madness familiar in modern conceptions of femininity. Significantly, Lady Macbeth is finally unable to relinquish her maternality. She remains one who has 'given suck' and knows 'How tender 'tis to love the babe that milks me' (1.7.55); she is prey to the ravings of guilt and feminine remorse. Maternality as it is figured in human women rather than in supernatural witches is benign, symptomatic of the innate moral sensibility of the mother which is so characteristic of her appearance in nascent modernity's newly created public sphere.[13]

Yet it is also the public sphere which helps to construct paternity, and this is one of the reasons why 3.4 is such a pivotal moment in the play. When Banquo's ghost appears at the banquet, Macbeth loses his composure in a public setting. Lady Macbeth's disapproval is immediate, asking first, 'Are you a man?' (3.4.55) and then chiding him with '[s]hame itself. / Why do you make such faces?' (3.4.63–4). Notably, when the ghost disappears, Macbeth answers, 'Why so, being gone / I am a man again' (3.4.105–6). It is as if Lady Macbeth is frustrated with her husband's childishness; rather than accusing him of becoming feminized when she asks, 'Are you a man?', she is in fact implying that he is acting like a young boy.

However, this dichotomy is not always consistent throughout the play. When Macduff hears of his family being slaughtered, he says, 'O, I could play the woman with mine eyes' (4.3.233), implying that he should weep, but instead he plots revenge. Malcolm concurs that action is required, replying, 'This time goes manly' (4.3.238). This equation of agency and masculinity reminds us of Lady Macbeth's desire to be unsexed, but also her frustration with her husband. As Kott argues, 'Lady Macbeth plays a man's part. She demands that Macbeth commit murder as a confirmation of his manhood'.[14] Janet Adelman continues this line of argument but develops the idea that fantasies of gendered power are rooted not merely within the initial gender binary but also within the differing states of childhood and adulthood:

> Maternal power in Macbeth is not embodied in the figure of a particular mother (as it is, for example, in *Coriolanus*); it is instead diffused throughout the play, evoked primarily by the figures of the witches and Lady Macbeth. Largely through Macbeth's relationship to them, the play becomes (like *Coriolanus*) a representation of primitive fears about male identity and autonomy itself; about those looming female presences who threaten to control one's actions and one's mind, to constitute one's very self, even at a distance [...] The fears of female coercion, female definition of the

> male, that are initially located cosmically in the witches thus find their ultimate locus in the figure of Lady Macbeth, whose attack on Macbeth's virility is the source of her strength over him and who acquires that strength [...] partly because she can make him imagine himself as an infant vulnerable to her.[15]

The power Lady Macbeth wields over her husband is not merely the taunt of emasculation; it seems far closer to infantalization. In fact, both gender and age need to be taken together when constructing identities in this period. Before reaching breeching age, boys would wear the same dress-like garments as girls, and we may recall Aufidius' mock at Coriolanus that he is a 'boy of tears' (5.6.103). Clearly, gender is not a simple binary here: the construction of early modern masculinity is also rooted in bridging the gap between childhood and adulthood. This point is augmented by the fact that the Macbeths are childless, and therefore, in the words of Alvin Kernan, 'have no future'.[16] Despite their success in killing Duncan, their status as sovereigns is insecure. As Kathryn L. Lynch notes, 'Macbeth's great fear is that, despite his audacity and force, his hand will ultimately be ineffective, that his "barren sceptre" will be wrenched from it "with an unlineal hand" [...] Lady Macbeth's version of this fear seems to be the guilt that causes the compulsive hand-rubbing'.[17] The difference, however, is that Lady Macbeth's shame is private, not public. Joan Larsen Klein argues this case:

> Unlike Macbeth, however, who revealed his guilt before the assembled nobility of Scotland, Lady Macbeth confesses hers when she is alone. She does so because she has always been, as women were supposed to be, a private figure, living behind closed doors. She also reveals her anguish in sleep partly because she has no purposeful waking existence and partly, as Banquo said, because in repose the fallen, unblessed nature 'gives way' to 'cursed thoughts' [...] Macbeth's guilty soul is as public as his acts. Lady Macbeth's is as private

as memory, tormented by a self whose function is only to remember in isolation and unwillingly the deeds done by another.[18]

This gendered sense of public and private space is one of the few binaries that seems to remain intact in the play. Furthermore, it reinforces how the act of seeing and the theatricality accompanying actions such as gesture are crucial elements in any attempt to construct their meaning.

The gesture of handwashing as a signifier of apparent innocence is discussed by Bulwer and shown in Figure 11. Referring to it as 'innocentia ostendo', or 'the show of innocence', Bulwer notes:

TO IMITATE THE POSTURE OF WASHING THE HANDS BY RUBBING THE BACK OF ONE IN THE HOLLOW OF THE OTHER WITH A KIND OF DETERSIVE MOTION, is a gesture sometimes used by those who would professe their innocency, and declare they have no Hand in that foule businesse, not so much as by their manuall assent; as it were assuring by that gesture, that they will keepe their Hands undefiled, and would wash their Hands of it: nor have any thing to doe therein. A gesture very significant, for the Hands naturally imply, as it were in Hieroglyphique, mens acts and operations; and that cleansing motion denotes the cleannesse of their actions. As this expression is heightened by the addition of water, 'tis made by the Aegyptians the Hieroglyphique of innocency.[19]

The action of washing the hands is taken as an embodied metaphor for ridding oneself of a negative association, literally cleansing it from their hands, and by association, their sense of responsibility. Perhaps one of the most noteworthy examples of this cultural gesture is the moment of Pilate washing his hands after condemning Christ to death. James Hall notes that this action is included by Matthew (27.11–26), Mark (15.2–15), Luke (23.13–25), and John (18.28–40), and that although

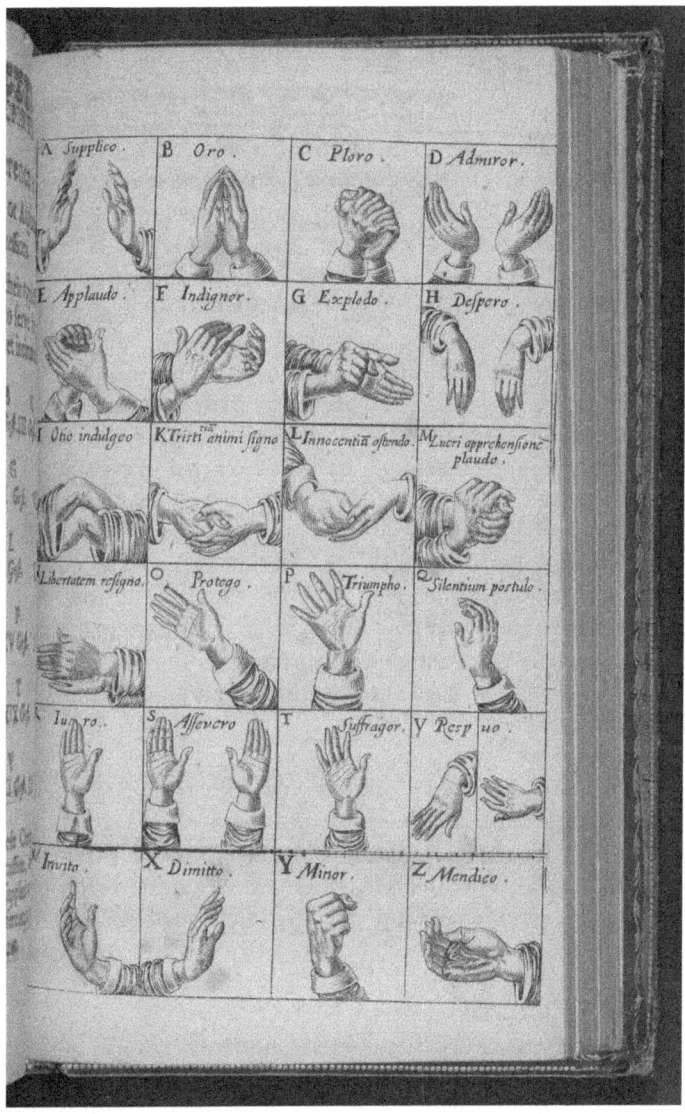

FIGURE 11 *Gesture plate, featuring 'Innocentia ostendo', from Bulwer's* Chirologia *(London, 1644), 151.* © *The British Library Board.*

Pilate had questioned Christ and found him 'innocent of any civil crime', the pressure from the local Jewish community ensured a death sentence.[20] After condemning Christ to death, Pilate, 'fearing a riot, gave way, but thereupon washed his hands in public to signify his refusal to be morally implicated in the decision'.[21] Hall also notes in his *Dictionary of Subjects and Symbols in Art* that 'a young woman washing her hands stands for innocence personified', and we may also note a reference in Psalm 26.6, 'I wash my hands in innocence.'[22] Of course, the issue with applying these cultural associations to Lady Macbeth is that she is *not* innocent: while she did not personally kill Duncan, she encourages her husband to do so, and covers the king's guards with blood in order to frame them for the murder. Her gesture of apparent innocence, played out in her sleepwalking state, is a paranoid repetition which both symbolizes and *is* her descent into madness.

There are also associations between Lady Macbeth's handwashing gesture and a collection of stories called *Gesta Romanorum* published in 1606, incidentally the same year *Macbeth* was written. Beatrice Daw Brown made this connection between the two texts in 1935, noting the similarity between the play and one of the stories contained within the *Gesta*:

> A woman of queenly station and hitherto of blameless report murders, in the interests of her own security, an innocent person. The blood of her victim falls upon her hand, and although she makes repeated efforts to remove the stain, it remains. Oppressed by the burden of her guilty secret, she finally makes confession to a priest and the stain vanishes.[23]

Kinney adds to this discussion by noting how the murder of Duncan also alludes to the killing of Christ, drawing on Brown's other observation that an indelible bloodstain is also reminiscent of the mark of Cain.[24] Such biblical associations are further compounded by the more intensely psychological workings of guilt and shame. In his essay 'Of Conscience', Montaigne observes:

> Whoever expects punishment, suffereth the same, and whosoever deserveth it, he doth expect it. Impietie doth invent, and iniquitie doth frame torments against it selfe [...] Even as the waspe stingeth and offendeth others, but her selfe much more; for, in hurting others, she loseth her force and sting for ever.
>
> – itasque in ulnere ponunt – VIRG. *Georg.* Iv. 238
> They, while they others sting,
> Death to themselves doe bring.[25]

Montaigne uncannily summarizes the fear-sickness and subsequent downfall of the Macbeths, and he also quotes Lucretius to elucidate how those with guilty minds may reveal themselves:

> *Quippe ubi se multi per somnia saepe loquentes,*
> *Aut morbo delirantes procraxe ferantur,*
> *Et celata diu in medium peccata dedisse.* – LUCR. v. 1168.
>
> Many in dreames oft speaking, or unhealed,
> In sicknesse raving have themselves revealed,
> And brought to light their sinnes long time concealed.[26]

Florio's translation of these lines, consciously or not, evoke the dark magic of triple rhyme also present in Shakespeare's play: 'When the hurly-burly's done, / When the battle's lost, and won, / That will be ere the set of sun' (1.1.3–5). Lucretius' observation that many 'in sicknesse raving have themselves revealed' is a disturbing reminder of Lady Macbeth's somnambulance, where her fear that her guilt will be revealed becomes a self-fulfilling prophecy.

Bloody hands provide an arresting dramatic image. The sheer level of gore when Macbeth murders Duncan is documented by

Simon Forman, who was present at a performance of the play in 1611: 'When Macbeth had murdered the king, the blood on his hands could not be washed off by any means, nor from his wife's hands, which handled the bloody daggers in hiding them, by which means they became much amazed and affronted.'[27] Interestingly, James' own love of hunting was rooted in similar levels of bloodthirstiness, with the king known to slit the throat of a stag and open its stomach, before plunging his hands into the beast's entrails and besmearing his courtiers' faces.[28] The sight of bloody hands in a play like *Macbeth*, especially when they besmear the faces of the sleeping grooms outside the king's chamber, would have been a familiar sight to James. However, the association of the hands in *Macbeth* with regicide becomes, in this instance, far more disturbing, particularly since the Gunpowder Plot had been such a recent attempt on James' life.

Macbeth's first instance of bloody hands – and the fear that they cannot be washed clean – occurs directly after Duncan's murder:

MACBETH
    Will all great Neptune's ocean wash this blood
    Clean from my hand? No, this my hand will rather
    The multitudinous seas incarnadine,
    Making the green, one red.
LADY MACBETH
    My hands are of your colour, but I shame
    To wear a heart so white.

(2.2.61–6)

Lady Macbeth contrasts their hands and their hearts and explicitly shames her husband for his concerns. She is, for the moment, steadfast in her resolution and mocks him for his fear that his hands will never be clean. Her tragedy is that she too succumbs to this fear and is driven to madness by it. The irony, of course, is that she herself counsels her husband that '[t]hese deeds must not be thought / After these ways; so, it will make us mad' (2.2.34–5). By 5.1 her trauma is manifest, as she constantly relives the moment of the murder. She is aghast that Duncan should have 'so much blood in him' (5.1.40). As Kinney notes, young men were thought to be full of blood, whereas older men were supposed to be drier in the humoural sense;[29] hence, Lady Macbeth's reaction is one of horror, with Duncan's plentiful blood creating a sense of traditional masculinity being in flux. Callaghan furthers this idea of blood being gendered, arguing that, '[b]lood in the play, notably Duncan's "golden Blood" (2.3.110) symbolizes patriarchy and can be equated with the life blood of a nation ("Bleed, bleed, poor country!" [4.3.32])'.[30] That blood should symbolize patriarchy may be a cruel joke at Lady Macbeth's expense, given her initial wish to be 'unsexed' as a nourishing female. The mark of patriarchy, Duncan's blood itself, cannot be unseen once it has been upon her hands. She is haunted by the very sign of sovereignty that she sought to overthrow, but, more than this, she is haunted by the blood's gendered symbolism of patriarchal power that she desired in the first place.

It is this obsession with blood throughout the play which leads Lady Macbeth to compulsively wash her hands, convinced of bloodstains. Critics such as Arthur F. Kinney see the exploration of motifs such as blood as 'a hypertextual exercise: it is not merely image-clustering but rather a vital network of kinship practices and of social formations that for 1606 have immediate and vital significance'.[31] The handwashing scene remains a disturbing episode for audiences, as it is the moment where Lady Macbeth unwillingly reveals her murderous past:

DOCTOR
   What is it she does now? Look how she rubs her hands.
GENTLEWOMAN
   It is an accustomed action with her, to seem thus washing her hands. I have known her continue in this a quarter of an hour.
LADY
   Yet here's a spot.
DOCTOR
   Hark, she speaks. I will set down what comes from her, to satisfy my remembrance the more strongly.

LADY

> Out, damned spot: out, I say. One; two. Why then 'tis time to do't. Hell is murky. Fie, my lord, fie, a soldier and afeared? What need we fear? Who knows it when none can call our power to account? Yet who would have thought the old man to have had so much blood in him?

DOCTOR

> Do you mark that?

LADY

> The Thane of Fife had a wife. Where is she now? What, will these hands ne-er be clean? No more o'that, my lord, no more o'that. You mar all with this starting.

DOCTOR

> Go to, go to. You have known what you should not.

GENTLEWOMAN

> She has spoke what she should not, I am sure of that. Heaven knows what she has known.

LADY

> Here's the smell of blood still. All the perfumes of Arabia will not sweeten this little hand. Oh, oh, oh.

(5.1.26–52)

Lady Macbeth's unconscious gestures throughout this scene re-enact the initial moment after the murder itself. Her line 'Fie, my lord, fie, a soldier and afeared? What need we fear?' recalls her chastising comment to her husband (2.2.65–6), once again referencing the equation of manhood with military agency. But her horror at the sight of bloodied hands is also reminiscent of an earlier literary text, as Spenser's *The Faerie Queene* also features this trope. In Book II, canto ii, Guyon finds that the child Ruddymane's hands cannot be cleansed of blood:

> He washt them oft and oft, yet nought they beene
> For all his washing cleaner. Still he stroue,
> Yet still the litle hands were bloody seene;

The which him into great amaz'ment droue,
And into diuerse doubt his wauering wonder cloue.[32]

The following stanza describes the bloodstains on the child's hands as a 'great contagion direful deadly stonck',[33] and we may also think of Claudius in *Hamlet*, who describes his murder of Old Hamlet as 'rank: it smells to heaven' (3.3.36). Claudius even goes on to express a similar fear to Lady Macbeth:

What if this cursed hand
Were thicker than itself with brother's blood?
Is there not rain enough in the sweet heavens
To wash it white as snow?

(3.3.43–6)

Throughout Shakespeare's works, bloody hands feature as a haunting sign. Michael Neill argues that 'the bloodstained hand [is] a recurrent symbol – not merely of guilt but of the necessary intimacy of violence and power', and he notes the image is prevalent in history plays in addition to the tragedies.[34] *Richard II* ends with the newly crowned Bolingbroke promising, 'I'll make a voyage to the Holy Land / To wash this blood off from my guilty hand' (5.6.49–50). He does this in order to seek divine forgiveness after Exton murders the imprisoned Richard II against orders, and it is interesting to note that although Bolingbroke is not the murderer, he takes responsibility for the act given that he is the new head of state.

Returning to *The Faerie Queene*, Evelyn B. Tribble notes how Ruddymane's bloodstained hands indicate a curious crisis of semiotics. When Guyon is unable to wash Ruddymane's hands of the blood, there is a degree of uncertainty over whether the stain represents guilt or innocence, and the failure to remove the blood 'causes a kind of crisis in the text'.[35] Tribble's reading of this section focuses on how symbols, such as bloody hands, complicate meaning rather than explain it, 'provoking a kind of crisis in reading, calling attention to the treacheries and the possibilities of figurative language'.[36] Rather than 'solving' the sign into a corresponding interpretation, it is the difficulty of such questions rather than the answerability of them that becomes the primary focus of analysis. But to do so involves a collapse in the relationship between the signifier and the signified, rendering symbols into madness rather than meaning. Although there is no doubt of Lady Macbeth's implication in Duncan's murder and no question of her guilt, like Ruddymane's hands, the image of Lady Macbeth's handwashing gesture cannot be easily (re)solved. She sees the blood upon her hands, but it does not actually remain there, and even as she fears the crime will be discovered, she reveals her own part in it. The symbols become more than mere dramatic irony in 5.1: they become the symbols of madness as the certainty of signs break down their meanings.

Lorraine Helms acknowledges the theatricality of gesture in order to 'distinguish between social and theatrical roles, between theatre and the theatricality of everyday life, between role-playing as theatrical transformation and role-playing as social subordination'.[37] Yet it is these very distinguishing features which start to blur within the gesture of Lady Macbeth washing her hands. The Doctor in the scene refers to the Lady's 'other actual performances' (5.1.12), with the gentlewoman observing the sleepwalker by saying, 'This is her very guise' (5.1.19). Lady Macbeth's gestures in this scene are simultaneously social and theatrical: the handwashing action is enacted with the social knowledge of its implication of innocence, and yet it is performance, first, because Lady Macbeth is re-enacting the moment from its initial occurrence, and second, because there is no actual blood on her hands at all. The incident of her sleepwalking almost becomes a play-within-a-play, a performance of a previous moment within the performance of *Macbeth* itself. Of course, the fact that Lady Macbeth performs while she is asleep complicates matters. Earlier in the play, when Macbeth and Lady Macbeth emerge from killing Duncan with blood on their hands, the blood is part of the theatrical performance and therefore the audience accepts the fake blood on the hands of the actors as a signifier for the real thing. Yet in 5.1, Lady Macbeth (and the actor playing the character) is still acting as though she has real blood on her hands, but only she is able to accept or perceive a signifier for the blood that, to an audience's mind, is not there at all. It becomes difficult to pinpoint exactly what an audience is looking at when this gesture is performed. On this matter, Stuart Clark notes the crucial role of 'the fallibility of seeing', and how the play 'adds a kind of hypocrisy of the eyes, where what appears as one thing might very well be (and thus mean) another, where images as well as words "palter with us in a double sense" (5.8.20)'.[38] Despite this, he neglects to mention Lady Macbeth's sleepwalking scene and the blood she appears to see on her hands.[39] It is vitally important to acknowledge the ephemerality of the gesture's initial enactment, in the sense that it loses its very existence as soon as the action is finished, with the only proof of its performance locked within the memory of the spectator. Such gestures are, like the witches, ghostly appearances: 'what seemed corporal, / Melted, as breath into the wind' (1.3.81–2).

It is this sense of memorial re-enaction and reconstruction – of what was seen, or may have been seen – which haunts Lady Macbeth and becomes epitomized by her action of handwashing. Having seen her bloody hands, it is as if she cannot see anything else. Joan Larsen Klein writes how, '[l]ike the damned in the *Inferno*, [Lady Macbeth] exists solely within the present memory of past horrors'.[40] This trauma is remarkably similar to the workings of personal shame itself, wherein the mind replays an upsetting moment over and over again in an endlessly self-accusing fashion. It is this personal act which takes over Lady Macbeth's mind in her somnambulance. In his *Discourse on the Preseruation of the Sight* of 1599, André Du Larens examines the action of sleepwalking:

> in melancholike persons, the materiall is wanting [...] the minde is not at rest, the braine is distempered, the minde is in continuall restlessness: for the feare that is in them doth continually set before them tedious & grieuous things,

which so gnaw and pinch them as that they hinder them from sleeping. But if at one time [...] they be overtaken with a little slumber, it is then but a trouble-some sleep, accompanied with a thousand of false and fearful apparitions, and dreams so dreadfull, as that it were better for them to be awake.[41]

This contemporary account considers the underlying mental disorders behind the physical act of somnambulance, and the language emphasizes the anguish of the mind: 'grieuous things, which so gnaw and pinch'. Mental turmoil is described in terms of physical pain. This is the horror of shameful fear-sickness: it is continuously self-inflicted harm, the mind turning on itself to enact continual punishment, except the ensuing emotional turmoil only rekindles the guilt still further.

As I argued in my Introduction, gestures are the embodied epitome of the political as personal (and vice versa). So in Lady Macbeth's representation of mental disorder, we see a reflection of the play's political moment. Alvin Kernan's observation that, for Shakespeare, 'treason becomes not only demonic possession, it is derangement and madness' strikes at the heart of the issue.[42] He continues:

Macbeth was the Stuart play, celebrating [James'] ancient lineage, portraying the critical event in it and in Scotland's history, and making divine-right kingship identical with nature and sanity.[43]

Madness and the gestures which convey it are political. The act of seeing, followed by the act of questioning what was seen, creates the fundamental crisis behind the paranoid gestures in *Macbeth*. The play reveals how fear-sickness is necessarily embodied, of which the gestures conveying such a state of mind are further embodiments.

The question of agency in *Macbeth* is inherently tied to the related issues of manhood and madness within the play – issues which are encompassed within Lady Macbeth's somnambulant handwashing and link with such issues of responsibility and personal guilt. This confusion of Lady Macbeth is embodied in her hands: she sees a signifier which is not really there, but the act of her seeing it is enough to signify her guilt. Read in this way, madness becomes a treason of the mind, rebelling against reason. These actions of handwashing, as with the *cornutu*, haunt those who see them, or those who believe they are being seen. Such moments, real or hallucinated, live on in the imagination, the signified moment becoming an invisible signifier within the mind itself, remaining unseen except by those tormenting themselves with shameful memories.

7

Kneeling: Passive Aggression in *Coriolanus*

The Peacham drawing (Figure 12), the only known contemporary illustration of Shakespearean performance, depicts one of the opening tableaux in *Titus Andronicus*.[1] Underneath the sketch reads, 'Enter Tamora pleadinge for her sonnes going to execution.' The drawing itself does not, however, depict her entrance; rather, it depicts the static act of asking for mercy through the gesture of kneeling and holding out her conjoined hands in supplication. Her two sons behind her visually echo her stance as they wait on their knees to learn of their fate. What is curious, however, is the altered perspective in the image. Tamora appears to be ever so slightly upstage of Titus, and presenting herself kneeling, and yet they are the same height. While the drawing is not meant to be a full artistic rendering of the scene, the lack of perspective is an intriguing oversight, especially given other detailing, such as the costuming, so perhaps this detail tells us something crucial about the way the scene may have been viewed by the early modern spectator. Despite the discrepancy of the power dynamic, represented physically by Titus' upright stance and open, declarative arms and Tamora's gesture of submission, in terms of height, at least, she remains Titus' equal.

There are three reasons why this potential disparity might have occurred. First, whoever drew the illustration may

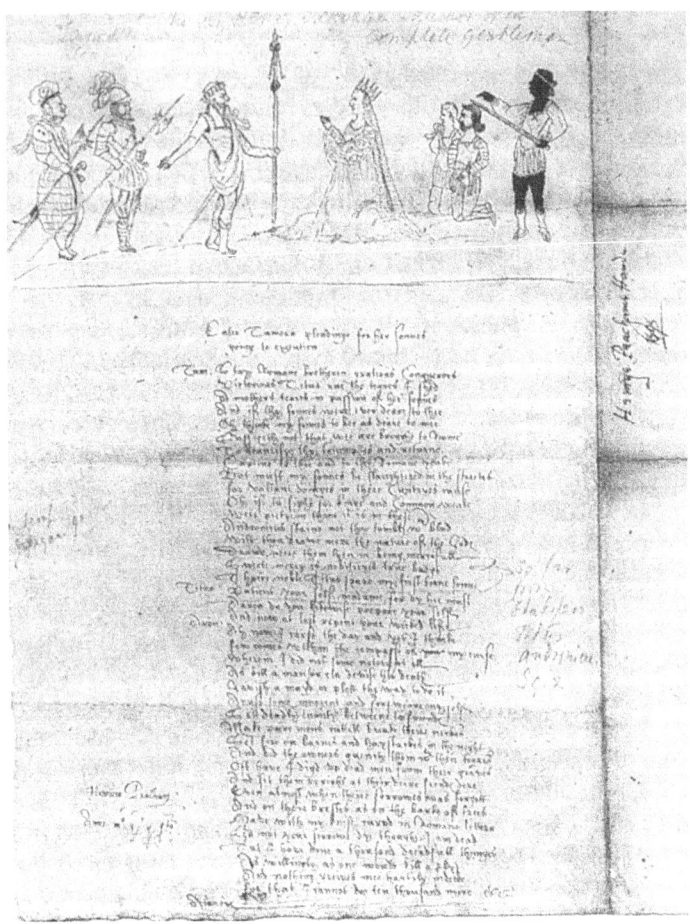

FIGURE 12 *Henry Peacham,* Titus Andronicus, *drawing, c.1595. Courtesy of Wikimedia (https://commons.wikimedia.org/wiki/File:Peacham_Drawing.jpg).*

have used artistic license based on a memory of the scene's performance, rather than the illustration being a rendering of the scene sketched while it occurs. Second, the drawing could have been composed with the artist's knowledge of the rest of the play. While Tamora begins in a position of apparent weakness ('O cruel, irreligious piety!' (1.1.133)), she does not remain so for long, helping to destroy the Andronicus clan before her own death. Thirdly, and more pertinently for the purposes of this chapter, the act of submission through the gesture of kneeling does not necessarily invoke a relationship of inequality between the two parties. Or rather, it can, but we should not necessarily be reading the kneeling Tamora as the weaker figure of the two.

If we look at his canon as a whole, Shakespeare's deployment of the act of kneeling in his *mise en scene* might appear somewhat ambivalent. But if we separate his plays by time period – in this case, into Elizabethan and Jacobean – an intriguing pattern emerges in the way that he approaches this gesture of apparent submission. This chapter contends that submissive stage acts, such as kneeling, take on a new power during the reign of James I. While many of the gestures discussed so far in this book have their roots in masculine aggression or the desire to 'feminize' unruly behaviour, these final two chapters concerns how shaming gestures in Jacobean drama not only incorporate more passive forms of shaming but also serve to reveal how successful such gestures can be.

Coriolanus might seem like an odd choice for a chapter taking passive-aggression as its theme. At its heart is a soldier bent on doing nothing more or less than his bloody duty by his country. He is simply aggressive: passivity angers him, as we see when he curses his fellow soldiers:

> All the contagion of the south light on you,
> You shames of Rome! You herd of – boils and plagues
> Plaster you o'er, that you may be abhorred
> Farther than seen, and one infect another
> Against the wind a mile! You souls of geese
> That bear the shapes of men, how have you run
> From slaves that apes would beat! Pluto and hell!
>
> (1.4.31–7)

But what this passage also tells us is that, when passivity is before him, he is emotionally riled. Such passivity spurs *him* on to further action. However, it is in the play's final act that his emotional response to passivity has fatal consequences. Turning his back on Rome, Coriolanus joins forces with the Volscian enemy and prepares to lead an attack on his former home. The eponymous character even says that 'I'll never / Be such a gosling as to obey instinct' (5.3.34–5), by which he means he will not be moved by his prior attachment to Rome. This reference to goslings is in itself a curious recollection of his earlier anger towards the timid Roman soldiers earlier in the play ('You souls of geese'); now, in the final act, Coriolanus wants to remain as resolute as he has always been, only this time his determination is bent on destroying Rome rather than urging the city onto further glory. All seems lost, until an intervention from Coriolanus' mother, Volumnia.

Volumnia, joined by her daughter-in-law Virgilia and grandson Young Martius, initially tries to persuade her son from battle by using words. Only, it does little to dissuade him, with an anguished Volumnia moaning, 'There's no man in the world / More bound to's mother, yet here he lets me prate / Like one i'th' stocks' (5.3.158–60). When Coriolanus turns away from his family (5.3.168), Volumnia turns to more drastic measures, as she, Virigilia, and Young Martius kneel to him. But this is what successfully stops Coriolanus' violence: seeing his family upon bended knees is what proves ultimately most persuasive. Rather than viewing this as an act of submission, however, it is in fact utilized by Volumnia as a show of strength: it may indicate passivity, but its loaded meaning is passive-aggressive. This gesture of *seeming* humility is anything but: it uses the submissive act of kneeling to shame Coriolanus for forcing his mother into such a position. It is a calculated move of emotional blackmail, which is as cunning as it is effective, and reveals how the patriarchal expectations of women as inherently submissive can be, in turn, wielded against the patriarchy as a weapon of its own.

In Josie Rourke's 2013 production of *Coriolanus* at the Donmar Warehouse, when Volumnia (Deborah Findlay) entreats her alliance of women (and Coriolanus' young son) to 'shame him with our knees', it is not merely a straightforward act of kneeling which is performed but a full on child's pose with knees, head, and outstretched arms all touching the ground. Coriolanus (Tom Hiddleston) turns away so as not to have to see the spectacle before him, but the knowledge of reducing his family to such a pitiful state brings tears to his eyes, particularly as the scene is played out in front of the Volsceans. This moment of emotion from Coriolanus recalls the image used in the production's publicity: a snapshot of a topless, vulnerable Hiddleston, obviously muscular but reduced by emotional might to the extent that a tear runs down his cheek. Perhaps this indicates that, for Rourke, this scene is the play's dramatic crux: for all Coriolanus' strength and manly vigour, he still becomes a 'boy of tears' before his mother. As the scene concludes and his family rises from their knees, Coriolanus (Hiddleston) finally, slowly, goes and takes his mother by the hand to concede defeat to her higher power.

Shakespeare had often used the spectacle of kneeling to create dramatic tension. One of his earliest comedies, *The Taming of the Shrew*, ends with the shrew in question, Katherina, declaring:

> I am ashamed that women are so simple
> To offer war where they should kneel for peace,
> Or seek for rule, supremacy and sway
> When they are bound to serve, love and obey.
>
> (5.2.167–70)

The play's resolution has troubled critics and audiences for its potential to be read as anti-feminist, with some productions taking care to ensure that the tone of the scene still manages to undercut patriarchal expectations. But reading the conclusion of Katherina's speech, and Petruccio's response to it, raises a variety of questions about how this moment can be performed:

KATHERINA
> But now I see our lances are but straws,
> Our strength as weak, our weakness past compare,
> That seeming to be most which we indeed least are.
> Then vail your stomachs, for it is no boot,
> And place your hands below your husband's foot:
> In token of which duty, if he please,
> My hand is ready, may it do him ease.
>
> PETRUCCIO
> Why, there's a wench. Come on, and kiss me, Kate.
>
> (5.2.179–86)

Frances E. Dolan notes that this custom of performing a 'courtesy' to a husband's foot had been outlawed for around forty years by the play's composition, which either 'marks Petruccio and Katherine's union as obviously anachronistic or endows it with the nostalgic prestige of a recently lost custom'.[2] So how might we read this episode? Is it a moment when the original audience, who might have been laughing along with the not-so-casual misogyny up until this point, are caught in the act of endorsing gendered cruelty that has only *now* gone too far?

We should also pause to consider how the script gives us no indication as to whether or not Katherina's hand actually touches Petruccio's foot. We know that she *offers* her hand, but it remains unclear whether Petruccio chooses to place his foot within her grasp or not.[3] It becomes a choice for the performers of the scene to make. We could turn to Petruccio's response in the following line in the hope of finding a hint of what happens. He says, 'Why, there's a wench. Come on, and kiss me, Kate.' Does he say, 'Why, there's a wench' while putting his hand into her hand, before drawing her up to him into a kiss? Does he simply pull her into a kiss and not give her his foot at all? Is he being sincere with his words, or is he embarrassed at Katherina calling his bluff, having spent the duration of the play trying to 'tame' her? We might even consider the nature of the kiss itself. Is it a moment of genuine desire and passion between the two of them? Does Petruccio kiss a sarcastic, unenthusiastic Kate, uninterested in returning his affection? Is Katherina's speech about respecting men genuine, sarcastic, tongue-in-cheek, or is it all an act so that she and her husband can win the wager that she has been tamed? These, as we have seen, are the nuances of gesture. They are a performance, but what they are performing and to what purpose is more than meets the eye.

The Two Gentlemen of Verona also makes reference to the kneeling of a female character; in this case, we hear a report of Silvia kneeling to her father after her lover, Valentine, is banished:

> she hath offered to the doom,
> Which unreserved stands in effectual force,
> A sea of melting pearl, which some call tears;
> Those at her father's churlish feet she tendered,
> With them, upon her knees, her humble self,
> Wringing her hands, whose whiteness so became them
> As if but now they waxed pale for woe.
> But neither bended knees, pure hands held up,
> Sad sighs, deep groans, nor silver-shedding tears
> Could penetrate her uncompassionate sire,
> But Valentine, if he be ta'en, must die.
> Besides, her intercession chafed him so,
> When she for thy repeal was suppliant,
> That to close prison he commanded her,
> With many bitter threats of biding there.
>
> (3.1.220–34)

Here, Silvia's gestural act does not placate her father, but exacerbates the situation. Rather than persuading him to cease hostilities against Valentine, her kneeling irritates him to the extent that she is locked away. Gestures of submission can clearly anger as well as placate. While Silvia displays feminine humility through an act such as kneeling, she is using it to the end of saving Valentine, revealing to her father that her filial loyalty has been usurped by her romantic feelings. She is punished accordingly.

Shakespeare's early history plays also serve to reinforce the hierarchy we might expect in a scene of kneeling. In *1 Henry VI*, John Talbot kneels before his father to encourage him to fly the battle and let him, the younger soldier, remain: 'Here on my knee I beg mortality, / Rather than life preserved with infamy' (4.4.32–3). In the face of his father's fear that his son will die, John replies, 'Ay, rather than I'll shame my mother's womb' (4.4.35). The familial duty here is clear: if John is to entreat his father to change his mind, he must approach with pious body language and an argument that his desired actions will honour the family. Talbot Senior is persuaded, but unfortunately, both father and son are dead before the next hundred lines have been spoken. The act of kneeling here, above all else, conjures up a sense of futility: rather than a decisive gesture of persuasion, John Talbot submits himself to death in battle, breaking his old father's heart.

In *3 Henry VI* Warwick and Edward kneel before each other to confirm their pact to avenge Warwick's brother's death:

WARWICK
> Why stand we like soft-hearted women here,
> Wailing our losses whiles the foe doth rage,
> And look upon, as if the tragedy
> Were played in jest by counterfeiting actors?
> Here on my knee I vow to God above:
> I'll never pause again, never stand still,
> Till either death hath closed these eyes of mine
> Or Fortune given me measure of revenge.

EDWARD
> O Warwick, I do bend my knee with thine,
> And in this vow do chain my soul to thine.

(2.3.29–34)

Their exchange is self-consciously rooted in performative action that is eager to gender itself as masculine: keen not to respond like 'soft-hearted women', they refuse to stand idly by and watch as if 'counterfeiting actors' were playing out history before them. Here, both Warwick and Edward kneel and, in doing so, make a pact to 'chain [their] soul[s]' together, binding their constancy and devotion to each other. Their act of kneeling is not one of submission, but one of power and comradeship.

A similar moment of solidarity occurs in *Measure for Measure*, only this time it is between two women. In the play's final scene, Mariana entreats Isabella to assist her in creating a persuasive spectacle:

> Isabel,
> Sweet Isabel, do yet but kneel by me;
> Hold up your hands, say nothing; I'll speak all.
> They say, best men are moulded out of faults;
> And, for the most, become much more the better
> For being a little bad: so may my husband.
> O Isabel, will you not lend a knee?
>
> (5.1.334–40)

As will have been apparent earlier on in the play, Isabella's constancy, as seen through her arguments to Angelo and in her submissive kneeling gestures, proves very effective. In her exchanges with Angelo, Lucio urges her to '[g]ive't not o'er so: to him again, entreat him; / Kneel down before him, hang upon his gown' (2.2.43–4). Isabella and Mariana's display of kneeling in the final scene once again constitutes an act of female solidarity lacking in the play until this point and reveals the persuasive power of women helping each other against the threat of powerful men.[4]

In *Richard II* the spectacle of kneeling becomes an almost farcical act. This instance is intriguing given the play's medieval context of chivalry and codes of civility, and while the play's earlier scenes have more orthodox presentations of kneeling as a solemn performance, by Act Five, its treatment as a gestural moment has shifted towards parody. In 5.3, Aumerle, York, and the Duchess of York all beseech Bolingbroke on their knees, with Bolingbroke himself noting the shift in generic tone: 'Our scene is altered from a serious thing, / And now changed to "The Beggar and the King"' (5.3.78–9). Marjorie Garber comments on this episode by noting that

> York, professing loyalty to the king over loyalty to flesh
> and blood, claims that his own kneeling means something
> different – means obeisance rather than supplication,
> compliance rather than revolt [...] In these scenes, as
> indeed throughout Shakespeare's staging, public / private
> hierarchies are troubled by the knee-work.[5]

The ambivalence of kneeling's meaning in the scene, given that York and his wife are both kneeling to different ends, is part of its comedy. Yet what should also be noted in this scene is Bolingbroke's response to the Duchess of York. Despite her pleading coming third after Aumerle and York, she is the first to be referred to in a derogatory manner: 'What shrill-voiced suppliant makes this eager cry?' (5.3.74). She is asked by the new king to rise from her knees no fewer than three times ('Rise up, good aunt!' 'Good aunt, stand up.' 'Good aunt, stand up' (5.3.91; 109; 128)), while her husband and son are not asked to rise. There is something in the duchess' submission that Bolingbroke does not like. It may be explained by her relentless speech in this scene, particularly from line 100, where she begins to speak in rhyme, adding to the sense of self-conscious performance in the scene. But rather than her suiting her action to her words, she is suiting her words to her action: Bolingbroke is unnerved by a woman kneeling before him and how this scene looks to a spectator from a gendered perspective of power. A woman kneeling to the new king is more troubling and disturbing than a man performing the same action.

Another of Shakespeare's Jacobean plays, *King Lear*, uses its tragic ending to subvert the gendered stereotype of kneeling. Lear, desperate to reconcile with his daughter Cordelia, says,

> We two alone will sing like birds i' th' cage.
> When thou dost ask me blessing I'll kneel down
> And ask of thee forgiveness.
>
> (5.3.9–11)

In promising to kneel before her, he capitulates his power in two ways. First, by being a father kneeling to a daughter, and second by being a king kneeling to a subject. This gesture seems to mirror an earlier moment of semi-parodic kneeling in the play, when Lear speaks to Regan: 'On my knees I beg / That you'll vouchsafe me raiment, bed and food' (2.2.344–5). She is unmoved: 'Good sir, no more. These are unsightly tricks' (2.2.346). In Act Two, Lear kneels almost sarcastically, and his daughter's response (or lack thereof) leaves him furious. In Act Five, by contrast, Lear's desire to kneel is genuinely respectful. These two moments, looked at side by side, reveal his emotional journey over the course of the plot.

The act of kneeling is far closer to a ceremonial performance than vulgar street gestures such as the fig or the thumb-bite. Ceremony is linked to, but not analogous with, decorum: something intrinsically connected with the preservation of honour and the antithesis of shame. T. McAlindon observes,

> Because of their grave and traditional nature, ceremonies constitute that area of speech and action where propriety is most expected; they are formal orderings of speech and gesture, of costume and movement, in which departures from accepted style are instantly perceptible and either offensive or ridiculous. Ceremonies are also reminders that all the world's a stage on which every man must accept his part and play it with the maximum of propriety.[6]

McAlindon's use of the male person is not accidental. Castiglione's *The Book of the Courtier* records the perceived seemliness of men, whose actions 'should display a certain robust and sturdy manliness', as opposed to women, who should 'have a certain soft and delicate tenderness, with an air of feminine sweetness in her every movement'.[7] Ceremony and pageantry on the Jacobean stage, as we shall see, evoke complex notions of what I might call 'gender decorum', by which I mean the 'formal orderings of speech and gesture' that are permissible or expected for male or female figures on display. Russell West-Pavlov, too, notes that new codes of civility emerging in the Renaissance were having a profound effect on the performance and practice of bodily refinement and how it was gendered.[8] This change had a particular effect on masculinity, with West-Pavlov noticing how early modern spectacle places as many points of decorum on men as it does on women, creating 'new pressures upon the male body' as the world of ceremony became more influenced by earlier pageantry.[9] However, far from creating a strong, achievable sense of performative masculinity, it led to men 'striving to attain an impossible ideal of manhood – and opened them up [to] the charge of merely performing manliness'.[10]

Yet while masculinity in performance was under pressure, the confusion surrounding male behaviour in Shakespeare's late plays contrasts with a new surety in feminine performance. In plays such as *Coriolanus* and *The Winter's Tale*, static gesture becomes not only more iconographical and ceremonial in tone, but more persuasive to the other characters onstage. There is a sense that, being charged with 'merely performing' certain roles, scenes become filled instead with a *lack* of physical movement as a way of surpassing critiques of theatricality. What is more, female passive-aggression reveals the alleged power of masculinity as something which is also a socially-constructed performance. It is for this reason that Volumnia's kneeling supplication to her son Coriolanus is the only thing that can save him from sacking Rome.

In the act of kneeling, Renaissance women are aligning themselves with a plethora of iconographic foremothers, and in doing so, they reference and retell the stories of previous women whose submission lent them honour and power. One example of this would be Esther, who we see in Figure 13 in an engraving by Lucas van Leyden, depicting her before her husband, Ahasuerus. Ahasuerus was a Persian king who selected his wife due to her humility as well as her beauty (the latter may well have been enhanced by the former). The scene shown here is of her interceding after learning that her

FIGURE 13 *Lucas van Leyden,* Esther before Ahasuerus, *engraving, 1518. Gift of Harry J. Friedman to the Metropolitan Museum of Art, New York (1962).*

husband's minister Haman had devised a plot to kill all those of Jewish heritage: a heritage that she also shared, although she had not made this knowledge known to her husband until this point. In the image, Ahasuerus touches Esther with his sceptre, moved by her submission to him and almost kneeling to her himself while still seated on his throne; he then sends Haman to death. Esther's humility wields power, preventing her own destruction.

I do not wish to imply that women such as Esther are empowered by their 'feminine' qualities, nor that such feminine qualities when freely chosen cannot be in themselves a sign of strength, nor that women who do not demonstrate 'feminine' qualities are undeserving of mercy; rather, my argument is that women use what performative means they can within a patriarchal social structure to ensure their survival, and in the Renaissance, this strategy involved the use of passive gestures for political purposes.

Esther's function in such images is that of peacemaker, described by H. Diane Russell as 'one of the most important roles that women could have in the political sphere'.[11] But depictions of this scene have precedents before van Leyden, appearing in medieval devotional books and offering a similar example to the Virgin Mary in her role as intercessor for mankind.[12] Indeed, the iconography of kneeling is probably most associated with Mary, who was a subject of apotheosis up until the Protestant Reformation. She was seen to have many admirable qualities which could serve as examples for other women, including her religious obedience, devotion to her children, honour for her husband, and readiness to help others even if it meant suffering for their sake.[13] For many in this period, '[t]he ideal woman withdrew from the world, she was not a leader in it'.[14] Despite this norm, texts reprinted many times in the Renaissance period, such as Boccaccio's *De claris mulieribus* (*Concerning Famous Women*), expound the lives of women who managed to humiliate men, often through vice.[15] But this detail is precisely what is so interesting about the efficacy of the gestures of Shakespearean characters such as Volumnia: despite not being a leader, nor using vice of any kind, she is the key focus of agency that serves to shame Coriolanus as the male protagonist in 5.3.

FIGURE 14 The Annunciation, *charcoal drawing by Federico Barocci (1528–1612), Italy, sixteenth century. Photo by Dea / G. Nimatallah/ Getty images.*

Federico Barocci's *The Annunciation* is an exemplary work showing the kneeling gesture associated with the Virgin Mary (Figure 14). What is perhaps most noteworthy is that the angel Gabriel is also kneeling, but he is very much kneeling to her to convey appreciation for her willingness to do God's work, as implied by her submissive stance. Albrecht Dürer's

FIGURE 15 The Assumption and Coronation of the Virgin, *1510 (1906), Albrecht Durer. Photo by The Print Collector/Getty Images.*

The Assumption and Coronation of the Virgin (Figure 15) is similarly striking. While Mary kneels before God, the male earthly figures depicted below kneel before her, in reverence of her duty to a greater good. Here, in the Virgin iconography, we see a woman assert her power through more traditionally submissive gestures, gestures that are also used to similar effect in Shakespeare's late works.

Visual depictions of Eve offer a more ambivalent narrative of female power. Born of Adam's rib and, therefore, inherently derivative of him, her story (and the iconography representing it) portrays her as initially subservient but ultimately capable of resistance to heavenly power. This is figured in Gislebertus' Eve, where she is depicted kneeling while simultaneously reaching back to pick the forbidden fruit (Figure 16). Such an image of Eve as a kneeling figure is all the more interesting given her ultimate role in the story of the Fall of Man. She is depicted both as passive and subservient, yet with agency enough to set the Fall in motion and, in doing so, bringing both knowledge and, crucially, the emotion of shame into the world. It is this sense of shame and its ramifications both in self-exploration and the role it plays in the public sphere that is the crux of the scene between Volumnia and Coriolanus.

As we shall see, Volumnia's kneeling to Coriolanus is a scene which draws on the play's wider tropes about gender and the body politic, as well as theatricality and the potential shame of spectatorship. From the play's opening focus on the starving

FIGURE 16 Temptation of Eve, *lintel by Gislebertus or Gisleberto, French sculptor active during the early decades of twelfth century. Photo by DeAgostini/Getty Images.*

citizens and Menenius' fable of the belly to Volumnia's claim that 'Action is eloquence, and the eyes of th'ignorant / More learned than the ears' (3.2.77–8), *Coriolanus* is preoccupied with the body, not only in how it works but in how it is seen by others. In fact, Volumnia's supplication to her son in 5.3 is foreshadowed by Menenius in the opening scene. Speaking to the rebellious citizens, Menenius declares, 'For the dearth, / The gods, not the patricians, make it, and / Your knees to them, not arms, must help' (1.1.67–9). His emphasis on a performed act of submission being the only way to respond to suffering anticipates what Volumnia will go on to do, and such a gesture is entirely in keeping with a Roman sense of duty before authority. For instance, Coriolanus himself kneels before his mother when returning from battle, with her urging him, 'Nay, my good soldier, up' (2.1.166).

But her later performance of kneeling to him is too much for Coriolanus to bear. Antonella Piazza writes that when Volumnia implores her son in this way, 'she recognizes and emphasizes Coriolanus's weakness, inability and failure rather than his heroic military success'.[16] In the other cases of kneeling we see, in this play and elsewhere, the kneeling represents a capitulation *to* power; in this scene, the act serves to *undermine* the person being kneeled to. It is the expectations behind specific gender roles which, crucially, re-shape the 'submissive' gesture of kneeling into something that has a subversive effect. We see this re-appropriation in the startling image Volumnia invokes:

> thou shalt no sooner
> March to assault thy country than to tread –
> Trust to't, thou shalt not – on thy mother's womb
> That brought thee to this world.
>
> (5.3.122–5)

In equating the state of Rome with her own womb, she implies that his identity as her son is analogous with his identity as a Roman, and that both her womb and his country have nourished, protected, and shaped him to be the man he is. The success of her kneeling stance, matched in the tableau by kneeling from Virgilia, Valeria, and Young Martius, is such that to conclude the scene, Coriolanus speaks these words:

> Ladies, you deserve
> To have a temple built you; all the swords
> In Italy and her confederate arms
> Could not have made this peace.
>
> (5.3.206–9)

To build a temple might be apt. In his essay 'Acting the Roman', Manfred Pfister observes how 'Volumnia performs the role of Roman matron in language and gesture to perfection, narcissistically identifying with Rome's tutelary goddess Juno (4.2.56), and so does Virgilia that of the submissive and taciturn wife, dedicated to her domestic needlework like any Penelope (1.3.85)'.[17] Yet Volumnia's power is very much rooted in her understanding of earthly relationships and particularly in how they are gendered. Antonella Piazza astutely notes that Volumnia has 'all the patriarchal power of a mother as well as of a father. All the virtues of classical old age — expediency, experience, flexibility – are projected onto Volumnia making her the only Roman statesman, a Jacobean Machiavellian governor'.[18] When we consider her power versus that of the ageing and ineffective patricians Menenius and Lartius, we see precisely how her agency as Coriolanus' mother serves to offer an authority unmatched by any other member of Roman society. Chikako D. Kumamoto is partly correct in arguing that Volumnia succeeds 'not only as a mother, but also as a now-penitent community member, in convincing Coriolanus of a new vision of heroism comprised not of an isolationist, avenging sword of anger […] but of the ability to learn to feel others' suffering and compassion as something that matters'.[19] However, I would argue that it is Volumnia's status as a mother that is entirely what renders her as the ultimate authority over Coriolanus. Her support of her son throughout his life is not an act of subservience, but an acknowledgement of her authorship of him that he, too, is obliged to acknowledge.

Volumnia's power within the Roman body politic emerges at an interesting point in Shakespeare's career. Written sometime between 1605 and 1608, the play marks Shakespeare's movement into the Jacobean period, which was in itself still in the process of being formed as the country shifted from being ruled by an unmarried Queen Elizabeth to the Scottish James and his wife, Anna of Denmark. Shakespeare's Roman plays often give an insight into contemporary politics: Pfister argues that the narrative of the Roman plays 'reflects the new upsurge of republican ideas and ideals in the politically critical period of the final decades of Elizabeth's reign with its insecurities about the future of the realm and the problematic transition from the late Tudor policy of negotiation and compromise to Stuart absolutism'.[20] The transition between monarchs as being a crucial influence on *Coriolanus* is further explored by Piazza. She writes that Volumnia, as the menopausal figure who is able to create peace from a warlike situation, is 'Shakespeare's suggestion to the contemporary James to look back to "prudent" Elizabeth I for advice'.[21] What is curious, although perhaps unsurprising, is that despite the prudence of the Virgin Queen, misogynistic tropes still undermine the gender politics of the era. One of the ways this sentiment manifests itself is in Coriolanus' refusal to reveal his battle wounds, and how Lisa S. Starks-Estes equates this 'dread of vulnerability, of openness' with the 'misogyny that underlies notions of masculinity and femininity'.[22] Jennifer Low contributes to this discussion, arguing that, in the early modern period, being on display was believed to subject the individual to a penetrating effeminacy. Examining how spatial elements control the subject, and the transaction between actors and their audience, Jennifer A. Low contends that the intrusive thrust stage of outdoor amphitheatres such as the Globe would have had a crucial effect on spectators.[23] Low contests that Coriolanus refuses to open himself up to public spectacle or 'figurative penetration':[24] of course, this fear reveals an insecurity that leads to his entire *modus operandi* to be questioned. Philosophers of the early seventeenth-century advised that Roman notions of Republicanism and Stoicism should be the recommended norms for 'civil discipline and responsibility, patriotic pride, and manly self-control and courage',[25] and perhaps this expectation is pertinent to Coriolanus being moved by his mother's kneeling. To change his mind so publicly is the ultimate failure of Stoicism and 'manly self-control'; however, such behaviour follows in the footsteps of 'civil discipline' and 'patriotic pride'. Being on display seems to have an ambivalent effect on Coriolanus' identity as a Roman man, but Volumnia's affect as a Roman woman is clear.

The sense of spectacle in 5.3 is crucial to the efficacy of Volumnia's action, and turning to how the staging of this scene enhances the idea of 'framing' that recurs throughout the play helps to further unpick the scene's ultimate power in performance. What we have in these later plays is a sense of the stage properties themselves being re-framed. While there is evidence that *Coriolanus* was also performed at the Globe, the emergence of the indoor playhouses as a rival performance space inevitably has an effect on the way in which theatrical spectacles became conceived.

The development of the Blackfriars theatre in the Jacobean period has long been associated with a change in Shakespeare's later style. Felix C. H. Sprang is one of many critics who observe this phenomenon:

> Blackfriars may have encouraged Shakespeare and his collaborators to further explore the spatial semantics of both stages. Thus, a case can be made for arguing that changes in lighting, stage design and acting styles, taken together, played a crucial role in the episodic structure and specific form of multiperspectivism, both visual axes and ideological perspectives, which we encounter in Shakespeare's late plays.[26]

The use of candlelight in the indoor playhouses significantly affected the onstage spectacle. Everything felt, quite literally, closer, in stark contrast to an outdoor performance being conducted in broad daylight, and in a far larger space.[27] As we might expect, plays written for these indoor spaces often make use of themes that ensure visual spectacle. The candles held by sconces, and perhaps also held in the hands of the actors,[28] would have literally highlighted the costumes and the faces of the characters, and this combined with the audience's overall proximity to the stage would have given a far more 'close up' effect than at somewhere like the Globe. These different properties of the indoor stage give a distinct re-framing of the dramatic action performed upon it, and this can be seen in the way spectacle is described in plays such as *Coriolanus*. The kneeling tableau in 5.3 is a prime example of this: the more intimate indoor setting and the softness of the candlelight combined with the stillness of four characters upon their knees make the scene appear particularly arresting. While there are undoubtedly picturesque scenes performed on the outdoor stages, the pictorial quality of this moment in *Coriolanus* seems wholly fitting with the nature of the play itself, which, as we shall see, occupies itself with the idea of taking ancient heroes out of their framing devices (of history or visual culture) and seeing how they respond to a more unpalatable reality.

'Framing', in addition to meaning a sense of enclosure, can also convey a sense of adjusting or accommodating, in addition to its connotations of spectacle. The word 'frame' is used more times in *Coriolanus* than any other of Shakespeare's plays. For instance, it occurs when Coriolanus must put on an act of humility to receive votes, with Cominius saying, 'I think 'twill serve, if he / Can thereto frame his spirit' (3.2.97–8). In order to receive a consulship, Coriolanus must frame, or adjust, his behaviour so that his public performance is more palatable to the people. The word recurs in the crucial scene of 5.3 when Coriolanus catches sight of his mother, whom he refers to as 'the honoured mould / Wherein this trunk was framed' (5.3.22–3). This usage is especially telling, given that later in the same speech, he is rousing himself not to be moved by his family's submissive performance ('What is that curtsy worth? Or those doves' eyes, / Which can make gods forsworn?' (5.3.27–8)). In doing so, he wishes that 'man were author of himself' (5.3.36): he wants no other creator, no other artist who has framed his being. But his mother is having none of it: 'Thou art my warrior. / I holp to frame thee' (5.3.62–3). Coriolanus is trapped in a frame not of his making: his agency is never his own.

This lack of freedom is the reason why Coriolanus feels intense shame when he is the centre of a spectacle such as the one his mother creates by her kneeling, so much so that he advises his son to retain his innate nobility 'that thou mayst prove / To shame unvulnerable' (5.3.72–3). Pfister argues persuasively of Coriolanus as an 'in-born actor trained in acting the Roman from his earliest childhood', whose moments of conflict occur when 'his internalized scripts clash with each other'.[29] His mother's kneeling is one such internalized script, because it cues him to react with respect and revise his actions. He has only one available response to Volumnia's kneeling; in fact, he cannot *not* respond mercifully: he has been culturally conditioned to do so above all else. Such gestural knowledge of how we respond to the performance acts of others is a script we learn without realizing it, as we grow up within a society and cannot help but be affected when we are cued to perform an appropriate action. No one is an island, entire of itself; similarly, Coriolanus has not grown up in private, but within Rome's public spaces: 'the market-place, the Capitol, the battle field or theatre of war ... [the Romans'] mode of speaking is primarily the rhetoric of public address'.[30] But it is not just the mode of speaking that is affected: the non-verbal language of gesture also develops in this mode.

The world of *Coriolanus* is therefore inherently performative, which is further reflected when the eponymous hero remarks how his shame makes him feel '[l]ike a dull actor now, / I have forgot my part and I am out, / Even to a full disgrace' (5.3.40–2). There is an echo here of his inability to perform in public, as noted earlier when he refuses to show his wounds and then has difficulty feigning humility before the citizens. Lisa

S. Starks-Estes wisely notes how Coriolanus associates 'the very idea of acting' with femininity, explaining how this link 'corresponds to Western concepts of mimesis and imitation, truth and falsity, honesty and deception – "the feminine" as the faulty imitation, the seductive illusion – the antithesis of manly valor'.[31] What we may recognize here is performance anxiety – or, essentially, stage fright – for the crucially humiliating element of the scene is that it happens in front of an audience. In fact, Coriolanus draws our attention to the fact that his family is not alone on stage: 'Aufidius and you Volsces, mark, for we'll / Hear nought from Rome in private' (5.3.92–3).

While Markku Peltonen argues that this scene hinges on 'mighty power of words',[32] it is rather the spectacle of being submitted to, not the language used, that shames Coriolanus into a change of plan. It is only when he begins to turn away that Volumnia takes full control of the *mise en scene*:

> Down, ladies; let us shame him with our knees.
> To his surname 'Coriolanus' 'longs more pride
> Than pity to our prayers. Down! An end,
> This is the last.
>
> (5.3.169–72)

To the sight presented before him, Coriolanus utters these words:

> O, mother, mother!
> What have you done? Behold, the heavens do ope,
> The gods look down, and this unnatural scene
> They laugh at. [...]
> Aufidius, though I cannot make true wars,
> I'll frame convenient peace.
>
> (5.3.183–5; 190–1)

While the Volscian soldiers watching the scene may or may not have been able to hear the words spoken by Volumnia, all are able to see the gesture of supplication. Once again, the word 'frame' appears: Coriolanus knows he is on display, framed by the situation and appearing as someone rendered static, trapped in the dramatic moment. His mother's supplication indicates that he is not enough as he is; he has been found wanting, and must do better.

Earlier in the scene, Volumnia reasons that Coriolanus must choose between destroying his homeland or 'as a foreign recreant be led / With manacles through our streets' (5.3.114–15), going on to say that he 'lets me prate / Like one i' the' stocks' (5.3.159–60). These references to public punishment are hardly accidental: they reinforce the shame inherent in such a spectacle as the one Coriolanus finds himself in. While Coriolanus says that he wants to 'stand / As if a man were author of himself' (5.3.35–6), the real power lies with a woman not standing, but kneeling: her doing so before his fellow warriors and rivals is the one attack he can never recover from. In the play's final scene, Aufidius tauntingly refers to Coriolanus as 'boy' as he puts him to death, completing the shaming ritual of his former rival. There is a sense, perhaps, that having seen Coriolanus shamed publically by his mother, his previous performance of manhood in battle has been cancelled out. His status as a strong warrior has been called into question; what is never called into question, however, is the fact that Volumnia's matriarchal status wields its own strength, not through further acts of violence, but through constancy and the unshakeable bond of motherhood. Volumnia's power is to act as a mother not just to her son – guiding him and showing him his errors – but as a mother to Rome itself by protecting all her citizens from harm.

8

Stillness: Female Constancy in *The Winter's Tale*

When Hermione's statue is revealed in the final scene of *The Winter's Tale*, her husband Leontes is struck dumb with astonishment. Paulina comments, 'I like your silence; it the more shows off / Your wonder' (5.3.21–2). Leontes' inability to speak echoes the silence between him and his wife lasting the previous sixteen years. As Hermione 'coldly stands' (5.3.36), Leontes marvels at her 'natural posture' (5.3.23), recalling how 'thus she stood' (5.3.34) all those years ago. The stance and gesture of the statue match her likeness exactly.

Of course, there is a simple explanation for why this spectacle is so uncanny: the statue is not a statue, but Hermione herself. The sculptor has not mimicked Hermione's natural gesture: they *are* her natural gestures. I acknowledge that critics have often been more ambivalent in their treatment of the statue and whether or not it comes to life, or if it was living all along. However, Huston Diehl's argument that the statue 'functions as a visual rebuke' takes us to the real pertinence of the issue.[1] The role of this 'statue' scene as shaming spectacle is to bring about the reunion of Hermione with Leontes and Perdita at the conclusion of *The Winter's Tale* and provides us with a crucial example of the subversion of gender politics through the act of public shaming.

While earlier sections of this book have considered gestural movement as actions of rebuke, the final scene of one of Shakespeare's latest plays deploys a rebuke through stillness. Rather than underwhelming the dramatic moment, it arrests it. Paul Menzer argues persuasively that 'physical stasis was quite clearly part of the early English stage's performance technology' and contends that the depiction of 'emotional regulation' through stillness

> idealized the *mastery*, not the defeat, of passion. Such a regimen enabled a language of affect in which the lack of discernable passion could denote not dispassion but precisely the opposite [...] By scripting the restraint of internal perturbation, playwrights could code the lack of evident passion as passion itself. In doing so, the stage infused stillness with significance, whereby to do nothing was to do something indeed.[2]

The dramatic efficacy of Hermione's spectacle in the play's final scene renegotiates the traditional binary of women as passive and men as active by showing the poignant emotional affect of stillness. Hermione's 'statue' reveals a persuasive power which defies the patriarchy by calling it out: in acting still and inactive, it emphasizes Leontes' controlling nature, as she has been reduced to the static blazon of love poetry which is, in fact, a means of male dominance. Graham Holderness writes that *The Winter's Tale* depicts how 'masculine power is subordinated to the art, magic, and power of the female',[3] but while on the surface, this scene appears to endow women with artistic power, a more feminist reading would focus less on the female mystique. Instead, we can re-evaluate this scene as a moment where Hermione and Paulina play the patriarchy at its own game in order to reveal its inconsistencies and inherent hypocrisy.

Cheek By Jowl's 2016 production of the play, as directed by Declan Donnellan, created an uncanny doubling in the trial scene of Act Three by showing Hermione (Natalie Radmall-Quirke) give her defence directly to the audience while a close-up camera recording her every gesture projected a relay of her speech onto a huge screen behind her. It confronted the audience with the unnerving level of scrutiny she was being subjected to by Leontes (Orlando James), and as the scene crescendoed, Leontes' rage led him to grab his wife's head and hold their faces close together. In this act, he controlled her gaze and tapped his fingers upon her temples on the line 'those of your fact are so', recalling two things: first, his own fear that horns are growing on the exact same position on his own head; and second, the fact that his belief in her infidelity is a trick of the mind.

In the final scene of reconciliation, Donnellan's production abbreviated a good deal of Shakespeare's text, with the final tableau, rather than showing all the characters being led away, featuring a standing Hermione embraced by Leontes and Perdita (Eleanor McLoughlin), both of whom remained on their knees. Curiously, in the production's final moments, the boy Mamillius (Tom Cawte) returned to the stage to observe the reunion and placed his hand upon his father's head, before going away with the figure of Time (Grace Andrews). It is ambiguous what this act of touch might convey, but in this moment of resolution, the boy's reappearance reminds us of the play's casualties who, unlike Hermione and Perdita, will not be revived or rediscovered. Is this moment of touch an act of forgiveness, of remembrance? Is it permission to forget previous troubles, to allow Leontes to forgive himself and move on? It is an ambiguous climax to the production, but nonetheless a terribly moving one, reminding us how the physical act of touch is itself *emotionally* touching, with its ability to move, reconcile, and disturb all at once.

In this chapter, as in the previous one, I refer to examples of women who have deployed power through the performance of submissive gestures; however, these instances do not necessarily imply an inherent 'power of the female'. Rather, they are indicative of the negotiations that must be made within existing gender norms. While Cristina León Alfar's work on justice in *The Winter's Tale* contends that it is the power of verbal speech acts that bring about Leontes' deserved shame,[4] both Paulina and Hermione's attempts to speak out against the charge of infidelity go ignored, and it is only Hermione's silence as a statue (not to mention her silence over the past sixteen years) which brings about the final reconciliation. If anything, their speech acts are seen by Leontes as confirmation of Hermione's promiscuity. Only by Hermione remaining still and silent in the final scene can Leontes recognize her as a subject and himself as a tyrant; paradoxically, the only way she can win back agency (or at least, prove her innocence) is to demonstrate her lack of agency within a patriarchal dynamic. The spectacle of stasis in *The Winter's Tale* is a keen contrast to what Maria Del Sapio Garbero calls the 'destructive masculinity' of Leontes;[5] indeed, such an assessment reminds us of Chapter 3 of this book, which argued that Richard III's grotesque masculinity must be neutralized in Anne's act of spitting upon him as an act of feminization. By *The Winter's Tale*, one of Shakespeare's last plays, he is still writing about the problem of masculinity, only now his approach is different. Del Sapio Garbero argues that Hermione's body 'turns male anxiety into a furious distortive perspectivalism', in particular when Leontes picks over the gestures she is seen making with Polixines (the 'paddling palms' and 'pinching fingers', which he takes as ocular proof).[6] As I have written elsewhere, this play obsessively misreads gestures and reveals the danger of reading bodily action at face value.[7] While we have seen male Shakespearean characters act in this manner before – as with *Much Ado about Nothing* and *Othello* – it is only in one of Shakespeare's final plays where the sense of voyeurism ends up travelling in both directions. Leontes' decision to put Hermione on trial in 3.2 is reprised in the final scene, where Hermione's statue takes on the role of rebuking *him* in a public performance. The final scene of *The Winter's Tale* is a two-way spectacle: Hermione may be on display, but Leontes is the one now on trial. Scene 5.3 serves not only as a loaded visual allegory for the objectified status of women in the period but also as a moment in which to interrogate the patriarchs who have perpetuated the silencing of women.

Shame needs an audience. To quote Ewan Fernie, shame 'brings a strong sense of exposure, producing an urgent desire to be concealed and hidden'.[8] This powerful emotion is why public shaming is such a potent civilizing process in the early modern period. These moments in Shakespeare's later work evoke not only these spectacles of shame but the audience that they require to humiliate. The incidents I have explored in *Coriolanus* and *The Winter's Tale* do not occur privately, but in view of a staged public. Coriolanus and Leontes are both being watched by their fellow characters onstage as well as the public audience around it. The justice of public shaming in this scene is matched by the sense of spectacle inherent in the dramatic staging itself. As we also saw in the previous chapter, the voyeuristic quality of looking would be intensified in a smaller, indoor theatre such as Blackfriars, where this play would have been performed in addition to the Globe.[9] Being that much closer to the action lends far greater intimacy, creating the moment where perhaps, for the first time, Leontes understands that women are people who feel, not objects to be used. The closer audience proximity to her statuesque figure is further enhanced by the candlelight of the indoor theatre. Farah Karim-Cooper notes how the candles in the statue scene as staged in Blackfriars perform 'a kind of lighting *ekphrasis*. It is a visual process that highlights, paradoxically, the deceptive nature of spectacle even while it works to elevate it'.[10] This comment astutely captures the trap that is laid for Leontes: just as he came to the wrong conclusion when viewing Hermione's gestures to Polixines, he sees a statue rather than a person and is then tutored in his error.

The use of statuesque figures is not limited to Shakespeare, nor to the public theatre. Clare McManus finds that Thomas Campion's *The Lord's Masque* (*c.*1607) involves four silver female statues as part of the court spectacle. This was performed two years before *The Winter's Tale*, and McManus connects the 'masque-like' ending of Shakespeare's play with the private court performances played before James I.[11] In *The Lord's Masque*, as in *The Winter's Tale*, the statues come to life: 'animated by Prometheus from clay models by stolen divine fire', and then 'transformed into statues by Jove as a punishment for this theft', the anger of the god finally begins to lessen: 'Lo, how fix'd they stand; / So did Jove's wrath so long, but now at least / It by degrees relents'.[12] This emotional journey reminds us of Leontes' transition from anger to remorse, and how it enables us to watch the movement of Hermione 'coming back to life'. But it also recalls to us the Stuart age's desire to inaugurate a period of peace through the myth of the Jacobean Golden Age, and this objective was often effected through the performance of pageantry. C. B. Hardman writes of the accession of James I and the iconography surrounding it, noting:

> When James I made his splendid triumphal entry into London in March 1603 he was welcomed as a second Brute fulfilling the ancient prophecy that the island would be united under a single ruler. Contemporary image-makers reinvigorated and reapplied Tudor myths of the Arthurian past and of the Golden Age.[13]

Here, the classical past is being appropriated by the present in an attempt to create a legacy for the future, attempting to convince the citizens of the new monarch's authority. But as we see in *The Winter's Tale*, the inclusion of medieval and classical pageantry is something which is also seen in the plays Shakespeare wrote in this period, reflecting a time of insecurity and the need for overcompensation through the compelling use of nostalgic visual culture. Naturally, such an iconographic shift has ramifications for how these spectacles are processed by the spectator and where they fit in among the categories of the real and the artificial. It has long been noted that a play like *The Winter's Tale* 'repeatedly draws attention to its own artificiality',[14] and the final scene even evokes notions of idolatry. Gillian Woods, in her study *Shakespeare's Unreformed Fictions*, explains the final scene's potential for staging Catholic idol-worship:

> Kneeling for parental blessing was an ideologically sound demonstration of filial respect in the post-Reformation period, yet it also provided a visual pun with behaviour that Perdita acknowledges as 'superstitious'. Kneeling at communion was a contentious issue; but when performed before images it was the defining marker of idolatry [...] As far as Perdita and first-time audiences of the play are aware, at 5.3.44 Perdita kneels to a statue, not a parent, and therefore the gesture looks more like idolatry than filial humility.[15]

Woods' pertinent observation reveals the play's dalliance with Catholic levels of iconography, and how it may have proved contentious for a contemporary audience. Perdita's act of kneeling before Hermione's 'statue' is a gesture that risks blasphemy, and it is only Hermione's revelation of her own performance that acquits her daughter of such an accusation.

Reading 5.3 in greater detail helps to connect the allusions to artistry evoked by Hermione's statue-like gesture, and it is in this way that we shall we able to see the wider concerns about the gendering of both artifice and power. At the start of 5.3, Leontes reminds the audience that Paulina has shown him and his party a number of artworks already: 'Your gallery / Have we passed through, not without much content / In many singularities' (5.3.10–12). When Paulina announces, 'prepare / To see the life as lively mocked as ever / Still sleep mocked death' (5.3.18–20), we may (like Leontes) overlook her repetition of the verb 'mock' in our excitement to see the statue, but it is an important inclusion which recalls the shaming process that the whole spectacle is set up to evoke. By this point in the play, plenty of time – not to mention a distracting pastoral act –

has passed since Hermioine's trial, but her apparent death and the lack of resolution within the family maintains an air of unease. No amount of singing swains can overshadow the fact that the show trial of 3.2 is one of the most uncomfortable and disturbing scenes Shakespearean performance has to offer, and even by Act Five, the audience may still have Leontes' words ringing in their ears:

> Your actions are my dreams.
> You had a bastard by Polixenes,
> And I but dreamed it. As you were past all shame –
> Those of your fact are so – so past all truth.
>
> (3.2.80–3)

The words 'so past all truth' are sickeningly ironic: while Leontes accuses his wife of being past all truth, it is his own accusations which lack credulity. This has a particular resonance in our current 'post-truth' age, underscoring how women have spent centuries not being believed: whether they are falsely accused of infidelity or sexually assaulted, a woman's voice carries less weight than a man saying the opposite.

Upon hearing of Hermione's sudden 'death', Leontes responds

> Go on, go on.
> Thou canst not speak too much. I have deserved
> All tongues to talk their bitterest.
>
> (3.2.211–13)

A few lines later, Paulina responds, 'Take your patience to you, / And I'll say nothing' (3.2.228–9). Leontes' expectation of verbal chastisement is met instead by Paulina first apologizing for showing 'too much / The rashness of a woman' (3.2.217–18) and then a descent into silence. But it is, of course, the silent eloquence of Hermione's stillness in 5.2 which shows up Leontes' previously tyrannical behaviour. This female silence recalls the belief of St Paul, as written in 1 Timothy 2.11–14 of the King James Bible:

Let the woman learn in silence with all subjection. But I suffer not a woman to teach, nor to usurp authority over the man, but to be in silence. For Adam was first formed, then Eve. And Adam was not deceived, but the woman being deceived was in the transgression.

St Paul indicates that women must be silent and not be teachers, but Hermione and Paulina's wordless spectacle of stillness reveals their hitherto unseen authority and didacticism. The process starts to work as soon as Leontes sees Hermione, his first words being

> Her natural posture.
> Chide me, dead stone, that I may say indeed
> Thou art Hermione – or, rather, thou art she
> In thy not chiding; for she was as tender
> As infancy and grace.
>
> (5.3.23–7)

Once again we are presented with a visual paradox: Hermione's statuesque pose shames Leontes in her not shaming him. The illusion of her artifice is maintained for several more lines, with Paulina crediting 'our carver's excellence' (5.3.30) for the statue's realism, and then once again the spectacle is turned back onto Leontes when he reveals, 'I am ashamed. Does not the stone rebuke me / For being more stone than it?' (5.3.37–8). In this moment, we see him caught: he has become part of the spectacle, equating himself with sculptor's stone and is on display as a heartless husband. The artistry of Hermione's gestic position is highlighted by the references to the cosmetics worn by the actor in the scene: she is described as 'but newly fixed; the colour's / Not dry' (5.3.46–7), and Paulina further warns Leontes:

> The ruddiness upon her lip is wet.
> You'll mar it if you kiss it, stain your own
> With oily painting. Shall I draw the curtain?
>
> (5.3.81–3)

Such a performance puts theatricality at the midpoint between nature and art. Leonard Barkan, recalling the play's allusion to the Pygmalion myth, reminds us that

> From antiquity onwards [the Pygmalion] transformation has been at once a triumph of nature, in the appearance of flexibility, liveliness, and love out of hard stone, and a triumph of art in that it has celebrated the genius of the sculptor in capturing an essence and equaling or even perfecting God's creation.[16]

Barkan's article seems to begin the trend of Shakespearean critics making the argument about how nature ultimately bests art. However, Karim-Cooper notes how nature and art are combined in the application of cosmetics. Writing about the role of cosmetics in the indoor theatres, she notes how

> the face was viewed as a map to the self; once painted, it could no longer be read, thus hypocrisy, vanity and corrupt sexuality (usually female) were all linked to the painted face – at once epitomized by the iconic notion of the painted harlot. But we know that women of all social ranks, especially nobility, used facial cosmetics, including, notoriously, Queen Elizabeth I.[17]

By drawing on notions about beauty and artificiality, the cultural moment of Shakespeare's later plays embodies wider concerns about illusion, persuasion, and the anti-theatrical movement, in addition to a nostalgia for the Elizabethan era which, while at the time was steeped in cultural insecurities, in retrospect appeared like a golden age of stability. Huston Diehl concurs that the statue scene's concern with artistry draws parallels with both Protestantism and anti-theatricality. She writes: 'Shakespeare exploits the actor's own aliveness, simultaneously creating the illusion that a statue is coming to life and calling attention to the fictitious nature of that illusion'.[18] Of course, there *is* artifice at play on the early modern stage. With Hermione being played by a boy actor or a young man, in female costume and cosmetics, we have the epitome of theatrical controversy by Puritanical standards. But in the moment of Leontes possibly marring his own lips 'with oily painting', perhaps we see a mirror held up to nature. Leontes, as the man who banished Hermione from his sight – and therefore, from life, in a theatrical sense, for in the theatre, being off-stage is a kind of death – did so over his fears of her inconstancy. Now, at the play's finale, the 'realness' of her fixity moves him to love. Perhaps then, there is a sense of Leontes as a Puritan-figure who, in finally realizing the magic of spectacle, sees the error of his ways. The final words of the play are his:

> Good Paulina,
> Lead us from hence, where we may leisurely
> Each one demand and answer to his part
> Performed in this wide gap of time since first
> We were dissevered. Hastily lead away. *Exeunt.*
>
> (5.3.151–5)

Paulina is selected to lead everyone away: out of the gallery, out of the play, out of the framing device of performance itself. The theatrical language repeats again: everyone must 'answer to his part / Performed in this wide gap of time', and there is a sense that Leontes finally begins to realize that he too is an actor playing a role, and he has an obligation to his audience and his fellow actors to play the part well.

Without Hermione's statuesque gestural performance, Leontes would not have learnt this lesson about the power of performance and the performance of power. As Jörg Hasler notes, Hermione's reunion with Leontes 'is allowed gestic expression only';[19] they do not speak to each other, but they do embrace voluntarily. This touch is what convinces him that she is alive: Evelyn Tribble reminds us that it is 'only when the touch passes between them in the final scene [...] that gesture in turn enliven[s] him'.[20] An embrace is a gesture that is violence's opposite, with bodies touching each other out of love, recognition, and acceptance. This final movement goes beyond gesture itself, becoming eloquent action.

The gestures in these final chapters have centred around the often-contradictory notions of passive aggression and female agency. But if they do, at times, seem paradoxical, it is only a wider reflection of the Jacobean political moment framing Shakespeare's late work. In an age where a male monarch is on the English throne for the first time since 1553, the curiosity in Jacobean drama towards the power wielded by women in a patriarchal society begins to come to the fore. The power of these gestures, unlike the more openly aggressive, sexualized ones of the 1590s, such as the thumb-bite and the fig, lies ultimately in their performance of measured calmness and restraint. It is this shift that shows the earlier, more vulgar gestures for what they are: ciphers of insecurity and empty bravado. The gestures of kneeling and statue-like posture are revealed to be the most effective shaming performance of all, because in the end, it is no performance: it is constancy itself, with nothing further to prove.

EPILOGUE

This book has progressed through Shakespeare's plays, and in doing so maps a journey from movement to stasis. It may be tempting to read this shift as Shakespeare turning to a more reflective and reconciliatory mood in his later works, abandoning the gung-ho action of his younger plays. However, the development of Shakespeare's work in this direction is likely to be less about the slippery process of biographical mapping onto an author's output – that as Shakespeare himself matures, his writing becomes more conciliatory – and more about his later work looking to stage new and different kinds of spectacle. With the emergent popularity of indoor playhouses, Shakespeare was now regularly writing for two very distinct theatrical spaces. The candle-lit intimacy of Blackfriars offered dramatists the opportunity to play with the staged exhibition of the actor's body and its effects. In a play like *The Winter's Tale*, the player taking on the role of Hermione would have worn stage cosmetics such as turpentine and white lead, dusted with powdered pearl; the same materials would have been used in the painting of portraiture. So when Leontes thinks he is looking at a piece of sculpture, there is actually an uncanny overlap between theatrical performance and static art, which makes the audience question what can be read onto the body itself. In a way, gesture has an overlapping relationship with art: both involve the creation of symbols, only in the case of gesture the body is both the artist and the medium.

This book's purpose has been to show how these bodily gestures are crucial for four reasons. First, they create tension in a dramatic scene in a way which words cannot, and this tension is exacerbated by the presence of an audience who contribute to the meaning-making process through their own interpretations of and associations with everyday bodily codes. Second, they reveal how such behavioural codes are often reliant on constructions of gender presentation in order to understand whether action is deemed inappropriate or not. Third, they present the importance of the context of social anxieties and codes in the Elizabethan and Jacobean periods in shaping the presentation of authority. Finally, they reveal a secret history behind everyday bodily action, reminding us of the norms which shape our behaviour and interactions.

This book has argued for the importance of gesture in Renaissance theatre, but of course, all the world's a stage. Over the process of writing this book, my method of reading the meanings behind gestures in early modern drama has begun to have all-too-relevant mirrorings in current events. The 'OK' hand gesture - joining the thumb and first finger together into a circle, with the remaining three fingers splayed above - has been appropriated by supporters of Donald Trump.[1] The gesture is sometimes performed by people while wearing red baseball caps emblazoned with the phrase 'Make America Great Again', but it has also been used by suited members of the Republican establishment. The gesture's meaning has been disputed, but its ambiguity and potential deniability is what has lent it social power. On the surface, the action is a simple symbol denoting that things are 'OK'. But when the gesture is performed by the left hand, the letters 'W' and 'P' – standing for 'White Power' – can be traced over the fingers. These kind of gestures are not merely an American phenomenon, nor are they only linked to white supremacists: French comedian Dieudonné M'Bala M'Bala's creation and repeated performance of the 'quenelle' gesture spread rapidly to his anti-establishment fans and supporters. The 'quenelle' features the arm and palm stretched downwards, with the top of the arm being touched by the opposite hand. Described by the *New York Times* as a 'downward-facing Nazi salute', it has been widely perceived as anti-Semitic, with the gesture being performed outside synagogues and Holocaust memorials.[2]

These gestures have become symbols of hate, but gestural movement has also been used as a show of resilience. American Football player Colin Kaepernick kneeled during the US national anthem as a silent protest against police brutality, and his action was copied by a number of other players in support of the Black Lives Matter movement.[3] This act of kneeling caused a national furore, with Kaepernick being accused of a lack of patriotism, and the NFL announcing that teams would be fined if their players continued to perform the action. Around the world, women have dressed in costumes described in Margaret Atwood's 1985 novel *The Handmaid's Tale* and have marched or stood with heads bowed in stoic acts of solidarity with women from Argentina to Ireland demanding abortion rights. These quiet acts of revolution have drawn the world's attention to the inequality of power structures: by performing submission, campaigners for change demonstrate how current social norms are actively complicit in the oppression of others.

These recent gestural trends are not down to Shakespeare or the performative legacy of his dramatic scenes. Rather, they reinstate the importance of gesture and its ability to embody social tensions, be it actions like the fig, the thumb-bite, or racist spitting performed in moments of conservative fear and latent insecurity or kneeling and stillness as a show of resilience in the face of such anxieties. In both Shakespeare's age and our own, these gestures reveal the performance of power for what it is – a symbolic fiction – and how we must regain control of the narrative before the story ends in darkness.

Shaming gestures occupy an intriguing space in the imagination: performed in the heat of the moment, they live on in the memory, perhaps being repeated over and over in the mind of the person shamed. There is no physical violence, possibly not even a fleeting moment of touch or bodily contact, yet the effect of that moment lives on. This lends to the gestures I have been examining – a kind of emotional violence that is at the very root of drama's capacity to provoke, question, and move. Not only that: they preserve 400-year-old tensions in a way that language alone does not. So, when we read Shakespeare's language, we must also read the bodies of his characters: those strange figures, spectral on the page, reanimated on the stage, whose physical actions may prove ephemeral in the instance of performance, but simultaneously retain vestiges of a different age while re-planting these plays in the gender politics of the present day.

NOTES

Introduction

1 Ewan Fernie, *Shame in Shakespeare* (London and New York: Routledge, 2002), 60.
2 Jennifer Jacquet, *Is Shame Necessary? New Uses for an Old Tool* (Great Britain: Allen Lane, 2015), 13.
3 Martin Henig, *Religion in Roman Britain* (London: B. T. Batsford Ltd, 1984), 186.
4 Jacques Lecoq, *Theatre of Gesture and Movement* (ed. David Bradby) (New York and London: Routledge, 2006), 20.
5 Michel de Certeau, *The Practice of Everyday Life* (trans. Steven F. Rendell) (Berkeley, Los Angeles, and London: University of California Press, 1988 [1984]), 42.
6 Lecoq, *Theatre of Gesture and Movement*, 27.
7 Alan Stewart, *Shakespeare's Letters* (Oxford: Oxford University Press, 2008), 75.
8 Andrew Gurr, *The Shakespearean Stage 1574–1642* (Cambridge: Cambridge University Press, 1995 [1992]), 97.
9 John H. Astington, *Actors and Acting in Shakespeare's Time: The Art of Stage Playing* (Cambridge: Cambridge University Press, 2011 [2010]), 47.
10 Thomas M. Conley, *Rhetoric in the European Tradition* (Chicago and London: University of Chicago Press, 1990), 138–139.
11 Thomas Wilson, *The Arte of Rhetorique* (London, 1553), Gg2v.
12 Wilson, *The Arte of Rhetorique*, Gg2v.
13 Phillip Stubbes, *The Anatomie of Abuses* (London, 1583), L8r.
14 Michel de Montaigne, 'An Apology for Raymond Sebond', in *Montaigne's Essays in Three Volumes: Volume Two* (trans. John Florio) (London and New York: Everyman's Library, 1965 [1910]), 144.

15 John Bulwer, *Chirologia, or, The Naturall Language of the Hand Composed of the Speaking Motions, and Discoursing Gestures Thereof: Whereunto Is Added Chironomia, or, The Art of Manuall Rhetoricke* (London, 1644), 8–9.

16 Keith Thomas, 'Introduction', in *A Cultural History of Gesture from Antiquity to the Present Day* (eds. Jan Bremmer and Herman Roodenburg) (Cambridge: Polity Press, 1993 [1991]), 1–14, 11.

17 Lecoq, *Theatre of Gesture and Movement*, 22.

18 Farah Karim-Cooper, *The Hand on the Shakespearean Stage: Gesture, Touch and the Spectacle of Dismemberment* (London: Arden, 2016), 3.

19 See Karim-Cooper and Darren Tunstall, *Shakespeare and Gesture in Practice* (London: Palgrave Macmillan, 2016).

20 Karen Newman, '"And Wash the Ethiop White": Femininity and the Monstrous in Othello', in *Shakespeare Reproduced: The Text in History and Ideology* (eds. Jean E. Howard and Marion F. O'Connor) (New York and London: Routledge, 1993 [1987]), 143–162, 157.

21 Thomas More, *Utopia*, in *Three Early Modern Utopias* (ed. Susan Bruce) (Oxford: Oxford University Press, 1999), 71.

22 Jacquet, *Is Shame Necessary?* 9–11.

23 Michel Foucault, *Discipline and Punish* (trans. Alan Sheridan) (London: Penguin, 1991 [1977; originally published as *Surveiller et punir*, 1975]), 58.

24 Foucault, *Discipline and Punish*, 94.

25 Fernie, *Shame in Shakespeare*, 9.

26 C. B. Watson, as quoted by Elizabeth A. Foyster, *Manhood in Early Modern England: Honour, Sex and Marriage* (London and New York: Longman, 1999), 6.

27 Foyster, *Manhood in Early Modern England*, 6.

28 Jean-Claude Schmitt, 'The Rationale of Gestures in the West: Third to Thirteenth Centuries', in *A Cultural History of Gesture from Antiquity to the Present Day* (eds. Jan Bremmer and Herman Roodenburg) (Cambridge: Polity Press, 1993 [1991]), 59–70, 62.

29 For instance, Caska's reporting of gestures at 1.2.220–2 emphasizes Caesar's denial of the crown as a 'necessary

theatrical scene', whereas Portia's gestural descriptions of Brutus (2.1.236–46) reveal his sincerity. See Miranda Fay Thomas, 'Political Acts and Political Acting: Roman Gesture in *Julius Caesar*', *Early Modern Literary Studies* (Special Issue: Rome and Home, 2016), 1–24.

30 David Bevington, *Action Is Eloquence: Shakespeare's Language of Gesture* (Cambridge, MA, and London: Harvard University Press, 1984), vii.

31 Quoted in Simon Palfrey and Tiffany Stern, *Shakespeare in Parts* (Oxford: Oxford University Press, 2007), 324.

32 Adam Kendon, *Gesture: Visible Action as Utterance* (Cambridge: Cambridge University Press, 2005 [2004]), 1.

33 Kendon, *Gesture*, 15.

34 Karim-Cooper, *The Hand on the Shakespearean Stage*, 7.

35 Stephen Greenblatt, *Renaissance Self-Fashioning: From More to Shakespeare* (Chicago and London: Chicago University Press, 2005 [1980]), 140–141.

36 Foyster, *Manhood in Early Modern England*, 2.

37 Foyster, *Manhood in Early Modern England*, 3.

38 Foyster, *Manhood in Early Modern England*, 4.

39 Foyster, *Manhood in Early Modern England*, 2.

40 Judith Butler, *Gender Trouble: Feminism and the Subversion of Identity* (New York and London: Routledge, 2006 [1990]), 186.

41 Will Fisher, *Materializing Gender in Early Modern English Literature and Culture* (Cambridge: Cambridge University Press, 2006), 6.

42 Fisher, *Materializing Gender in Early Modern English Literature and Culture*, 6.

43 Fisher, *Materializing Gender in Early Modern English Literature and Culture*, 2.

44 Karim-Cooper, *The Hand on the Shakespearean Stage*, 10.

45 Allison P. Hobgood, 'Feeling Fear in *Macbeth*', in *Shakespearean Sensations: Experiencing Literature in Early Modern England* (eds. Katharine A. Craik and Tanya Pollard) (Cambridge: Cambridge University Press, 2013), 29–46, 34.

Chapter 1

1. Robert Coe, 'Verona, Mississippi', *American Theatre*, 6:2 (May, 1989): 14–21, 52–57, 16.
2. William Shakespeare, *Romeo and Juliet* (ed. James N. Loehlin) (Cambridge: Cambridge University Press, 2002), 91.
3. Shakespeare, *Romeo and Juliet* (ed. Loehlin), 91.
4. Romana Lefevre, *Rude Hand Gestures of the World: A Guide to Offending without Words* (San Francisco: Chronicle Books, 2011), 110.
5. Desmond Morris, Peter Collett, Peter Marsh, and Marie O'Shaughnessy, *Gestures: Their Origins and Distribution* (London: Jonathan Cape, 1979), 148–155.
6. Fritz Graf, 'Gestures and Conventions: The Gestures of Roman Actors and Orators', in *A Cultural History of Gesture from Antiquity to the Present Day* (eds. Jan Bremmer and Herman Roodenburg) (Cambridge: Polity Press, 1993 [1991]), 36–58, 52.
7. William Shakespeare, *The First Quarto of Romeo and Juliet* (ed. Lukas Erne) (Cambridge: Cambridge University Press, 2007), 1.1.1–48.
8. William Shakespeare, *The Most Excellent and Lamentable Tragedie of Romeo and Juliet* (London: 1599), A3v.
9. Alexandra Shepard, *Meanings of Manhood in Early Modern England* (Oxford: Oxford University Press, 2006 [2003]), 140.
10. Thomas Dekker, *The Dead Tearme*, as quoted in *The Plays and Poems of William Shakespeare* (ed. Edmond Malone) (New Street, London: 1821), 10.
11. Shepard, *Meanings of Manhood in Early Modern England*, 146.
12. Shepard, *Meanings of Manhood in Early Modern England*, 141.
13. Shepard, *Meanings of Manhood in Early Modern England*, 150.
14. Charles Edelman, *Brawl Ridiculous: Swordfighting in Shakespeare's Plays* (Manchester and New York: Manchester University Press, 1992), 174–175.
15. William Shakespeare, *Romeo and Juliet* (ed. Jill L. Levenson) (Oxford: Oxford University Press, 2000), 35–36.

16 Lawrence Stone, *The Crisis of the Aristocracy, 1558–1641* (Oxford: Oxford University Press, 1965), 245.

17 Edelman, *Brawl Ridiculous*, 173.

18 Murray J. Levith, *Shakespeare's Italian Settings and Plays* (Hampshire and London: Macmillan, 1989), 57.

19 Edelman, *Brawl Ridiculous*, 173.

20 Shakespeare, *Romeo and Juliet* (ed. Levenson), 146.

21 John Walter, 'Gesturing at Authority: Deciphering the Gestural Code of Early Modern England', in *The Politics of Gesture: History Perspectives* (ed. M. Braddick), *Past and Present*: Supplement 4 (2009), 96–127, 126.

22 Kendon, *Gesture*, 9.

23 'thumb, n.'. Oxford English Dictionary Online (Oxford University Press).

24 'thumb, n.'. OED Online.

25 Morris et al., *Gestures*, 199.

26 Morris et al., *Gestures*, 199.

27 William Shakespeare, *The Variorum Shakespeare: Romeo and Juliet* (ed. H. H. Furness) (Philadelphia: Press of the J. B. Lippincott Company, 1899), 9.

28 William Shakespeare, *Romeo and Juliet* (ed. G. Blakemore Evans) (Cambridge: Cambridge University Press, 1984), 70.

29 William Shakespeare, *Romeo and Juliet* (ed. René Weis) (London: Arden, 2012), 127.

30 Isidore, as quoted by Anthony Corbeill, *Nature Embodied: Gesture in Ancient Rome* (Princeton and Oxford: Princeton University Press, 2004), 43.

31 Montaigne, 'Of Thumbs', *Montaigne's Essays in Three Volumes (II)* (trans. John Florio) (London and New York: Everyman's Library, 1965 [1910]), 416–417.

32 Plutarch, *The Lives of the Noble Grecians and Romanes Compared Together by that Graue Learned Philosopher and Historiographer, Plutarke of Chaeronea; Translated out of Greeke into French by Iames Amyot; and out of French into Englishe, by Thomas North* (London, 1579), 56.

33 John Bulwer, *Chirologia and Chironomia* (London, 1644), 183.

34 Bulwer, *Chirologia and Chironomia*, 162.

35 Bulwer, *Chirologia and Chironomia*, 176.

36 Bulwer, *Chirologia and Chironomia*, 161.

37 Bulwer, *Chirologia and Chironomia*, 161.

38 Peter Burke, *The Historical Anthropology of Early Modern Italy: Essays on Perception and Communication* (Cambridge: Cambridge University Press, 1987), 96.

39 Anonymous, *Dick of Devonshire* (eds. James G. and Mary R. McManaway) (Oxford: Malone Society, 1955), lines 1713–1714.

40 John Walter, 'Gesturing at Authority: Deciphering the Gestural Code of Early Modern England', in *The Politics of Gesture: History Perspectives* (ed. M. Braddick), *Past and Present*: Supplement 4 (2009), 96–127, 113.

41 George Croke, *The Reports of Sir George Croke, Knight* (London: Printed by J.S. and sold by the Stationers of London, 1657), 242.

42 Raymond Tallis, *The Hand: A Philosophical Inquiry into Human Being* (Edinburgh: Edinburgh University Press, 2003), 85.

43 Stephen Greenblatt, 'Mutilation and Meaning', in *The Body in Parts* (eds. David Hillman and Carla Mazzio (New York and London: Routledge, 1997), 221–241, 229.

44 Ralph Berry, *Shakespeare and Social Class* (Atlantic Highlands, New Jersey: Humanities Press International, Inc., 1988), 41.

45 Jean-Paul Sartre, *Critique of Dialectical Reason I. Theory of Practical Ensembles* (trans. Alan Sheridan-Smith, ed. Jonathan Rée) (London: NLB, 1976), 816.

46 Corbeill, *Nature Embodied*, 47.

47 Quintilian, *The Orator's Education in Five Volumes: Volume 5: Books 11–12* (ed. and trans. Donald A. Russell) (Cambridge, MA and London: Harvard University Press, 2001), 139.

48 Corbeill, *Nature Embodied*, 49.

49 Henk Driessen, 'Gestured Masculinity in Rural Andalusia', in *A Cultural History of Gesture from Antiquity to the Present*

Day (eds. Jan Bremmer and Herman Roodenburg) (Cambridge: Polity Press, 1993 [1991]), 237–252, 248.

50 Bulwer, *Chirologia and Chironomia*, 77.

51 Corbeill, *Nature Embodied*, 49–50.

52 Gregory S. Aldrete, *Gestures and Acclamations in Ancient Rome* (London: Johns Hopkins University Press, 2002), 90–91.

53 Corbeill, *Nature Embodied*, 66.

54 Levith, *Shakespeare's Italian Settings and Plays*, 58.

55 Arthur Laurents and Stephen Sondheim, *West Side Story* (New York: Bantam Doubleday Dell, 1965 [1956]), 137.

56 Laurents and Sondheim, *West Side Story*, 137–138.

57 Laurents and Sondheim, *West Side Story*, 138.

58 Judith Buchanan, *Shakespeare on Film* (Essex: Routledge, 2005), 231–232.

59 Peter Holding, *Romeo and Juliet: Text and Performance* (Hampshire and London: Palgrave Macmillan, 1992), 63.

60 Karim-Cooper, *The Hand on the Shakespearean Stage*, 178.

61 Karim-Cooper, *The Hand on the Shakespearean Stage*, 175.

Chapter 2

1 Bulwer, *Chirologia and Chironomia*, 183.

2 W. L. Hildburgh, 'Images of the Human Hand as Amulets in Spain', *Journal of the Warburg and Courtauld Institute*, 18:1/2 (January–June, 1955), 67–89, 68–69.

3 Andrew Gurr, *Playgoing in Shakespeare's London* (Cambridge: Cambridge University Press, 2005 [1987]), 19–21.

4 William Shakespeare, *The Chronicle History of Henry the Fift, with His Battell Fought at Agin Court in France. Togither with Auntient Pistoll* (London: 1600), A1v.

5 Nicholas Grene, *Shakespeare's Serial History Plays* (Cambridge: Cambridge University Press, 2002), 199.

6 Shakespeare, *The Chronicle History of Henry the Fift,* D1r.

7   William Shakespeare, *The Life of King Henry Fift*, in *Mr William Shakespeare's Comedies, Histories, & Tragedies* (London, 1623), 80.

8   Steven Mullaney, *The Place of the Stage: License, Play, and Power in Renaissance England* (Michigan: University of Michigan Press, 1995 [1988]), 131–132.

9   Eric J. Griffin, *English Renaissance Drama and the Specter of Spain: Ethnopoetics and Empire* (Philadelphia: University of Pennsylvania Press, 2009), 1.

10 Griffin, *English Renaissance Drama and the Specter of Spain*, 13.

11 Eric Griffin, 'Shakespeare, Marlowe, and the Stranger Crisis of the Early 1590s', in *Shakespeare and Immigration* (eds. Ruben Espinosa and David Rutter) (Surrey and Burlington: Ashgate, 2014), 13–36, 13.

12 Griffin, 'Shakespeare, Marlowe, and the Stranger Crisis of the Early 1590s', 13–14.

13 Edward Daunce, *A Brief Discourse of the Spanish State* (London, 1590), 35–36; as quoted by Griffin, 'Shakespeare, Marlowe, and the Stranger Crisis of the Early 1590s', 30.

14 In Lording Barry's play *Ram Alley*, the braggart Lieutenant Beard makes repeated references to figs, although Martin Wiggins notes that out of the four words of Italian and French spoken in the play, Beard speaks half of them. Of course, this statistic remains a very small amount of foreign language. In itself, these details give us little to go on, but perhaps Beard's use of fig references in addition to these other elements place him in a category of European Otherness. See Martin Wiggins (in association with Catherine Richardson), *British Drama 1533–1642: A Catalogue (Volume V: 1603–1608)* (Oxford: Oxford University Press, 2015), 458–459.

15 Geneva version (1599).

16 Kenneth Clark, *The Nude: A Study of Ideal Art* (London: John Murray, 1956), 301.

17 J. David Velleman, 'The Genesis of Shame', *Philosophy and Public Affairs*, 30:1 (Winter, 2001), 27–52, 31.

18 Dante, *The Divine Comedy* (trans. Peter Dale) (London: Anvil Press Poetry Ltd, 2004 [1996]), *Inferno*: Canto 25, lines 1–3.

19 Dante, *Inferno*: Canto 24, lines 137–139.

20 Benjamin Blech and Roy Doliner, *The Sistine Secrets: Michelangelo's Forbidden Messages in the Heart of the Vatican* (New York: HarperOne, 2008), 136.

21 Georgia Illetschko, Michelangelo Buonarroti, and Christopher Wynne, *I, Michelangelo* (Munich: Prestel, 2004), 45.

22 Tallis, *The Hand*, 158.

23 Benedict Anderson, *Imagined Communities: Reflections on the Origin and Spread of Nationalism* (London and New York: Verso, 1991 [1983]), 6.

24 Anderson, *Imagined Communities*, 7.

25 Robin Headlam Wells, *Shakespeare on Masculinity* (Cambridge: Cambridge University Press, 2000), 35.

26 Wells, *Shakespeare on Masculinity*, 36; see also Robert Devereux, 2nd Earl of Essex, *An Apologie of the Earl of Essex* (London, 1603).

27 Wells, *Shakespeare on Masculinity*, 35–36.

28 Claire McEachern, '*Henry V* and the Paradox of the Body Politic', *Shakespeare Quarterly*, 45:1 (Spring, 1994), 33–56, 35.

29 Katherine Eggert, 'Nostalgia and the Not Yet Late Queen: Refusing Female Rule in *Henry V*', *ELH*, 61:3 (Autumn, 1994), 523–550, 544.

30 E. A. M. Colman notes that 'Part 1 runs to 2993 lines, of which only about twenty-one are demonstrably indecent. Part 2, a longer piece by nearly 10 per cent (3229 lines), has some seventy-four instances of bawdy'. In E. A. M. Colman, *The Dramatic Use of Bawdy in Shakespeare* (London: Longman, 1974), 99.

31 Jean E. Howard and Phyllis Rackin, *Engendering a Nation: A Feminist Account of Shakespeare's English Histories* (London and New York: Routledge, 1997), 165.

32 Colman, *The Dramatic Use of Bawdy in Shakespeare*, 104.

33 Howard and Rackin, *Engendering a Nation*, 8.

34 Coppélia Kahn, *Man's Estate: Masculine Identity in Shakespeare* (Berkeley, Los Angeles, and London: University of California Press, 1981), 80–81.
35 The apotropaic nature of the thumb is also alluded to in *Macbeth*: 'By the pricking of my thumbs, / Something wicked this way comes' (4.1.44–45).
36 Hildburgh, 'Images of the Human Hand as Amulets in Spain', 68.
37 Jan Kott, *Shakespeare Our Contemporary* (trans. Boleslaw Taborski) (New York: W. W. Norton and Company Inc, 1974 [1964]), 108.

Chapter 3

1 Michèle H. Richman, 'Spitting Images in Montaigne and Bataille for a Heterological Counterhistory of Sovereignty', *Diacritics*, 35:3 (Autumn, 2005), 46–61, 47.
2 Shepard, *Meanings of Manhood*, 146.
3 Hilda Johnstone (ed.), *Churchwarden's Presentments (17th Century), Part 1: Archdeaconry of Chichester* (Lewes: Sussex Record Society, 1948), 49.
4 Janet Adelman, *Suffocating Mothers: Fantasies of Maternal Origin in Shakespeare's Plays, Hamlet to the Tempest* (New York: Routledge, 1992), 29.
5 Rachel Trubowitz, '"But Blood Whitened": Nursing Mothers and Others in Early Modern Britain', in *Maternal Measures: Figuring Caregiving in the Early Modern Period* (eds. Naomi J. Miller and Naomi Yavneh) (Aldershot and Burlington: Ashgate, 2000), 82–101.
6 Edward Topsell, *The Historie of Serpents* (London, 1608), 50.
7 Topsell, *The Historie of Serpents*, 21–22.
8 Denzell S. Smith, 'The Credibility of the Wooing of Anne in *Richard III*', *Papers on Language and Literature*, 7:2 (Spring, 1971), 199–202 (200).

9 Michael Torrey, '"The Plain Devil and Dissembling Looks": Ambivalent Physiognomy and Shakespeare's *Richard III*', *English Literary Renaissance*, 30:2 (Spring, 2000), 123–153, 144.

10 Katherine Schaap Williams, 'Enabling Richard: The Rhetoric of Disability in *Richard III*', *Disability Studies Quarterly*, 29:4 (2009), no page numbers.

11 Ian Frederick Moulton, '"A Monster Great Deformed": The Unruly Masculinity of *Richard III*', *Shakespeare Quarterly*, 47:3 (Autumn, 1996), 251–268, 262–263.

12 Fernie, *Shame in Shakespeare*, 96.

13 David T. Mitchell and Sharon L. Snyder, *Narrative Prosthesis: Disability and the Dependencies of Discourse* (Ann Arbor: University of Michigan Press, 2000), 101.

14 Torrey, 'The Plain Devil and Dissembling Looks', 141.

15 Torrey, 'The Plain Devil and Dissembling Looks', 147.

16 Derek Dunne, 'Blushing on Cue: The Forensics of the Blush in Early Modern Drama', *Shakespeare Bulletin*, 34:2 (Summer, 2016), 233–252.

17 Antony Sher, *Year of the King: An Actor's Diary and Sketchbook* (London: Nick Hern Books, 2012 [1985]), 236.

18 Scott Colley, *Richard's Himself Again: A Stage History of Richard III* (Westport, CT: Greenwood Press, 1992), 216.

19 Colley, *Richard's Himself Again*, 201.

20 Brett Greatley-Hirsch, 'The Taming of the Jew: Spit and the Civilizing Process in *The Merchant of Venice*', in *Staged Transgression in Shakespeare's England* (eds. Rory Loughnane and Edel Semple) (New York: Palgrave, 2013), 136–152, 136–137.

21 Antoine de Courtin, *Nouveau traite de civilité*, 273, as quoted by Norbert Elias, *The Civilizing Process* (trans. Edmund Jephcott) (MA, Oxford, Victoria: Blackwell Publishing, 2000 [1994]), 130.

22 Michel de Montaigne, 'Of Custom', in *Essays in Three Volumes: Volume One* (trans. John Florio) (London and New York: Everyman's Library, 1965 [1910]), 109.

23 Walter Darrell, *A Short Discourse of the Life of Seruingmen Plainly Expressing the Way That Is Best to Be Followed, and the Meanes Wherby They May Lawfully Challenge a Name and Title in That Vocation and Fellowship. With Certeine Letters Verie Necessarie for Seruingmen, and Other Persons to Peruse. With Diuerse Pretie Inuentions in English Verse. Hereunto Is Also Annexed a Treatise, Concerning Manners and Behauiours* (London, 1578), 120.

24 Mateo Alemán, *The Rogue: or The life of Guzman de Alfarache. Written in Spanish by Matheo Aleman, Seruant to His Catholike Maiestie, and Borne in Seuill* (London, 1623), 219.

25 Greatley-Hirsch, 'The Taming of the Jew', 140.

26 Erasmus, *The Ciuilitie of Childehode with the Discipline and Institucion of Children* (London, 1560), B1v.

27 Erasmus, *The Ciuilitie of Childehode*, B1v–B2r.

28 Erasmus, *The Ciuilitie of Childehode*, B1v.

29 Erasmus, *Lingua*, from *The Collected Works of Erasmus, Volume 29* (eds. Elaine Fantham and Erika Rummel with the assistance of Jozef Ijsewijn) (Toronto/Buffalo/London: University of Toronto Press, 1989), 250.

30 Erasmus, *Lingua*, 285.

31 Erasmus, *Lingua*, 268–269.

32 Marcel Griaule, 'CRACHAT-crachat-âme', *Dictionnaire, Documents* 1 (1929), 381–382.

33 Elias, *The Civilizing Process*, 134.

34 Elias, *The Civilizing Process*, 133.

35 Wayne A. Rebhorn, 'Baldesar Castiglione, Thomas Wilson, and the Courtly Body of Renaissance Rhetoric', *Rhetorica: A Journal of the History of Rhetoric*, 11:3 (Summer, 1993), 241–274, 242.

36 Mikhail Bakhtin, *Rabelais and His World* (trans. Helene Iswolsky) (Massachusetts and London: MIT Press, 1968 [1965, in Russian]), 319.

37 Bakhtin, *Rabelais and His World*, 317.

38 Bakhtin, *Rabelais and His World*, 318.

39 Carla Mazzio, 'Sins of the Tongue in Early Modern England', *Modern Language Studies*, 28:3/4 (Autumn, 1998), 93–124, 98.

40 Bakhtin, *Rabelais and His World*, 26.

41 Julia Kristeva, *Powers of Horror: An Essay on Abjection* (trans. Leon S. Roudiez) (New York: Columbia University Press, 1982), 2.

42 Peter Stallybrass, 'Patriarchal Territories: The Body Enclosed', in *Rewriting the Renaissance: The Discourses of Sexual Difference in Early Modern Europe* (eds. Margaret Fergusan, Maureen Quilligan, and Nancy J. Vickers) (Chicago: University of Chicago Press, 1986), 123–142, 123.

43 Stallybrass, 'Patriarchal Territories', 125.

44 Foucault, *Discipline and Punish*, 43.

45 Foucault, *Discipline and Punish*, 90.

46 Edward Hall, *The Union of the Two Noble and Illustre Families of Lancastre and Yorke* (London: 1548), L1r.

47 Peter Stallybrass and Allon White, *The Politics and Poetics of Transgression* (Ithaca, NY: Cornell University Press, 1986), 47.

48 Richard Overton, *A New Bull-bayting: or, A Match Play'd at the Tovvn-bull of Ely. By Twelve Mungrills. Viz. 4 English 4 Irish 4 Scotch Doggs. Iohn Lilburn, Richard Overton, Thomas Prince, and William Walwyn, to Stave and Nose. With His Last Will and Testament, and Several Legacies Bequeathed to the Iuncto, the Councel of State, and Army. Too Him My Dogge; Ha-loe There; Now Hee's Down: Bayted to Death, and Forfeit to the Crown* (London: 1649), 5.

49 Thomas Middleton and Thomas Dekker, *The Roaring Girl* (eds. Simon Barker and Hilary Hinds, in *The Routledge Anthology of Renaissance Drama*) (London: Routledge, 2003), 343.

50 Thomas Middleton, *The Roaring Girle, or Moll Cut-purse* (London: 1611), A3r.

51 Ellen Samuels, 'Critical Divides: Judith Butler's Body Theory and the Question of Disability', *NSWA Journal*, 14:3: Feminist Disability Studies (Autumn, 2002), 58–76, 65.

52 Moulton, 'A Monster Great Deformed', 265.

53 Moulton, 'A Monster Great Deformed', 255.

54 Lynda E. Boose, 'Scolding Brides and Bridling Scolds: Taming the Woman's Unruly Member', *Shakespeare Quarterly*, 42:2 (Summer, 1991), 179–213, 189.

55 Moulton, 'A Monster Great Deformed', 257.

56 As Mitchell and Snyder note, *Richard III* has 'a scapegoat patterning to the play reiterates exile as a culturally sanctioned historical solution to the social disruption that disabled people are perceived to present to an otherwise harmonious social order' (*Narrative Prosthesis*, 105).

Chapter 4

1 Maddy Costa, '"The Cast All Abused Me": The Pain of Playing Shylock.' *The Guardian*, 8 May 2011. http://www.guardian.co.uk/stage/2011/may/08/playing-shylock-patrick-stewart-sher.

2 Costa, 'The Cast All Abused Me'.

3 Costa, 'The Cast All Abused Me'.

4 See the entry in the *Oxford English Dictionary*, whereby 'apology' can be used as a vindication as opposed to an expression of contrition. 'apology, n.'. OED Online. Oxford University Press.

5 John Philpot, *An Apologie of Iohan Philpot Written for Spitting upon an Arrian, with an Inuectiue against the Arrians (the Very Natural Chyldren of Antichrist) with an Admonition to All That Be Faythfull in Christ, to Beware of Them, and of Other Late Sprong Heresies, as of the Most Enemies of the Gospell* (Emden: E. van der Erve, 1556[?]), C1r.

6 Philpot, *An Apologie of Iohan Philpot*, A2v.

7 Philpot, *An Apologie of Iohan Philpot*, A5r.

8 Philpot, *An Apologie of Iohan Philpot*, A6r.

9 Foucault, *Discipline and Punish*, 43.

10 John Hale, *The Civilization of Europe in the Renaissance* (London: HarperCollins, 1994 [1993]), 167.

11 Hale, *The Civilization of Europe in the Renaissance*, 168.

12 Hale, *The Civilization of Europe in the Renaissance*, 168.

13 Aaron Kitch, 'Shylock's Sacred Nation', *Shakespeare Quarterly*, 59:2 (Summer, 2008), 131–155, 145.

14 W. D. Howells, *Venetian Life* (Marlboro, VT: The Marlboro Press, 1989), 151–159, 153–154.

15 James Shapiro, *Shakespeare and the Jews* (New York: Columbia Press, 1996), 11.

16 Shapiro, *Shakespeare and the Jews*, 62.

17 Shapiro, *Shakespeare and the Jews*, 71.

18 Shapiro, *Shakespeare and the Jews*, 82.

19 Gillian Woods, '"Strange Discourse": The Controversial Subject of *Sir Thomas More*', *Renaissance Drama New Series*, 39 (2011), 3–35, 10.

20 Shapiro, *Shakespeare and the Jews*, 187.

21 Woods, 'Strange Discourse', 10.

22 Hale, *The Civilization of Europe in the Renaissance*, 168.

23 Greatley-Hirsch, 'The Taming of the Jew', 149.

24 Bruce Boehrer, 'Shylock and the Rise of the Household Pet: Thinking Social Exclusion in *The Merchant of Venice*', *Shakespeare Quarterly*, 50:2 (Summer, 1999), 152–170, 63.

25 Greatley-Hirsch, 'The Taming of the Jew', 148. However, in the case of Richard, all three apply: he is the loyal brother to George, who does not suspect his malice; he is treated abjectly due to his physical appearance; and he is predatory in his race for the crown.

26 Emma Smith, 'Was Shylock Jewish?' *Shakespeare Quarterly*, 64:2 (Summer, 2013), 188–219, 208.

27 Smith, 'Was Shylock Jewish?' 203.

28 William Shakespeare, *The Merchant of Venice* (ed. John Russell Brown) (Surrey: Metheun and Co., 1955), xi.

29 Jonathan Gil Harris, *Foreign Bodies and the Body Politic: Discourses of Social Pathology in Early Modern England* (Cambridge: Cambridge University Press, 1998), 79.

30 Harris, *Foreign Bodies and the Body Politic*, 79.

31 Harris, *Foreign Bodies and the Body Politic*, 105.

32 Shapiro, *Shakespeare and the Jews*, 51.

33 Thomas Calvert, *The Blessed Jew of Marocco; or, A Blackamoor Made White*, as quoted by David S. Katz, 'Shylock's Gender:

Jewish Male Menstruation in Early Modern England', *The Review of English Studies New Series*, 50:200 (November, 1999), 440–462, 441.

34 Harris, *Foreign Bodies and the Body Politic*, 79.

35 Katz, 'Shylock's Gender', 443.

36 Katz, 'Shylock's Gender', 459.

37 Trubowitz, 'But Blood Whitened', 90.

38 Gail Kern Paster, *The Body Embarrassed: Drama and the Disciplines of Shame in Early Modern England* (New York: Cornell University Press, 1993), 25.

39 Boose, 'Scolding Brides and Bridling Scolds', 193.

40 Trubowitz, 'But Blood Whitened', 91.

41 Robert Cleaver, *A Briefe Explanation of the Whole Booke of the Proverbs of Salomon*, as quoted by Trubowitz, 96.

42 Katz, 'Shylock's Gender', 451.

43 William Shakespeare, *The Merchant of Venice* (ed. Charles Edelman) (Cambridge: Cambridge University Press, 2002), 238.

44 Thomas Adams, *The Happines of the Church, or, A Description of Those Spirituall Prerogatiues Wherewith Christ Hath Endowed Her Considered in Some Contemplations upon Part of the 12. Chapter of the Hebrewes: Together with Certain Other Meditations and Discourses upon Other Portions of Holy Scriptures, the Titles Wherof Immediately Precede the Booke: Being the Summe of Diuerse Sermons Preached in S. Gregories* (London, 1619), 85.

45 Bruce R. Smith, *Phenomenal Shakespeare* (Malden and Oxford: Wiley-Blackwell, 2010), 168.

46 Adams, *The Happines of the Church*, 183.

Chapter 5

1 *The Resolution of the Women of London to the Parliament* (London: 1642), A2r.

2 *The Resolution of the Women of London to the Parliament*, A2r.

3   Smith, *Shakespeare and Masculinity* (Oxford: Oxford University Press, 2000), 131. Smith refers to the work of David Gilmore, especially *Manhood in the Making: Cultural Conceptions of Masculinity* (New Haven: Yale University Press, 1990).
4   Gilmore, *Manhood in the Making*, 17.
5   Smith, *Shakespeare and Masculinity*, 3.
6   Fernie, *Shame in Shakespeare*, 137.
7   Paul Menzer, 'The Actor's Inhibition: Early Modern Acting and the Rhetoric of Restraint', *Renaissance Drama New Series*, 35: Embodiment and Environment in Early Modern Drama and Performance (2006), 83–111, 90.
8   John Lidgate, *The Life and Death of Hector* (London, 1614), 41, 70.
9   *Julius Caesar* is a particularly rich case in point. When Caesar refuses the crown in a gestural dumbshow before the Roman people, he does so in an attempt to prove that he is not ambitious, despite his other pretensions to a more absolutist state of sovereignty. See Thomas, 'Political Acts and Political Acting', 1–24.
10 Thomas, 'Political Acts and Political Acting', 3.
11 Stuart Clark, *Vanities of the Eye: Vision in Early Modern European Culture* (Oxford: Oxford University Press, 2007), 329.
12 Clark, *Vanities of the Eye*, 2.
13 William Shakespeare, *Much Ado about Nothing* (ed. Claire McEachern) (London: Arden Bloomsbury, 2014 [2007]), 43.
14 McEachern, *Much Ado about Nothing*, 48.
15 Bulwer, *Chirologia and Chironomia*, 182.
16 Bulwer, *Chirologia and Chironomia*, 183.
17 Richard Tarlton, *Tarltons Jests Drawne into These Three Parts* (London, 1638), B2v.
18 Anthony Copley, *Wits Fittes and Fancies, Fronted and Entermedled with Presidentes of Honour and Wisdome. Also: Loves Owl, an Idle Conceited Dialogue between Love, and an Olde Man* (London, 1595), 94.
19 W. Carew Hazlitt, *A Dictionary of Faiths and Folklore* (Volume 1) (London: Reeves and Turner, 1905), 160.

20 Hazlitt, *A Dictionary of Faiths and Folklore*, 327.

21 Hazlitt, *A Dictionary of Faiths and Folklore*, 328.

22 Hazlitt, *A Dictionary of Faiths and Folklore*, 328.

23 Hazlitt, *A Dictionary of Faiths and Folklore*, 328.

24 Kott, *Shakespeare Our Contemporary*, 123.

25 Alvin Kernan, *Shakespeare, the King's Playwright: Theater in the Stuart Court, 1603–1613* (New Haven and London: Yale University Press, 1995), 74.

26 Fernie, *Shame in Shakespeare*, 138.

27 Richard Jobson, *The Golden Trade* (ed. Walter Rodney) (London: Dawsons, 1968 [1623]), 65–67.

28 Newman, 'And Wash the Ethiop White', 152.

29 Edward Washington, '"At the Door of Truth": The Hollowness of Signs in *Othello*', in *Othello: New Essays by Black Writers* (ed. Mythili Kaul) (Washington, DC: Howard University Press, 1996), 167–187, 178.

30 McEachern, *Much Ado about Nothing*, 46.

31 We see a similar connection in *The Winter's Tale*; although, of course, what Leontes thinks he sees is not actually the truth. When Leontes believes that his wife has committed adultery with Camillo, he tells him:

Ha' you not seen, Camillo –

But that's past doubt; you have, or your eye-glass

Is thicker than a cuckold's horn[.] (1.2.265-7)

32 Douglas Bruster, 'The Horn of Plenty: Cuckoldry and Capital in the Drama of the Age of Shakespeare', *Studies in English Literature, 1500–1900*, 30:2: Elizabethan and Jacobean Drama (Spring, 1990), 195–215, 211.

33 Fernie, *Shame in Shakespeare*, 156.

34 Barbara Everett, '"Spanish" Othello: The Making of Shakespeare's Moor', in *Shakespeare and Race* (eds. Catherine M. S. Alexander and Stanley Wells) (Cambridge: Cambridge University Press, 2000), 64–81, 68.

35 Everett, '"Spanish" Othello', 66–67. Additionally, a pun in the final act of *Cymbeline* serves to reinforce the received idea that

an ancient or ensign might be an untrustworthy figure. When describing the noble deeds of Belarius, Posthumus speaks of him as 'an ancient soldier, / (An honest one, I warrant)' (5.3.15–16). Posthumus refers to Belarius' age, but because of the pun of 'ancient' with the military status of the ensign, his honesty needs to be confirmed before the accidental pun casts doubt upon his credentials.

36 Everett, '"Spanish" Othello', 76.

37 Juliet Dusinberre, *Shakespeare and the Nature of Women* (Hampshire and London: Macmillan Press Ltd, 1996 [1975]), 302.

38 Jyotsna Singh, 'The Interventions of History: Narratives of Sexuality', in *The Weyward Sisters: Shakespeare and Feminist Politics* (eds. Dympna Callaghan, Lorraine Helms, and Jyotsna Singh) (Oxford, UK and Cambridge, USA: Blackwell, 1994), 7–58, 46.

39 Singh, 'The Interventions of History', 46.

40 Hale, *The Civilization of Europe in the Renaissance*, 505.

41 Hale, *The Civilization of Europe in the Renaissance*, 505.

42 Singh, 'The Interventions of History', 49.

43 Singh, 'The Interventions of History', 47.

44 Madelon Gohlke, '"I Wooed Thee with My Sword": Shakespeare's Tragic Paradigms', in *The Woman's Part: Feminist Criticism of Shakespeare* (eds. Carolyn Ruth Swift Lenz, Gayle Greene, and Carol Thomas Neely) (Urbana, Chicago, and London: University of Illinois Press, 1980), 150–170, 156.

45 Margaret Atwood, *Second Words: Selected Critical Prose* (Toronto: Anansi, 2000), 413.

Chapter 6

1 Hobgood, 'Feeling Fear in *Macbeth*', 30.

2 Hobgood, 'Feeling Fear in *Macbeth*', 31.

3 Clark, *Vanities of the Eye*, 255.

4 Arthur F. Kinney, *Lies Like Truth: Shakespeare, Macbeth, and the Cultural Moment* (Detroit: Wayne State University Press, 2001), 68–69.

5 Kinney, *Lies Like Truth*, 74–75.

6 Mullaney, *The Place of the Stage*, 113.

7 Mullaney, *The Place of the Stage*, 114.

8 King James VI and I, *The Basilicon Doron of James VI* (ed. James Craigie) (Edinburgh and London: Blackwood and Sons, 1944), 162.

9 Kinney, *Lies Like Truth*, 151.

10 Kernan, *Shakespeare, The King's Playwright*, 75–76.

11 King James VI and I, as quoted by Joanna Levin, 'Lady Macbeth and the Daemonologie of Hysteria', *ELH*, 69:1 (Spring, 2002), 21–55 (p. 44).

12 Jonathan Goldberg, 'Speculations: *Macbeth* and Source', in *Shakespeare Reproduced: The Text in History and Ideology* (eds. Jean E. Howard and Marion F. O'Connor) (New York and London: Routledge, 1993 [1987]), 242–264, 258.

13 Dympna Callaghan, 'Wicked Women in *Macbeth*: A Study of Power, Ideology, and the Production of Motherhood', in *Reconsidering the Renaissance* (ed. Mario A. Di Cesare) (Binghamton, NY: Center for Medieval and Early Renaissance Studies, 1992), 355–369, 363.

14 Kott, *Shakespeare Our Contemporary*, 89.

15 Janet Adelman, 'Fantasies of Maternal Power in *Macbeth*', in *Cannibals, Witches, and Divorce: Estranging the Renaissance* (ed. Marjorie Garber) (Baltimore and London: Johns Hopkins University Press, 1987), 90–121, 90, 101.

16 Kernan, *Shakespeare, The King's Playwright*, 81.

17 Kathryn L. Lynch, '"What Hands Are Here?" The Hand as Generative Symbol in Macbeth', *The Review of English Studies*, 39:153 (February, 1988), 29–38, 37.

18 Joan Larsen Klein, 'Lady Macbeth: "Infirm of Purpose"', in *The Woman's Part: Feminist Criticism of Shakespeare* (eds. Carolyn Ruth Swift Lenz, Gayle Greene, and Carol Thomas Neely) (Urbana, Chicago, and London: University of Illinois Press, 1980), 240–255, 250.

19 Bulwer, *Chirologia and Chironomia*, 40.

20 James Hall, *Dictionary of Subjects and Symbols in Art* (London: John Murray Ltd, 1974), 308.

21 Hall, *Dictionary of Subjects and Symbols in Art*, 308.

22 Hall, *Dictionary of Subjects and Symbols in Art*, 144, 161.

23 *Gesta Romanorum* (trans. Herman Oesterley) (Berlin, 1872), 291; as cited in Beatrice Daw Brown, 'Exemplum Materials Underlying *Macbeth*', *PMLA* 50:3 (September, 1935), 700–714, 403.

24 Kinney, *Lies Like Truth*, 28.

25 Michel de Montaigne, 'Of Conscience', in *Essays in Three Volumes: Volume Two* (trans. John Florio) (London and New York: Everyman's Library, 1965 [1910]), 46.

26 Montaigne, 'Of Conscience', in *Essays* (2), 46.

27 Gamini Salgado (ed.), *Eyewitnesses of Shakespeare: First-hand Accounts of Performances 1590–1890* (London: Chatto and Windus, 1975), 31.

28 John Matusiak, *James I: Scotland's King of England* (Gloucestershire: The History Press, 2015), 193–194.

29 Kinney, *Lies Like Truth*, 190.

30 Callaghan, 'Wicked Women in *Macbeth*', 359.

31 Kinney, *Lies Like Truth,* 144.

32 Edmund Spenser, *The Faerie Queene* (ed. A. C. Hamilton) (Harlow: Pearson, 2007 [2001]), book II, canto ii, stanza iii, lines 5–9.

33 Spenser, *The Faerie Queene,* book II, canto ii, stanza iv, line 9.

34 Michael Neill, '"Amphitheatres in the Body": Playing with Hands on the Shakespearean Stage', *Shakespeare Survey*, 48: Shakespeare and Cultural Exchange (March, 2007), 23–50, 46.

35 Evelyn B. Tribble, 'The Partial Sign: Spenser and the Sixteenth-century Crisis of Semiotics', in *Ceremony and Text in the Renaissance* (ed. Douglas F. Rutledge) (Newark: University of Delaware Press, 1996), 23–34, 30.

36 Tribble, 'The Partial Sign', 32.

37 Lorraine Helms, 'Acts of Resistance: The Feminist Player', in *The Weyward Sisters: Shakespeare and Feminist Politics*

(eds. Dympna Callaghan, Lorraine Helms, and Jyotsna Singh) (Oxford, UK and Cambridge, USA: Blackwell, 1994), 102–156, 138.

38 Clark, *Vanities of the Eye*, 237, 255.

39 Clark does discuss the dagger as an apparition (236; 239), the sighting of the witches (247–249), and the ghostly spectacle of royal lineage in 4.1 (250–251).

40 Joan Larsen Klein, 'Lady Macbeth: "Infirm of Purpose"', 249.

41 André Du Larens, *A Discourse on the Preseruation of the Sight* (London, 1599), 95, as quoted by Kinney, *Lies Like Truth*, 185.

42 Kernan, *Shakespeare, The King's Playwright*, 88.

43 Kernan, *Shakespeare, The King's Playwright*, 88.

Chapter 7

1 June Schlueter and Richard Levin have debated the veracity of this claim; I remain persuaded by Levin's argument. Schlueter is of the opinion that the drawing does not represent *Titus Andronicus* at all, but in fact shows an early modern German play entitled *Eine sehr klägliche Tragaedia von Tito Andronico und der hoffertigen Käyserin* (A Very Lamentable Tragedy of Titus Andronicus and the Haughty Empress). Levin maintains that the drawing is of Shakespeare's *Titus Andronicus* and is 'an artist's reading' of the first scene (332). See Schlueter, 'Rereading the Peacham Drawing', *Shakespeare Quarterly*, 50:2 (Summer, 1999), 171–184, and Levin, 'The Longleat Manuscript and *Titus Andronicus*', *Shakespeare Quarterly*, 53:3 (Autumn, 2002), 323–340.

2 Frances E. Dolan (ed.), *The Taming of the Shrew: Bedford Texts and Contexts* (Boston: Bedford Books of St. Martin's Press, 1996), 35.

3 See Karim-Cooper, *The Hand on the Shakespearean Stage*, 1.

4 I have previously written about a similar moment in *The Two Noble Kinsmen*. See Miranda Fay Thomas, '"Tremble at Patience": Constant Queens and Female Solidarity in *The Two Noble Kinsmen* and *The Winter's Tale*', in *The Palgrave*

Handbook of Shakespeare's Queens (eds. Kavita Mudan Finn and Valerie Schutte) (Basingstoke: Palgrave Macmillan, 2018), 87–103, especially 97–100.

5 Marjorie Garber, 'Out of Joint', in *The Body in Parts: Fantasies of Corporeality in Early Modern Europe* (eds. David Hillman and Carla Mazzio) (New York and London: Routledge, 1997), 23–52, 26.

6 T. McAlindon, *Shakespeare and Decorum* (London and Basingstoke: Macmillan, 1973), 11.

7 Baldesar Castiglione, *The Book of the Courtier* (trans. George Bull) (London: Penguin Books, 2003 [1967]), 211.

8 Russell West-Pavlov, *Bodies and Their Spaces: System, Crisis and Transformation in Early Modern Theatre* (Amsterdam, New York: Rodolphi, 2006), 133.

9 Russell West-Pavlov, *Bodies and Their Spaces*, 128.

10 Russell West-Pavlov, *Bodies and Their Spaces*, 142.

11 H. Diane Russell (with Bernadine Barnes), *Eva/Ave: Woman in Renaissance and Baroque Prints* (New York: National Gallery of Art, Washington, and the Feminist Press at the City University of New York, 1990), 53.

12 Russell (with Barnes), *Eva/Ave*, 53.

13 Russell (with Barnes), *Eva/Ave*, 75.

14 Russell (with Barnes), *Eva/Ave*, 29.

15 Russell (with Barnes), *Eva/Ave*, 29.

16 Antonella Piazza, 'Volumnia, the Roman Patroness', in *Questioning Bodies in Shakespeare's Rome* (eds. Maria Del Sapio Garbero, Nancy Isenberg, and Maddalena Pennacchia) (Goettingen: V & R unipress, 2010), 121–134, 132.

17 Manfred Pfister, 'Acting the Roman: Coriolanus', in *Identity, Otherness and Empire in Shakespeare's Rome* (ed. Maria Del Sapio Garbero) (Surrey: Ashgate, 2009), 35–47, 44.

18 Piazza, 'Volumnia, the Roman Patroness', 129.

19 Chikako D. Kumamoto, 'Shakespeare's Achillean Coriolanus and Heraean Volumnia: Textual Contamination and Crossing of Homer's *Iliad* in *Coriolanus*', *Journal of the Wooden O Symposium*, 7 (2007), 51–63, 60–61.

20 Pfister, 'Acting the Roman: Coriolanus', 37.

21 Piazza, 'Volumnia, the Roman Patroness', 134.

22 Lisa S. Starks-Estes, 'Virtus, Vulnerability, and the Emblazoned Male Body in Shakespeare's *Coriolanus*', in *Violent Masculinities: Male Aggression in Early Modern Texts and Culture* (eds. Jennifer Feather and Catherine E. Thomas) (Hampshire: Palgrave Macmillan, 2013), 85–108, 96.

23 Jennifer A. Low, '"Bodied Forth": Spectator, Stage and Actor in the Early Modern Theatre', *Comparative Drama*, 39:1 (Spring, 2005), 1–29, 18.

24 Low, 'Bodied Forth', 19.

25 Pfister, 'Acting the Roman: Coriolanus', 36.

26 Felix C. H. Sprang, 'Never Fortune Did Play a Subtler Game: The Creation of "Medieval" Narratives in *Pericles* and *The Two Noble Kinsmen*', *European Journal of English Studies*, 15:2 (July, 2011), 115–128, 124.

27 Gurr, *Playgoing in Shakespeare's London*, 19–20.

28 Martin White, 'Light and Darkness in the Indoor Jacobean Theatre', in *Moving Shakespeare Indoors: Performance and Repertoire in the Jacobean Playhouse* (eds. Andrew Gurr and Farah Karim-Cooper) (Cambridge: Cambridge University Press, 2014), 115–136, 118, 127.

29 Pfister, 'Acting the Roman: Coriolanus', 43.

30 Pfister, 'Acting the Roman: Coriolanus', 42.

31 Starks-Estes, 'Virtus, Vulnerability, and the Emblazoned Male Body in Shakespeare's *Coriolanus*', 96.

32 Markku Peltonen, 'Political Rhetoric and Citizenship in *Coriolanus*', in *Shakespeare and Early Modern Political Thought* (eds. David Armitage, Conal Condren, and Andrew Fitzmaurice) (Cambridge: Cambridge University Press, 2009), 234–252, 244.

Chapter 8

1 Huston Diehl, '"Does Not the Stone Rebuke Me?" The Pauline Rebuke and Paulina's Lawful Magic', in *The Winter's Tale*,

Shakespeare and the Cultures of Performance (eds. Paul Yachnin and Patricia Badir) (Hampshire: Ashgate, 2008), 69–82, 81.

2 Menzer, 'The Actor's Inhibition', 84–85.

3 Graham Holderness, '*The Winter's Tale*: Country into Court', in *Shakespeare: Out of Court* (eds. Graham Holderness, Nick Potter, and John Turner) (Hampshire: Macmillan, 1990), 195–235, 233.

4 Cristina León Alfar, '"Proceed in Justice": Narratives of Marital Betrayal in *The Winter's Tale*', in *Justice, Women, and Power in English Renaissance Drama* (eds. Andrew Majeske and Emily Detmer-Goebel) (Madison, Teaneck: Fairleigh Dickinson University Press, 2009), 46–65.

5 Maria Del Sapio Garbero, 'A Spider in the Eye/I: The Hallucinatory Staging of the Self in Shakespeare's *The Winter's Tale*', in *Solo Performances: Staging the Early Modern Self in England* (ed. Ute Berns) (Amsterdam and New York: Rodolphi, 2010), 133–155, 133.

6 Del Sapio Garbero, 'A Spider in the Eye/I', 150.

7 Thomas, 'Tremble at Patience', 92–97.

8 Fernie, *Shame in Shakespeare*, 9.

9 For more on this, see Penelope Woods, 'The Audience of the Indoor Theatre', in *Moving Shakespeare Indoors: Performance and Repertoire in the Jacobean Playhouse* (eds. Andrew Gurr and Farah Karim-Cooper) (Cambridge: Cambridge University Press, 2014), 152–167, 154.

10 Farah Karim-Cooper, 'To Glisten in a Playhouse: Cosmetic Beauty Indoors', in *Moving Shakespeare Indoors: Performance and Repertoire in the Jacobean Playhouse* (eds. Andrew Gurr and Farah Karim-Cooper) (Cambridge: Cambridge University Press, 2014), 184–200, 200.

11 Clare McManus, *Women on the Renaissance Stage: Anna of Denmark and Female Masquing in the Stuart Court 1590–1619* (Manchester and New York: Manchester University Press, 2002), 150–151.

12 McManus, *Women on the Renaissance Stage*, 150.

13 C. B. Hardman, '*The Winter's Tale* and the Stuart Golden Age', *Review of English Studies New Series*, 45:178 (May, 1994), 221–229, 221.

14 Robin Headlam Wells, *Shakespeare, Politics and the State* (Hampshire: Macmillan, 1986), 19.

15 Gillian Woods, *Shakespeare's Unreformed Fictions* (Oxford: Oxford University Press, 2013), 179.

16 Leonard Barkan, '"Living Sculptures": Ovid, Michelangelo, and *The Winter's Tale*', *ELH*, 48:4 (Winter, 1981), 639–667, 664.

17 Karim-Cooper, 'To Glisten in a Playhouse', 190.

18 Huston Diehl, '"Strike All that Look upon with Marvel": Theatrical and Theological Wonder in *The Winter's Tale*', in *Rematerializing Shakespeare: Authority and Representation on the Early Modern English Stage* (eds. Bryan Reynolds and William N. West) (Hampshire: Palgrave Macmillan, 2005), 19–34, 27.

19 Jörg Hasler, 'Romance in the Theater: The Stagecraft of the "Statue Scene" in *The Winter's Tale*', in *Shakespeare: Man of the Theater* (eds. Kenneth Muir, Jay L. Halio, and D. J. Palmer) (Newark: University of Delaware Press, 1983), 203–211, 208.

20 Evelyn Tribble, '"O, She's Warm": Touch in *The Winter's Tale*', in *Knowing Shakespeare: Senses, Embodiment and Cognition* (eds. Lowell Gallagher and Shankar Raman) (Hampshire: Palgrave Macmillan, 2010), 65–81, 79.

Epilogue

1 Emily Pothast, 'Does the OK Sign Actually Signify "White Power," or What?' *Medium*, 5 September 2018. https://medium.com/s/story/does-the-ok-sign-actually-signify-white-power-or-what-6cf3309df985.

2 Scott Sayare, 'Concern over an Increasingly Seen Gesture Grows in France', *New York Times*, 2 January 2014. https://www.nytimes.com/2014/01/03/world/europe/concern-over-quenelle-gesture-grows-in-france.html.

3 Clark Mindock, 'Taking a Knee: Why Are NFL Players Protesting and When Did They Start to Kneel?' *Independent*, 4 September 2018. https://www.independent.co.uk/news/world/americas/us-politics/taking-a-knee-national-anthem-nfl-trump-why-meaning-origins-racism-us-colin-kaepernick-a8521741.html.

BIBLIOGRAPHY

Adams, Thomas, *The Happines of the Church, or, A Description of Those Spirituall Prerogatiues Wherewith Christ Hath Endowed Her Considered in Some Contemplations upon Part of the 12. Chapter of the Hebrewes: Together with Certain Other Meditations and Discourses upon Other Portions of Holy Scriptures, the Titles Wherof Immediately Precede the Booke: Being the Summe of Diuerse Sermons Preached in S. Gregories* (London, 1619).

Adelman, Janet, 'Fantasies of Maternal Power in *Macbeth*', in *Cannibals, Witches, and Divorce: Estranging the Renaissance* (ed. Marjorie Garber) (Baltimore and London: Johns Hopkins University Press, 1987), 90–121.

Adelman, Janet, *Suffocating Mothers: Fantasies of Maternal Origin in Shakespeare's Plays, Hamlet to the Tempest* (New York: Routledge, 1992).

Aldrete, Gregory S., *Gestures and Acclamations in Ancient Rome* (London: Johns Hopkins University Press, 2002).

Alemán, Mateo, *The Rogue: or The Life of Guzman de Alfarache. Written in Spanish by Matheo Aleman, Seruant to His Catholike Maiestie, and Borne in Seuill* (London, 1623).

Alfar, Cristina León, '"Proceed in Justice": Narratives of Marital Betrayal in *The Winter's Tale*', in *Justice, Women, and Power in English Renaissance Drama* (eds. Andrew Majeske and Emily Detmer-Goebel) (Madison, Teaneck: Fairleigh Dickinson University Press, 2009), 46–65.

Alighieri, Dante, *The Divine Comedy* (trans. Peter Dale) (London: Anvil Press Poetry Ltd., 2004 [1996]).

Anderson, Benedict, *Imagined Communities: Reflections on the Origin and Spread of Nationalism* (London and New York: Verso, 1991 [1983]).

Anonymous, *Dick of Devonshire* (eds. James G. and Mary R. McManaway) (Oxford: Malone Society, 1955).

Astington, John H., *Actors and Acting in Shakespeare's Time: The Art of Stage Playing* (Cambridge: Cambridge University Press, 2011 [2010]).

Atwood, Margaret, *Second Words: Selected Critical Prose* (Toronto: Anansi, 2000).

Bakhtin, Mikhail, *Rabelais and His World* (trans. Helene Iswolsky) (Massachusetts and London: MIT Press, 1968 [1965, in Russian]).

Barkan, Leonard, '"Living Sculptures": Ovid, Michelangelo, and *The Winter's Tale*', *ELH*, 48:4 (Winter, 1981), 639–667.

Berry, Ralph, *Shakespeare and Social Class* (Atlantic Highlands, NJ: Humanities Press International, Inc., 1988).

Bevington, David, *Action Is Eloquence: Shakespeare's Language of Gesture* (Cambridge, MA, and London: Harvard University Press, 1984).

Blec, Benjamin, and Roy Doliner, *The Sistine Secrets: Michelangelo's Forbidden Messages in the Heart of the Vatican* (New York: HarperOne, 2008).

Boehrer, Bruce, 'Shylock and the Rise of the Household Pet: Thinking Social Exclusion in *The Merchant of Venice*', *Shakespeare Quarterly*, 50:2 (Summer, 1999), 152–170.

Boose, Lynda E., 'Scolding Brides and Bridling Scolds: Taming the Woman's Unruly Member', *Shakespeare Quarterly*, 42:2 (Summer, 1991), 179–213.

Brown, Beatrice Daw, 'Exemplum Materials Underlying *Macbeth*', *PMLA*, 50:3 (September, 1935), 700–714.

Bruster, Douglas, 'The Horn of Plenty: Cuckoldry and Capital in the Drama of the Age of Shakespeare', *Studies in English* Literature, *1500–1900*, 30:2: Elizabethan and Jacobean Drama (Spring, 1990), 195–215.

Buchanan, Judith, *Shakespeare on Film* (Essex: Routledge, 2005).

Bulwer, John, *Chirologia, or, The Natural Language of the Hand Composed of the Speaking Motions, and Discoursing Gestures Thereof: Whereunto Is Added Chironomia, or, The Art of Manuall Rhetoricke* (London, 1644).

Burke, Peter, *The Historical Anthropology of Early Modern Italy: Essays on Perception and Communication* (Cambridge: Cambridge University Press, 1987).

Butler, Judith, *Gender Trouble: Feminism and the Subversion of Identity* (New York and London: Routledge, 2006 [1990]).

Callaghan, Dympna, 'Wicked Women in *Macbeth*: A Study of Power, Ideology, and the Production of Motherhood', in *Reconsidering the Renaissance* (ed. Mario A. Di Cesare) (Binghamton, New

York: Center for Medieval and Early Renaissance Studies, 1992), 355–369.

Castiglione, Baldesar, *The Book of the Courtier* (trans. George Bull) (London: Penguin Books, 2003 [1967]).

de Certeau, Michel, *The Practice of Everyday Life* (trans. Steven F. Rendell) (Berkeley, Los Angeles, and London: University of California Press, 1988 [1984]).

Clark, Kenneth, *The Nude: A Study of Ideal Art* (London: John Murray, 1956).

Clark, Stuart, *Vanities of the Eye: Vision in Early Modern European Culture* (Oxford: Oxford University Press, 2007).

Coe, Robert, 'Verona, Mississippi', *American Theatre*, 6:2 (May, 1989), 14–21, 52–57.

Colley, Scott, *Richard's Himself Again: A Stage History of Richard III* (Westport, CT: Greenwood Press, 1992).

Colman, E. A. M., *The Dramatic Use of Bawdy in Shakespeare* (London: Longman, 1974).

Conley, Thomas M., *Rhetoric in the European Tradition* (Chicago and London: University of Chicago Press, 1990).

Copley, Anthony, *Wits Fittes and Fancies, Fronted and Entermedled with Presidentes of Honour and Wisdome. Also: Loves Owl, an Idle Conceited Dialogue between Love, and an Olde Man* (London, 1595).

Corbeill, Anthony, *Nature Embodied: Gesture in Ancient Rome* (Princeton and Oxford: Princeton University Press, 2004).

Costa, Maddy, '"The Cast All Abused Me": The Pain of Playing Shylock', *The Guardian*, 8 May 2011. http://www.guardian.co.uk/stage/2011/may/08/playing-shylock-patrick-stewart-sher

Croke, George, *The Reports of Sir George Croke, Knight* (London: Printed by J.S. and sold by the Stationers of London, 1657).

Darrell, Walter, *A Short Discourse of the Life of Seruingmen Plainly Expressing the Way That Is Best to Be Followed, and the Meanes Wherby They May Lawfully Challenge a Name and Title in That Vocation and Fellowship. With Certeine Letters Verie Necessarie for Seruingmen, and Other Persons to Peruse. With Diuerse Pretie Inuentions in English Verse. Hereunto Is Also Annexed a Treatise, Concerning Manners and Behauiours* (London, 1578).

Daunce, Edward, *A Brief Discourse of the Spanish State* (London, 1590).

Devereux, Robert, *An Apologie of the Earl of Essex* (London, 1603).

Diehl, Huston, '"Strike All that Look upon with Marvel": Theatrical and Theological Wonder in *The Winter's Tale*', in *Rematerializing Shakespeare: Authority and Representation on the Early Modern English Stage* (eds. Bryan Reynolds and William N. West) (Hampshire: Palgrave Macmillan, 2005), 19–34.

Diehl, Huston, '"Does Not the Stone Rebuke Me?" The Pauline Rebuke and Paulina's Lawful Magic', in *The Winter's Tale, Shakespeare and the Cultures of Performance* (eds. Paul Yachnin and Patricia Badir) (Hampshire: Ashgate, 2008), 69–82.

Dolan, Frances E. (ed.), *The Taming of the Shrew: Bedford Texts and Contexts* (Boston: Bedford Books of St. Martin's Press, 1996).

Driessen, Henk, 'Gestured Masculinity in Rural Andalusia', in *A Cultural History of Gesture from Antiquity to the Present Day* (eds. Jan Bremmer and Herman Roodenburg) (Cambridge: Polity Press, 1993 [1991]), 237–252.

Dunne, Derek, 'Blushing on Cue: The Forensics of the Blush in Early Modern Drama', *Shakespeare Bulletin*, 34:2 (Summer, 2016), 233–252.

Dusinberre, Juliet, *Shakespeare and the Nature of Women* (Hampshire and London: Macmillan Press Ltd., 1996 [1975]).

Edelman, Charles, *Brawl Ridiculous: Swordfighting in Shakespeare's Plays* (Manchester and New York: Manchester University Press, 1992).

Eggert, Katherine, 'Nostalgia and the Not Yet Late Queen: Refusing Female Rule in *Henry V*', *ELH*, 61:3 (Autumn, 1994), 523–550.

Elias, Norbert, *The Civilizing Process* (trans. Edmund Jephcott) (MA, Oxford, Victoria: Blackwell Publishing, 2000 [1994]).

Erasmus, *The Ciuilitie of Childehode with the Discipline and Institucion of Children* (London, 1560).

Erasmus, *Lingua*, from *The Collected Works of Erasmus, Volume 29* (eds. Elaine Fantham and Erika Rummel with the assistance of Jozef Ijsewijn) (Toronto/Buffalo/London: University of Toronto Press, 1989).

Everett, Barbara, '"Spanish" Othello: The Making of Shakespeare's Moor', in *Shakespeare and Race* (eds. Catherine M. S. Alexander and Stanley Wells) (Cambridge: Cambridge University Press, 2000), 64–81.

Fernie, Ewan, *Shame in Shakespeare* (London and New York: Routledge, 2002).

Fisher, Will, *Materializing Gender in Early Modern English Literature and Culture* (Cambridge: Cambridge University Press, 2006).

Foucault, Michel, *Discipline and Punish* (trans. Alan Sheridan) (London: Penguin, 1991 [1977; originally published as *Surveiller et punir*, 1975]).

Foyster, Elizabeth A., *Manhood in Early Modern England: Honour, Sex and Marriage* (London and New York: Longman, 1999).

Garber, Marjorie, 'Out of Joint', in *The Body in Parts: Fantasies of Corporeality in Early Modern Europe* (eds. David Hillman and Carla Mazzio) (New York and London: Routledge, 1997), 23–52.

Gilmore, David, *Manhood in the Making: Cultural Conceptions of Masculinity* (New Haven: Yale University Press, 1990).

Gohlke, Madelon, '"I Wooed Thee with My Sword": Shakespeare's Tragic Paradigms', in *The Woman's Part: Feminist Criticism of Shakespeare* (eds. Carolyn Ruth Swift Lenz, Gayle Greene, and Carol Thomas Neely) (Urbana, Chicago, and London: University of Illinois Press, 1980), 150–170.

Goldberg, Jonathan, 'Speculations: *Macbeth* and Source', in *Shakespeare Reproduced: The Text in History and Ideology* (eds. Jean E. Howard and Marion F. O'Connor) (New York and London: Routledge, 1993 [1987]), 242–264.

Graf, Fritz 'Gestures and Conventions: The Gestures of Roman Actors and Orators', in *A Cultural History of Gesture from Antiquity to the Present Day* (eds. Jan Bremmer and Herman Roodenburg) (Cambridge: Polity Press, 1993 [1991]).

Greatley-Hirsch, Brett, 'The Taming of the Jew: Spit and the Civilizing Process in *The Merchant of Venice*', in *Staged Transgression in Shakespeare's England* (eds. Rory Loughnane and Edel Semple) (New York: Palgrave, 2013), 136–152.

Greenblatt, Stephen, *Renaissance Self-Fashioning: From More to Shakespeare* (Chicago and London: Chicago University Press, 2005 [1980]).

Greenblatt, Stephen, 'Mutilation and Meaning', in *The Body in Parts* (eds. David Hillman and Carla Mazzio) (New York and London: Routledge, 1997), 221–241.

Grene, Nicholas, *Shakespeare's Serial History Plays* (Cambridge: Cambridge University Press, 2002).

Griaule, Marcel, 'CRACHAT-crachat-âme', *Dictionnaire, Documents*, 1 (1929), 381–382.

Griffin, Eric J., *English Renaissance Drama and the Specter of Spain: Ethnopoetics and Empire* (Philadelphia: University of Pennsylvania Press, 2009).

Griffin, Eric, 'Shakespeare, Marlowe, and the Stranger Crisis of the Early 1590s', in *Shakespeare and Immigration* (eds. Ruben Espinosa and David Rutter) (Surrey and Burlington: Ashgate, 2014).

Gurr, Andrew, *The Shakespearean Stage 1574–1642* (Cambridge, Cambridge University Press, 1995 [1992]).

Gurr, Andrew, *Playgoing in Shakespeare's London* (Cambridge: Cambridge University Press, 2005 [1987]).

Hale, John, *The Civilization of Europe in the Renaissance* (London: HarperCollins, 1994 [1993]).

Hall, Edward, *The Union of the Two Noble and Illustre Families of Lancastre and Yorke* (London, 1548).

Hall, James, *Dictionary of Subjects and Symbols in Art* (London: John Murray Ltd., 1974).

Hardman, C. B., '*The Winter's Tale* and the Stuart Golden Age', *Review of English Studies New Series*, 45:178 (May, 1994), 221–229.

Harris, Jonathan Gil, *Foreign Bodies and the Body Politic: Discourses of Social Pathology in Early Modern England* (Cambridge: Cambridge University Press, 1998).

Hasler, Jörg, 'Romance in the Theater: The Stagecraft of the "Statue Scene" in *The Winter's Tale*', in *Shakespeare: Man of the Theater* (eds. Kenneth Muir, Jay L. Halio, and D. J. Palmer) (Newark: University of Delaware Press, 1983), 203–211.

Hazlitt, W. Carew, *A Dictionary of Faiths and Folklore* (Volume 1) (London: Reeves and Turner, 1905).

Helms, Lorraine, 'Acts of Resistance: The Feminist Player', in *The Weyward Sisters: Shakespeare and Feminist Politics* (eds. Dympna Callaghan, Lorraine Helms, and Jyotsna Singh) (Oxford, UK, and Cambridge, USA: Blackwell, 1994), 102–156.

Henig, Martin, *Religion in Roman Britain* (London: B. T. Batsford Ltd., 1984).

Hildburgh, W. L., 'Images of the Human Hand as Amulets in Spain', *Journal of the Warburg and Courtauld Institute*, 18:1/2 (January–June, 1955), 67–89.

Hobgood, Allison P., 'Feeling Fear in *Macbeth*', in *Shakespearean Sensations: Experiencing Literature in Early Modern England* (eds. Katharine A. Craik and Tanya Pollard) (Cambridge: Cambridge University Press, 2013), 29–46.

Holderness, Graham, '*The Winter's Tale*: Country into Court', in *Shakespeare: Out of Court* (eds. Graham Holderness, Nick Potter and John Turner) (Hampshire: Macmillan, 1990), 195–235.

Holding, Peter, *Romeo and Juliet: Text and Performance* (Hampshire and London: Palgrave Macmillan, 1992).

Howard, Jean E., and Phyllis Rackin, *Engendering a Nation: A Feminist Account of Shakespeare's English Histories* (London and New York: Routledge, 1997).

Howells, W. D., *Venetian Life* (Marlboro, VT: The Marlboro Press, 1989).

Illetschko, Georgia, Michelangelo Buonarroti, and Christopher Wynne, *I, Michelangelo* (Munich: Prestel, 2004).

Jacquet, Jennifer, *Is Shame Necessary? New Uses for an Old Tool* (Great Britain: Allen Lane, 2015).

James VI and I, *The Basilicon Doron of James VI* (ed. James Craigie) (Edinburgh and London: Blackwood and Sons, 1944).

Jobson, Richard, *The Golden Trade* (ed. Walter Rodney) (London: Dawsons, 1968 [1623]).

Johnstone, Hilda (ed.), *Churchwarden's Presentments (17th Century), Part 1: Archdeaconry of Chichester* (Lewes: Sussex Record Society, 1948).

Kahn, Coppélia, *Man's Estate: Masculine Identity in Shakespeare* (Berkeley, Los Angeles, and London: University of California Press, 1981).

Karim-Cooper, Farah, 'To Glisten in a Playhouse: Cosmetic Beauty Indoors', in *Moving Shakespeare Indoors: Performance and Repertoire in the Jacobean Playhouse* (eds. Andrew Gurr and Farah Karim-Cooper) (Cambridge: Cambridge University Press, 2014), 184–200

Karim-Cooper, Farah, *The Hand on the Shakespearean Stage: Gesture, Touch and the Spectacle of Dismemberment* (London: Arden, 2016).

Katz, David S., 'Shylock's Gender: Jewish Male Menstruation in Early Modern England', *The Review of English Studies New Series*, 50:200 (November, 1999), 440–462.

Kendon, Adam, *Gesture: Visible Action as Utterance* (Cambridge: Cambridge University Press, 2005 [2004]).

Kernan, Alvin, *Shakespeare, the King's Playwright: Theater in the Stuart Court, 1603–1613* (New Haven and London: Yale University Press, 1995).

Kinney, Arthur F., *Lies Like Truth: Shakespeare, Macbeth, and the Cultural Moment* (Detroit: Wayne State University Press, 2001).

Kitch, Aaron, 'Shylock's Sacred Nation', *Shakespeare Quarterly*, 59:2 (Summer, 2008), 131–155.

Klein, Joan Larsen, 'Lady Macbeth: "Infirm of Purpose"', in *The Woman's Part: Feminist Criticism of Shakespeare* (eds. Carolyn Ruth Swift Lenz, Gayle Greene, and Carol Thomas Neely) (Urbana, Chicago, and London: University of Illinois Press, 1980), 240–255.

Kott, Jan, *Shakespeare Our Contemporary* (trans. Boleslaw Taborski) (New York: W. W. Norton and Company Inc, 1974 [1964]).

Kristeva, Julia, *Powers of Horror: An Essay on Abjection* (trans. Leon S. Roudiez) (New York: Columbia University Press, 1982).

Kumamoto, Chikako D., 'Shakespeare's Achillean Coriolanus and Heraean Volumnia: Textual Contamination and Crossing of Homer's *Iliad* in *Coriolanus*', *Journal of the Wooden O Symposium*, 7 (2007), 51–63.

Du Larens, André, *A Discourse on the Preseruation of the Sight* (London, 1599).

Laurents, Arthur, and Stephen Sondheim, *West Side Story* (New York, 1965 [1956]).

Lecoq, Jacques, *Theatre of Gesture and Movement* (ed. David Bradby) (New York and London: Routledge, 2006).

Lefevre, Romana, *Rude Hand Gestures of the World: A Guide to Offending without Words* (San Francisco: Chronicle Books, 2011).

Levin, Joanna, 'Lady Macbeth and the Daemonologie of Hysteria', *ELH*, 69:1 (Spring, 2002), 21–55.

Levin, Richard, 'The Longleat Manuscript and *Titus Andronicus*', *Shakespeare Quarterly*, 53:3 (Autumn, 2002), 323–340.

Levith, Murray J., *Shakespeare's Italian Settings and Plays* (Hampshire and London: Macmillan, 1989).

Lidgate, John, *The Life and Death of Hector* (London, 1614).

Low, Jennifer A., '"Bodied Forth": Spectator, Stage and Actor in the Early Modern Theatre' in *Comparative Drama*, 39:1 (Spring, 2005), 1–29.

Lynch, Kathryn L., '"What Hands Are Here?" The Hand as Generative Symbol in Macbeth', *The Review of English Studies*, 39:153 (February, 1988), 29–38.

Matusiak, John, *James I: Scotland's King of England* (Gloucestershire: The History Press, 2015).
McAlindon, T., *Shakespeare and Decorum* (London and Basingstoke: Macmillan, 1973).
McEachern, Claire, '*Henry V* and the Paradox of the Body Politic', *Shakespeare Quarterly*, 45:1 (Spring, 1994), 33–56.
McManus, Clare, *Women on the Renaissance Stage: Anna of Denmark and Female Masquing in the Stuart Court 1590–1619* (Manchester and New York: Manchester University Press, 2002).
Mazzio, Carla, 'Sins of the Tongue in Early Modern England', *Modern Language Studies*, 28:3/4 (Autumn, 1998), 93–124.
Menzer, Paul, 'The Actor's Inhibition: Early Modern Acting and the Rhetoric of Restraint', *Renaissance Drama New Series*, 35: Embodiment and Environment in Early Modern Drama and Performance (2006), 83–111.
Middleton, Thomas, *The Roaring Girle, or Moll Cut-purse* (London, 1611).
Middleton, Thomas, and Thomas Dekker, *The Roaring Girl* (eds. Simon Barker and Hilary Hinds, in *The Routledge Anthology of Renaissance Drama*) (London: Routledge, 2003).
Mitchell, David T., and Sharon L. Snyder, *Narrative Prosthesis: Disability and the Dependencies of Discourse* (Ann Arbor: University of Michigan Press, 2000).
Mindock, Clark, 'Taking a Knee: Why Are NFL Players Protesting and When Did They Start to Kneel?' *Independent*, 4 September 2018. https://www.independent.co.uk/news/world/americas/us-politics/taking-a-knee-national-anthem-nfl-trump-why-meaning-origins-racism-us-colin-kaepernick-a8521741.html
de Montaigne, Michel, *Essays in Three Volumes: Volume Two* (trans. John Florio) (London and New York: Everyman's Library, 1965 [1910]).
de Montaigne, Michel, *Essays in Three Volumes: Volume Three* (trans. John Florio) (London and New York: Everyman's Library, 1965 [1910]).
More, Thomas, *Utopia*, in *Three Early Modern Utopias* (ed. Susan Bruce) (Oxford: Oxford University Press, 1999).
Morris, Desmond, Peter Collett, Peter Marsh, and Marie O'Shaughnessy, *Gestures: Their Origins and Distribution* (London: Jonathan Cape, 1979).

Moulton, Ian Frederick, '"A Monster Great Deformed": The Unruly Masculinity of *Richard III*', *Shakespeare Quarterly*, 47:3 (Autumn, 1996), 251–268.

Mullaney, Steven. *The Place of the Stage: License, Play, and Power in Renaissance England* (Michigan: University of Michigan Press, 1995 [1988]).

Neill, Michael, '"Amphitheatres in the Body": Playing with Hands on the Shakespearean Stage, *Shakespeare Survey*, 48: Shakespeare and Cultural Exchange (March, 2007), 23–50.

Newman, Karen, '"And Wash the Ethiop White": Femininity and the Monstrous in Othello', in *Shakespeare Reproduced: The Text in History and Ideology* (eds. Jean E. Howard and Marion F. O'Connor) (New York and London: Routledge, 1993 [1987]), 143–162.

Overton, Richard, *A New Bull-bayting: or, A Match Play'd at the Tovvn-bull of Ely. By Twelve Mungrills. Viz. 4 English 4 Irish 4 Scotch Doggs. Iohn Lilburn, Richard Overton, Thomas Prince, and William Walwyn, to Stave and Nose. With His Last Will and Testament, and Several Legacies Bequeathed to the Iuncto, the Councel of State, and Army. Too Him My Dogge; Ha-loe There; Now Hee's Down: Bayted to Death, and Forfeit to the Crown* (London: 1649).

Palfrey, Simon, and Tiffany Stern, *Shakespeare in Parts* (Oxford: Oxford University Press, 2007).

Paster, Gail Kern, *The Body Embarrassed: Drama and the Disciplines of Shame in Early Modern England* (New York: Cornell University Press, 1993).

Peltonen, Markku, 'Political Rhetoric and Citizenship in *Coriolanus*', in *Shakespeare and Early Modern Political Thought* (eds. David Armitage, Conal Condren, and Andrew Fitzmaurice) (Cambridge: Cambridge University Press, 2009), 234–252.

Pfister, Manfred, 'Acting the Roman: Coriolanus', in *Identity, Otherness and Empire in Shakespeare's Rome* (ed. Maria Del Sapio Garbero) (Surrey: Ashgate, 2009), 35–47.

Philpot, John, *An Apologie of Iohan Philpot Written for Spitting upon an Arrian, with an Inuectiue against the Arrians (the Very Natural Chyldren of Antichrist) with an Admonition to All That Be Faythfull in Christ, to Beware of Them, and of Other Late Sprong Heresies, as of the Most Enemies of the Gospell* (Emden: E. van der Erve, 1556 [?]).

Piazza, Antonella, 'Volumnia, the Roman Patroness', in *Questioning Bodies in Shakespeare's Rome* (eds. Maria Del Sapio Garbero, Nancy Isenberg, and Maddalena Pennacchia) (Goettingen: V & R unipress, 2010), 121–134.

Plutarch, *The Lives of the Noble Grecians and Romanes Compared Together by that Graue Learned Philosopher and Historiographer, Plutarke of Chaeronea; Translated out of Greeke into French by Iames Amyot; and out of French into Englishe, by Thomas North* (London, 1579).

Pothast, Emily, 'Does the OK Sign Actually Signify "White Power," or What?' *Medium*, 5 September 2018, https://medium.com/s/story/does-the-ok-sign-actually-signify-white-power-or-what-6cf3309df985

Quintilian, *The Orator's Education in Five Volumes: Volume 5: Books 11–12* (ed. and trans. Donald A. Russell) (Cambridge, MA and London: Harvard University Press, 2001).

Rebhorn, Wayne A., 'Baldesar Castiglione, Thomas Wilson, and the Courtly Body of Renaissance Rhetoric', *Rhetorica: A Journal of the History of Rhetoric*, 11:3 (Summer, 1993), 241–274.

The Resolution of the Women of London to the Parliament (London, 1642).

Richman, Michèle H., 'Spitting Images in Montaigne and Bataille for a Heterological Counterhistory of Sovereignty', *Diacritics*, 35:3 (Autumn, 2005), 46–61.

Russell, H. Diane (with Bernadine Barnes), *Eva/Ave: Woman in Renaissance and Baroque Prints* (New York: National Gallery of Art, Washington, and the Feminist Press at the City University of New York, 1990).

Salgado, Gamini (ed.), *Eyewitnesses of Shakespeare: First-hand Accounts of Performances 1590–1890* (London: Chatto and Windus, 1975).

Samuels, Ellen, 'Critical Divides: Judith Butler's Body Theory and the Question of Disability', *NSWA Journal*, 14:3: Feminist Disability Studies (Autumn, 2002), 58–76.

Del Sapio Garbero, Maria, 'A Spider in the Eye/I: The Hallucinatory Staging of the Self in Shakespeare's *The Winter's Tale*', in *Solo Performances: Staging the Early Modern Self in England* (ed. Ute Berns) (Amsterdam and New York: Rodolphi, 2010), 133–155.

Sartre, Jean-Paul, *Critique of Dialectical Reason I. Theory of Practical Ensembles* (trans. Alan Sheridan-Smith, ed. Jonathan Rée) (London: NLB, 1976).

Sayare, Scott, 'Concern over an Increasingly Seen Gesture Grows in France', *New York Times*, 2 January 2014. https://www.nytimes.com/2014/01/03/world/europe/concern-over-quenelle-gesture-grows-in-france.html

Schmitt, Jean-Claude, 'The Rationale of Gestures in the West: Third to Thirteenth Centuries', in *A Cultural History of Gesture from Antiquity to the Present Day* (eds. Jan Bremmer and Herman Roodenburg) (Cambridge: Polity Press, 1993 [1991]), 59–70.

Schlueter, June, 'Rereading the Peacham Drawing', *Shakespeare Quarterly*, 50:2 (Summer, 1999), 171–184.

Shapiro, James, *Shakespeare and the Jews* (New York: Columbia Press, 1996).

Sher, Antony, *Year of the King: An Actor's Diary and Sketchbook* (London: Nick Hern Books, 2012 [1985]).

Shakespeare, William, *The Most Excellent and Lamentable Tragedie of Romeo and Juliet* (London, 1599).

Shakespeare, William, *The Chronicle History of Henry the Fift, with His Battell Fought at Agin Court in France. Togither with Auntient Pistoll* (London, 1600).

Shakespeare, William, *The Life of King Henry Fift*, in *Mr William Shakespeare's Comedies, Histories, & Tragedies* (London, 1623).

Shakespeare, William, *The Plays and Poems of William Shakespeare* (ed. Edmond Malone) (New Street, London, 1821).

Shakespeare, William, *The Variorum Shakespeare: Romeo and Juliet* (ed. H. H. Furness) (Philadelphia: Press of the J. B. Lippincott Company, 1899).

Shakespeare, William, *The Merchant of Venice* (ed. John Russell Brown) (Surrey: Metheun and Co., 1955).

Shakespeare, William, *Romeo and Juliet* (ed. G. Blakemore Evans) (Cambridge: Cambridge University Press, 1984).

Shakespeare, William, *Antony and Cleopatra* (ed. John Wilders) (London: Arden Shakespeare, 1995).

Shakespeare, William, *King Lear* (ed. R. A. Foakes) (London: Arden Shakespeare, 1997).

Shakespeare, William, *Othello* (ed. E. A. J. Honigmann) (London: Arden Shakespeare, 1997).

Shakespeare, William, and John Fletcher, *The Two Noble Kinsmen* (ed. Lois Potter) (London: Arden Shakespeare, 1997).

Shakespeare, William, *Troilus and Cressida* (ed. David Bevington) (London: Arden Shakespeare, 1998).

Shakespeare, William, *Love's Labour's Lost* (ed. H. R. Woudhuysen) (London: Arden Shakespeare, 1998)

Shakespeare, William, *Romeo and Juliet* (ed. Jill L. Levenson) (Oxford: Oxford University Press, 2000).

Shakespeare, William, *The Merchant of Venice* (ed. Charles Edelman) (Cambridge: Cambridge University Press, 2002).

Shakespeare, William, *King Henry IV Part One* (ed. David Scott Kastan) (London: Arden Shakespeare, 2002).

Shakespeare, William, *Romeo and Juliet* (ed. James N. Loehlin) (Cambridge: Cambridge University Press, 2002).

Shakespeare, William, *King Henry IV Part Two* (ed. A. R. Humphreys) (London: Arden Shakespeare, 2004 [1981]).

Shakespeare, William, *Pericles* (ed. Suzanne Gossett) (London: Arden Shakespeare, 2006 [2004]).

Shakespeare, William, *All's Well That Ends Well* (ed. G. K. Hunter) (London: Arden Shakespeare, 2006 [1959]).

Shakespeare, William, *A Midsummer Night's Dream* (ed. Harold F. Brooks) (London: Arden Shakespeare, 2007 [1979]).

Shakespeare, William, *The First Quarto of Romeo and Juliet* (ed. Lukas Erne) (Cambridge: Cambridge University Press, 2007).

Shakespeare, William, *King John* (ed. E. A. J. Honigmann) (London: Arden Shakespeare, 2007 [1954]).

Shakespeare, William, *Cymbeline* (ed. J. M. Nosworthy) (London: Arden Shakespeare, 2007 [1955]).

Shakespeare, William, *Hamlet* (eds. Ann Thompson and Neil Taylor) (London: Arden Shakespeare, 2007 [2006]).

Shakespeare, William, *Timon of Athens* (eds. Anthony B. Dawson and Gretchen E. Minton) (London: Arden Shakespeare, 2008).

Shakespeare, William, *The Comedy of Errors* (ed. R. A. Foakes) (London: Arden Shakespeare, 2008 [1962]).

Shakespeare, William, *Measure for Measure* (ed. J. W. Lever) (London: Arden Shakespeare, 2008 [1965])

Shakespeare, William, *Titus Andronicus* (ed. Jonathan Bate) (London: Arden Shakespeare, 2009 [1995]).

Shakespeare, William, *Richard III* (ed. James R. Siemon) (London: Arden Shakespeare, 2009).

Shakespeare, William, *The Taming of the Shrew* (ed. Barbara Hodgdon) (London: Arden Shakespeare, 2010).

Shakespeare, William, *The Winter's Tale* (ed. John Pitcher) (London: Arden Shakespeare, 2010).

Shakespeare, William, *Romeo and Juliet* (ed. René Weis) (London: Arden, 2012).

Shakespeare, William, *King Henry VI Part 3* (eds. John D. Cox and Eric Rasmussen) (London: Arden Shakespeare, 2013 [2001]).

Shakespeare, William, *King Henry* (ed. T. W. Craik) (London: Arden Shakespeare, 2013 [1995]).

Shakespeare, William, *The Merchant of Venice* (ed. John Drakakis) (London: Arden Shakespeare, 2013 [2010]).

Shakespeare, William, *Coriolanus* (ed. Peter Holland) (London: Arden Shakespeare, 2013).

Shakespeare, William, *King Henry VIII* (ed. Gordon McMullan) (London: Arden Shakespeare, 2013 [2000]).

Shakespeare, William, *King Henry VI Part 1* (ed. Edward Burns) (London: Arden Shakespeare, 2014 [2000]).

Shakespeare, William, *Julius Caesar* (ed. David Daniell) (London: Arden Shakespeare, 2014 [1998]).

Shakespeare, William, *The Two Gentlemen of Verona* (ed. William C. Carroll) (London: Arden Shakespeare, 2014 [2004]).

Shakespeare, William, *As You Like It* (Juliet Dusinberre) (London: Arden Shakespeare, 2014 [2006]).

Shakespeare, William, *Twelfth Night* (ed. Keir Elam) (London: Arden Shakespeare, 2014 [2008]).

Shakespeare, William, *Much Ado about Nothing* (ed. Claire McEachern) (London: Arden Shakespeare, 2014 [2007]).

Shakespeare, William, *The Merry Wives of Windsor* (ed. Giorgio Melchiori) (London: Arden Shakespeare, 2014 [2000]).

Shakespeare, William, *The Tempest* (eds. Virginia Mason Vaughan and Alden T. Vaughan) (London: Arden Shakespeare, 2014 [1999]).

Shakespeare, William, *Macbeth* (eds. Sandra Clark and Pamela Mason) (London: Arden Shakespeare, 2015)

Shakespeare, William, *King Richard II* (ed. Charles R. Forker) (London: Arden Shakespeare, 2015 [2002]).

Shakespeare, William, *King Henry VI Part 2* (ed. Ronald Knowles) (London: Arden Shakespeare, 2015 [1999]).

Shepard, Alexandra, *Meanings of Manhood in Early Modern England* (Oxford: Oxford University Press, 2006 [2003]).

Singh, Jyotsna, 'The Interventions of History: Narratives of Sexuality', in *The Weyward Sisters: Shakespeare and Feminist Politics* (eds. Dympna Callaghan, Lorraine Helms, and Jyotsna

Singh) (Oxford, UK and Cambridge, USA: Blackwell, 1994), 7–58.

Smith, Bruce R., *Phenomenal Shakespeare* (Malden and Oxford: Wiley-Blackwell, 2010).

Smith, Denzell S., 'The Credibility of the Wooing of Anne in *Richard III*', *Papers on Language and Literature*, 7:2 (Spring, 1971), 199–202.

Smith, Emma, 'Was Shylock Jewish?' *Shakespeare Quarterly*, 64:2 (Summer, 2013), 188–219.

Spenser, Edmund, *The Faerie Queene* (ed. A. C. Hamilton) (Harlow: Pearson, 2007 [2001]).

Sprang, Felix C. H., 'Never Fortune Did Play a Subtler Game: The Creation of "Medieval" Narratives in *Pericles* and *The Two Noble Kinsmen*', *European Journal of English Studies*, 15:2 (July, 2011), 115–128.

Stallybrass, Peter, 'Patriarchal Territories: The Body Enclosed', in *Rewriting the Renaissance: The Discourses of Sexual Difference in Early Modern Europe* (eds. Margaret Fergusan, Maureen Quilligan, and Nancy J. Vickers) (Chicago: University of Chicago Press, 1986), 123–142.

Starks-Estes, Lisa S., 'Virtus, Vulnerability, and the Emblazoned Male Body in Shakespeare's *Coriolanus*', in *Violent Masculinities: Male Aggression in Early Modern Texts and Culture* (eds. Jennifer Feather and Catherine E. Thomas) (Hampshire: Palgrave Macmillan, 2013), 85–108.

Stewart, Alan, *Shakespeare's Letters* (Oxford: Oxford University Press, 2008).

Stallybrass, Peter, and Allon White, *The Politics and Poetics of Transgression* (Ithaca, NY: Cornell University Press, 1986).

Stone, Lawrence, *The Crisis of the Aristocracy, 1558–1641* (Oxford: Oxford University Press, 1965).

Stubbes, Phillip, *The Anatomie of Abuses* (London, 1583).

Tallis, Raymond, *The Hand: A Philosophical Inquiry into Human Being* (Edinburgh: Edinburgh University Press, 2003).

Tarlton, Richard, *Tarltons Jests Drawne into These Three Parts* (London, 1638).

Thomas, Keith, 'Introduction', in *A Cultural History of Gesture from Antiquity to the Present Day* (eds. Jan Bremmer and Herman Roodenburg) (Cambridge: Polity Press, 1993 [1991]), 1–14.

Thomas, Miranda Fay, 'Political Acts and Political Acting: Roman Gesture in *Julius Caesar*', *Early Modern Literary Studies* (Special Issue: Rome and Home, 2016), 1–24.

Thomas, Miranda Fay, '"Tremble at Patience": Constant Queens and Female Solidarity in *The Two Noble Kinsmen* and *The Winter's Tale*', in *The Palgrave Handbook of Shakespeare's Queens* (eds. Kavita Mudan Finn and Valerie Schutte) (Basingstoke: Palgrave Macmillan, 2018), 87–103.

Topsell, Edward, *The Historie of Serpents* (London, 1608).

Torrey, Michael, '"The Plain Devil and Dissembling Looks": Ambivalent Physiognomy and Shakespeare's *Richard III*', *English Literary Renaissance*, 30:2 (Spring, 2000), 123–153.

Tribble, Evelyn B., 'The Partial Sign: Spenser and the Sixteenth-century Crisis of Semiotics', in *Ceremony and Text in the Renaissance* (ed. Douglas F. Rutledge) (Newark: University of Delaware Press, 1996), 23–34.

Tribble, Evelyn, '"O, She's Warm": Touch in *The Winter's Tale*', in *Knowing Shakespeare: Senses, Embodiment and Cognition* (eds. Lowell Gallagher and Shankar Raman) (Hampshire: Palgrave Macmillan, 2010), 65–81.

Trubowitz, Rachel, '"But Blood Whitened": Nursing Mothers and Others in Early Modern Britain', in *Maternal Measures: Figuring Caregiving in the Early Modern Period* (eds. Naomi J. Miller and Naomi Yavneh) (Aldershot and Burlington: Ashgate, 2000), 82–101.

Tunstall, Darren, *Shakespeare and Gesture in Practice* (London: Palgrave Macmillan, 2016).

Velleman, J. David, 'The Genesis of Shame', *Philosophy and Public Affairs*, 30:1 (Winter, 2001), 27–52.

Walter, John, 'Gesturing at Authority: Deciphering the Gestural Code of Early Modern England', in *The Politics of Gesture: History Perspectives* (ed. M. Braddick), *Past and Present*: Supplement 4 (2009), 96–127.

Washington, Edward, '"At the Door of Truth": The Hollowness of Signs in *Othello*', in *Othello: New Essays by Black Writers* (ed. Mythili Kaul) (Washington, DC: Howard University Press, 1996), 167–187.

Wells, Robin Headlam, *Shakespeare, Politics and the State* (Hampshire: Macmillan, 1986).

Wells, Robin Headlam, *Shakespeare on Masculinity* (Cambridge: Cambridge University Press, 2000).

West-Pavlov, Russell, *Bodies and Their Spaces: System, Crisis and Transformation in Early Modern Theatre* (Amsterdam, New York: Rodolphi, 2006).

White, Martin, 'Light and Darkness in the Indoor Jacobean Theatre', in *Moving Shakespeare Indoors: Performance and Repertoire in the Jacobean Playhouse* (eds. Andrew Gurr and Farah Karim-Cooper) (Cambridge: Cambridge University Press, 2014), 115–136.

Wiggins, Martin (in association with Catherine Richardson), *British Drama 1533–1642: A Catalogue (Volume V: 1603–1608)* (Oxford: Oxford University Press, 2015).

Williams, Katherine Schaap, 'Enabling Richard: The Rhetoric of Disability in *Richard III*', *Disability Studies Quarterly*, 29:4 (2009), no page numbers.

Wilson, Thomas, *The Arte of Rhetorique* (London, 1553).

Woods, Gillian, '"Strange Discourse": The Controversial Subject of *Sir Thomas More*', *Renaissance Drama New Series*, 39 (2011), 3–35.

Woods, Gillian, *Shakespeare's Unreformed Fictions* (Oxford: Oxford University Press, 2013).

Woods, Penelope, 'The Audience of the Indoor Theatre', in *Moving Shakespeare Indoors: Performance and Repertoire in the Jacobean Playhouse* (eds. Andrew Gurr and Farah Karim-Cooper) (Cambridge: Cambridge University Press, 2014), 152–167.

INDEX

Adams, Thomas 106, 109
Alemán, Mateo
   The Rogue 81
amulets 5–6
ancient Rome 24, 32, 37–8
Andrews, Grace 189
Andronicus, Emperor 124
Anna of Denmark 180
anti-Spanish sentiment 19
anti-theatrical movement 196–7
apprentices 28
   apprentice riots 99
Arden of Faversham 54
Atwood, Margaret 139, 201
   The Handmaid's Tale 201

Bakhtin, Mikhail 84–5
Barbarossa 50
Barnfield, Richard
   A New Tragicall Comedie of Apius and Virginia 54
Barocci, Federico
   The Annunciation 175
Barrie, Hannah 78
Barrit, Desmond 93–4
Bates, Alan 78
bear-baiting 47
beards 96
Bedford, Brian 78
Blackfriars theatre 181–2, 191, 199
Black Lives Matter 201
Blake, William 60–1

blood 151–7
Boccaccio
   De claris mulieribus (Concerning Famous Women) 174
body politic 6, 19, 72, 86, 88, 97, 105, 142, 177, 180
Bogdanov, Michael 41
Boleyn, Anne 127
boundary panic 72, 95–6, 98, 101, 111–2
Boyd, Michael 23
braggart soldier 54–5, 69, 136, 210 n.14
Brando, Marlon 14
brawls 27, 37, 39
Brewer, Dominic 32
bull-baiting 128
Bulwer, John
   Chirologia and Chironomia 7, 33–4, 38, 45–6, 122–3, 148–9
Butler, Judith 16
Byrne, Anthony 45, 69

Calvert, Thomas
   The Blessed Jew of Marocco or *A Blackamoor Made White* 103
Campion, Thomas
   The Lord's Masque 191–2
Castiglione, Baldesar
   The Book of the Courtier 171

Catholicism 144, 193
Cawte, Tom 189
ceremony 171
Charles I, King 15
Cheek By Jowl 189
Christ, Jesus 56–8
   persecution of 95, 97,
      106–9, 150
   spitting on 106–9
Christian, King of Denmark 125
Christianity 95
   baptism 95, 109
   Cain 150
   Genesis 58–9
   Isaiah 80
   John, Gospel of 148
   Leviticus 103
   Luke, Gospel of 148
   Mark, Gospel of 106, 148
   Matthew, Gospel of 148
   1 Timothy 194
   Psalms 150
   Romans 109
Cicero 6
civilizing process 8, 11, 84, 88
class 28, 35, 37, 48–50, 62, 65,
   69, 81
Copley, Anthony
   Wits, Fittes and Fancies
      123–4
Cornerstone Theatre 23
cornutu. *See* cuckoldry
cosmetics 196–7, 199
costume 4, 171, 197
Cotgrave, Randl
   Dictionary of the French
      and English Tongues 32
Courtin, Antoine de
   Nouveau traite de civilité 81
Cranstoun, James 30

Crusades 124
cuckoldry 116
   and beasts 133
   Cuckold's Haven 135
   horns 14, 115–18, 124, 132,
      134, 189
   and masculinity 136
   and ornithology 124
   in *Othello* 6, 13, 19, 115–39
Cukor, George 39
'cutis' gesture 24

Dante
   The Divine Comedy 60–2
Darrell, Walter 81
Daunce, Edward
   A Brief Discourse of the
      Spanish State 52
Dekker, Thomas
   The Dead Tearme 27
   The Famous History of Sir
      Thomas Wyatt 54
   The Roaring Girl 89
disability 90
   and *Richard III* 19, 77–8,
      84–5, 216 n.56
dogs 88–9, 100–1, 112, 128
Donmar Warehouse 165
duels 8, 36
Dürer, Albrecht
   The Assumption and
      Coronation of the Virgin
      176

Edward the Confessor 145
Elizabeth I, Queen 18, 20, 28,
   51, 65–6, 90, 127, 142,
   180, 196
embodiment 1, 2, 15, 96, 148
English Civil War 116

ensign 136, 221 n.35
ephemerality 5, 13, 30, 118, 157, 202
Erasmus 82
  De Civilitate Morum Puerilium 82
  Lingua 82–3
Essex, Earl of 51, 65
Esther, wife of Ahasuerus 172–4
Eve 177
evil eye 47, 68

Fall of Man 58–9, 75, 177
fascinus 4–5
female solidarity 169
Field, Nathan 14
fig gesture 4–5, 19, 45–69, 136, 171, 198, 201, 210 n.14
  Fig for the Spaniard, A 52
  in *Othello* 68–9
  as used by Pistol 6, 19, 45, 48–69
Filmer, (Sir) Robert 16
Findlay, Deborah 165
Florence 97
Florio, John 151
Forman, Simon 152
Foucault, Michel 10–11, 87
fragile masculinity 117, 120, 132, 135, 139
Franken, Frans (II) 56–7

gaze 12, 51, 56, 116, 138, 145
gender
  and age 146–7, 185
  and anti-Semitism 103–4
  and blood 153
  as construction 15, 16, 117, 122, 138, 146–7, 172
  and decorum 171–2

gender 'difference' 15, 17, 20, 90, 104–5, 145–6
gendered violence 18–9, 37–8, 42, 48, 66–8, 138
gender politics 2, 15, 16, 24, 51, 79, 130, 145–6, 174, 180
  and honour 117
  as performance 2, 17, 55, 168, 172, 200
  and public space 148
Genoa 97
genre 14, 18
Gesta Romanorum 150
gesture 199–202
  classical gesture 6
  as culturally specific 1–2, 8, 14, 21, 29–30
  and deniability 29, 47–8
  and ephemerality 13
  as gendered 37, 64, 170
  in *Hamlet* 12
  and imagination 130–1, 135
  as intention 14, 120–1, 130–1, 167
  in *Julius Caesar* 13
  and misreading 125, 130
  reported gesture 13, 167, 204 n.29
  vulgar gesture 7, 50, 60, 69
Gislebertus
  Temptation of Eve 177
Globe Theatre, London 3–4, 23, 32, 47, 128, 180–2, 191
Gosson, Stephen 14
Gouge, William 16
grammar school syllabus 6
Gunpowder Plot 144, 152

INDEX

Hall, Edward
    The Union of the Two Noble and Illustre Families of Lancastre and Yorke 30–1, 88
Hall, Peter 23
hand-shaking 42
handwashing in *Macbeth* 6, 141–59
Hemessen, Jan Sanders Van 55–6
Henry VII (King) 27
Henry VIII (King) 27–8
hermaphrodites 17
Heywood, Thomas
    A Challenge for Beautie 54
Hiddleston, Tom 165
Hirsch, John 78
Holland, Philemon 81
humoural theory 16–17, 90

Ireland 51
Isidore 32

James I, King 18, 20, 125, 142–5, 152, 158, 163, 180, 192
James, Orlando 189
Jonson, Ben
    The Alchemist 50
Judaism 19, 81, 110
    anti-Semitism 95–105, 110, 173, 200

Kaepernick, Colin 201
King's evil. *See* scrofula
King's touch 145
kneeling 7, 21, 161–85, 198, 201
    in *Coriolanus* 6, 20, 163–85
    in *Titus Andronicus* 161
Koerbecke, Johann 106–7

Kramer, Daniel 23
Kristeva, Julia 86

Lecoq, Jacques 5, 8
Leyden, Lucas van 172–4
Lidgate, John
    The life and death of Hector 120–1
Limbourg, Pol de 58–9
Lodge, Thomas
    Wits Miserie 30
Lucretius 151
Luhrmann, Baz 40
Luther, Martin 97

Marlowe, Christopher
    Edward II 54
    The Jew of Malta 97, 100–4, 112
masculinity and the military 118, 125, 142, 144, 185
May Day riots 99
M'Bala M'Bala, Dieudonné 200
McLoughlin, Eleanor 189
menstruation 19, 103–5
Messkirch, Meister von 106–7
Michelangelo 63
Middleton, Thomas
    The Roaring Girl 89
Montaigne, Michel de 7, 32–3, 81, 151
More, Thomas
    Utopia 10
Moses 95

Naples 97
National Theatre 32
non-verbal communication 1, 8, 37

'OK' hand gesture 200
oratory 6
outsiders 19, 100
Overton, Richard
   A New Bull-Bayting 89

Pacino, Al 14
Paré, Ambroise
   Monsters and Marvels 17
passive-aggression 164, 172, 174, 188, 198
patriarchy 138, 188, 190
   as rooted in biblical belief 16
Peacham, Henry 161–2, 224 n.1
pendants 4
personal as political 1, 9, 158
Petrarchan love 134
Philpot, John 94–5
pigs 88
Pilate 98, 148, 150
Pliny
   Natural History 81
Plutarch 33
political as personal. *See* personal as political, the
post-truth 194. *See also* Trump, Donald
Protestant Reformation 174

'quenelle' gesture 200
Quintilian 6, 37

Radmall-Quirke, Natalie 189
Republicanism 180
reputation 12
Resolution of the Women of London to the Parliament, the 115–16
Rose Theatre 128
Rourke, Josie 165
Royal Shakespeare Company (RSC) 23, 32, 41, 45, 47, 77, 94
Rules of Civility, The 31

St Paul 194
Sam Wanamaker Playhouse 32
Sartre, John-Paul 37, 52
scrofula 145
Shakespeare, William
   All's Well That Ends Well 128
   A Midsummer Night's Dream 119–20
   As You Like It 79
   Comedy of Errors 79
   Coriolanus 6, 20, 146–7, 163–85, 191
   Cymbeline 3, 80, 126–7, 220 n.35
   First Folio 49–50
   Hamlet 12
   1 Henry IV 79, 100, 211 n.30
   2 Henry IV 6, 19, 45, 48, 51, 67, 69, 211 n.30
   1 Henry VI 168
   2 Henry VI 54
   3 Henry VI 168
   Henry V 4, 6, 19, 35, 48–50, 53, 60–2, 65–8, 69
      First Quarto 48, 49–51
   Henry VI 90
   Henry VIII 127, 144
   Julius Caesar 13, 204 n.29, 219 n.9
   King Lear 170
   Love's Labour's Lost 54

Macbeth 6, 19–20, 118, 141–59, 212 n.35
Measure for Measure 79, 169
Merchant of Venice, The 6, 19, 72, 78, 93–113
Merry Wives of Windsor, The 126
Much Ado About Nothing 126, 190
Othello 6, 12, 13, 19, 54, 68–9, 116–39, 144, 190
Richard II 79–80, 155, 169
Richard III 1, 6, 71–91, 135, 216 n.56, 217 n.25
Romeo and Juliet 1, 6, 19, 23–32, 34–42, 50, 135
  First Quarto 26
  Second Quarto 26
Taming of the Shrew, The 79, 165–7
Timon of Athens 80
Titus Andronicus 18–19, 161–3, 224 n.1
Troilus and Cressida 128
Two Gentlemen of Verona, The 167
Winter's Tale, The 1, 20, 172, 187–98, 220 n.31
shame 1, 2–3, 101
  and the Bible 177
  and the body 5
  as culturally defined 10
  and emotional pain 3, 11, 20, 116, 191, 201
  as gendered 19, 48, 104–5, 163
  gestural shaming 1, 9

public shaming 3, 10–12, 106, 131, 134, 183–5, 190–1, 193
  and Shakespeare 17–18
  as spectacle 3, 10–12, 27, 116, 133, 177, 181, 183, 193, 195
Sher, Antony 77, 94
Shirley, James
  The Maid's Revenge 54
sight 121–2, 142, 152, 157, 224 n.39
signifiers 118, 134, 156, 159
Sistine Chapel 63
Skelton, John 30
Slinger, Jonathan 78
Spain 36, 48, 50, 51, 54, 65, 68–9, 125, 136, 142–3
Spanish Armada 19, 48, 52, 66, 68–9, 72, 90, 125
Spanish fig. *See* fig gesture
Spenser, Edmund
  The Faerie Queene 142, 154–5
spitting 7, 19, 40, 201
  at Christ 106–9
  at dogs 88–9
  as feminizing 72, 89–90, 97, 190
  as grotesque 71, 84–6, 95
  and religion 94–5
  in *Richard III* 1, 6, 19, 71–90
  as taming 93
  in *The Merchant of Venice* 6, 19, 72, 78, 93–113
spittle 84, 93
  as healing 81
stage directions 13, 35, 75
Stationers' Register 102

Stewart, Patrick 93–4
stillness 19, 20, 21, 198–9
   in *The Winter's Tale* 1, 6, 20, 187–98
Stoicism 181
stranger crisis 52
Stratford Festival (Ontario) 78
Stubbes, Phillip 7
   Anatomie of Abuses 7

Tacitus 32
Tarlton, Richard 14, 123
thumbs 32–3, 212 n.35
thumb-biting 23–43, 47, 68, 171, 198, 201
   as audible 32
   in *Dick of Devonshire* 35
   in *Romeo and Juliet* 1, 6, 19, 23–43
Topsell, Edward
   The Historie of Serpents 74
toxic masculinity 19, 23, 28, 42
Treaty of London 143

Trojan war 128
Trump, Donald 200. *See also* toxic masculinity; white power

Venice 98, 112, 125
Virgin Mary 174–6

Wapull, George
   The Tyde Taryeth No Man 54
Wars of the Roses 76
Webster, John
   The Duchess of Malfi 54, 81
   The White Devil 54
West Side Story 40
white power 200
Wilson, Robert
   The Three Ladies of London 54
Wilson, Thomas 6–7
   The Arte of Rhetorique 6–7

Zeffirelli, Franco 40